To Uncle Frank
with love from
Graham. Annette.

in.

.92.

D0297125

COURAGE IN THE SKIES

COURAGE
IN THE SKIES

GREAT AIR BATTLES FROM
THE SOMME TO DESERT STORM

AIR VICE-MARSHAL J. E. 'JOHNNIE' JOHNSON
CB, CBE, DSO, DFC

WING COMMANDER P. B. 'LADDIE' LUCAS
CBE, DSO, DFC

STANLEY PAUL
LONDON

By the same authors

J.E. 'JOHNNIE' JOHNSON
Wing Leader
Full Circle
The Story of Air Fighting
Glorious Summer: The Story of the Battle of Britain
(with Laddie Lucas)

P.B. 'LADDIE' LUCAS
Five Up
The Sport of Prince's
Flying Colours: The Epic Story of Douglas Bader
Wings of War: Airmen of all Nations Tell their Stories (1939-45)
Out of the Blue: The Role of Luck in Air Warfare 1917-66
John Jacobs' Impact on Golf
Thanks for the Memory: Unforgettable Characters in Air Warfare 1939-45
Glorious Summer: The Story of the Battle of Britain
(with J.E. 'Johnnie' Johnson)
Malta: The Thorn in Rommel's Side

Stanley Paul & Co. Ltd

An imprint of Random House UK Limited
20 Vauxhall Bridge Road, London SW1V 2SA

Random House Australia (Pty) Ltd
20 Alfred Street, Milsons Point, Sydney, NSW 2061

Random House New Zealand Ltd
18 Poland Road, Glenfield, Auckland, New Zealand

Random House South Africa (Pty) Ltd
PO Box 337, Bergvlei 2012, South Africa

First published 1992

Set in ITC Cheltenham by SX Composing Ltd, Rayleigh, Essex

Printed in Great Britain by Butler & Tanner Ltd,
Frome and London

A catalogue record for this book is available upon request
from the British Library
ISBN 0 09 174676 0

CONTENTS

THE AUTHORS

AIR VICE-MARSHAL J. E. 'JOHNNIE' JOHNSON
CB, CBE, DSO, DFC

Johnnie Johnson, the Royal Air Force's outstanding wing leader in World War II, became the Allies' top scoring ace on the Western Front with a total of 38 enemy aircraft destroyed. Apart from his individual successes which brought him three DSOs and two DFCs, and several foreign decorations, Johnson's aggressive command of the brilliant Canadian formations, allied with his acute tactical mind, placed him at the forefront of fighter leaders of two World Wars.

Later, in the Korean War, Johnson, who had flown in Douglas Bader's wing in the Battle of Britain, operated with the United States Air Force and played a telling part in the advanced jet fighting high up over the north of the country. No Allied leader had a longer run of operational success.

It is not surprising that after so extensive a Service career this remarkable officer has been able to write three widely read books on the development of aerial combat. *Courage in the Skies*, his fifth published work, confirms the extent of his unrivalled experience.

WING COMMANDER P. B. 'LADDIE' LUCAS
CBE, DSO, DFC

Laddie Lucas rose in two years from Aircraftman 2nd Class, the lowest rank in the Royal Air Force, to command of No. 249 (Fighter) Squadron at the height of the Battle of Malta in 1942. He was then 26.

In three tours of operational flying, interspersed with two spells as a Command Headquarters staff officer, Lucas led two Spitfire squadrons and a wing on the Western Front in 1943 before switching to command a Mosquito squadron during the Allied drive through north-west Europe in 1944 and '45. He was awarded the DSO and bar, DFC and French Croix de Guerre.

A Tory MP for ten years in the 1950s, Lucas was one of the country's best-known amateur golfers, captaining Cambridge, England and Great Britain and Ireland against the United States.

He retired in 1976 from the chairmanship of a public company to turn again to writing. *Courage in the Skies* is Lucas's tenth published work in a successful run as an author, his early experience as a Fleet Street journalist standing him in good stead.

PHOTOGRAPH ACKNOWLEDGEMENTS

The authors and publishers are grateful to the following for permission to reproduce photographs and paintings:

Associated Press, pages 200 below and 202.
Bruno Barbey/Magnum, page 181.
Bomber Command Association, page 121.
Camera Press, page 180.
Gerald Coulson, pages 2/3 and 122.
Len Morgan Collection, DeGolyer Library, Dallas, page 124.
Fleet Air Arm Museum, Yeovilton, page 125 above.
Philip Jones Griffiths/Magnum, page 177.
John Hamilton/Imperial War Museum, page 83.
Hulton-Deutsch Collection, page 79 above.
Robert Hunt Picture Library, pages 16/17, 28 below, 32/33, 36, 37, 42/43, 54, 55, 64, 65 above, 68, 75 above, 77, 91, 102, 103, 123, 126, 131, 142, 153, 157, 162, 164 and 166.
Novosti Press Agency, pages 145, 147, 149, 150 and 151.
Popperfoto, pages 44, 97, 173, 174 and 175.
Marc Riboud/Magnum, pages 178 and 182.
Royal Air Force Museum, Hendon, pages 24/25, 63 above, 66 below left and right and 138.
Captain Todd Sheehy, page 201.
Frank Spooner Pictures, pages 10, 170/171, 183, 185, 186 below, 187, 189, 194 above and below, 195, 196, 197, 198 and 200 above.
United States Air Force, pages 179 and 188.

The photograph on page 72 is from *Royal Air Force 1939-1945*, Volume II, H.M.S.O. 1954.

The photographs on pages 87 and 89 are from the private collection of Laddie Lucas.

All other photographs are reproduced courtesy of the Imperial War Museum, London.

ACKNOWLEDGEMENTS

The authors thank those who have aided them in the writing of this story. They are particularly grateful to the two Air Chief Marshals, Sir Harry Broadhurst and Sir Kenneth Cross, practised exponents of the art of close air support for ground forces, who have, between them, allowed the weight of their experience to colour the accounts of the desert fighting in North Africa and, later, the annihilation of the German armour in the break-out of the Allied armies from Normandy.

They are indebted, too, to Air Vice-Marshal Frank Dodd and his wartime navigator, the journalist Eric Hill, for rehearsing again in detail their remarkable photographic mission to the German battleship, *Tirpitz*, as she lay alongside in the heavily-defended Alten Fjord of Norway in July 1944, a necessary prelude to the ship's destruction.

Likewise, they acknowledge warmly the contribution made by Air Commodore P. G. Jameson, the highly-regarded New Zealander, in describing at first hand the sinking of the aircraft carrier, *Glorious*, off the Norwegian coast in June 1940. The disclosure of his own and Bing Cross's subsequent ordeal, as they drifted with their other stricken survivors for days and nights on a Carley float in Arctic waters, is of historic importance.

The authors remember also the help they have received from Air Commodore J. Fenton whose experienced judgement has made him an ally in the preparation of this work. Further, they are mindful of the guidance willingly given by their old friend and former opponent, Lieutenant-General Adolf Galland, the Luftwaffe's General of the Fighters for much of World War II. His input has added strength to the descriptions of the German Air Force's prolonged wartime effort.

Collective thanks are also accorded to Lieutenant-Colonel 'Baz' Lawlor and Wing Commander Roderick I. A. Smith of the Royal Canadian Air Force, and similarly to Wing Commander R. Gibbes of the Royal Australian Air Force – and, again, to Lieutenant-Colonel James A. Goodson and Captain Todd K. Sheehy of the United States Air Force – for their ready assistance in securing the authority of telling passages in the narrative.

The authors also take this opportunity of thanking those who have added colour and realism to the important chapter on Desert Storm. They are particularly indebted to Robert F. Dorr for his interest and help. Likewise they remember gratefully the cooperation offered by Group Captain 'Jock' Stirrup, officer commanding Royal Air Force, Marham, in Norfolk, Squadron Leader G. Thwaites and the pilots of 27 and 617 Squadrons who, after the Gulf fighting, provided first-hand background.

Two other sources of support must be mentioned. The help dispensed by the Royal Air Force's Air Historical Branch, first, under Air Commodore Henry Probert and then under his successor, Group Captain Ian Madelin, has proved to be invaluable in marshalling the events which make up this story. By the same token, thanks are also due to John Andrews, Chief Librarian at the Ministry of Defence, and his patient staff, for sustaining so helpfully the research needed for the successful completion of this work.

THE SPREAD OF THE STORY

The epics of air warfare portrayed in this work cover a period of eight decades from 1916 and the Battle of the Somme to the recent fighting in the Gulf – a time of extraordinary advance in military aviation. Graphically illustrated, these signal operational events represent, in dramatic sequence, the rise of air power as the new and governing factor in modern war. They expose the development of the aeroplane, in all its varied roles and with its diversity of armament, as the twentieth century's most significant military weapon before the introduction of the range of ballistic missiles.

The arresting illustrations and the narrative which accompanies them, embrace the principal phases of land-based and carrier-borne air warfare . . . the primitive biplanes and the hand-to-hand combat of the first German war . . . the emergent monoplane with which Hitler's new Luftwaffe got its blooding in the Spanish Civil War . . . and the advent, in the Second World War, of the dive-bomber and *blitzkrieg* in the West, followed in 1940 by the fighter-dominated contest of the Battle of Britain . . . the bomber fleets of the United States Air Force and the Royal Air Force's Bomber Command which brought precision bombing and mass destruction into the heartland of Nazi Germany . . . North Africa and the Battle for Malta . . . The Battle of the Atlantic and the eventual mastery from the air of the U-boat threat . . . the heroic defence of Stalingrad . . . Germany's frustrated lead in jet and rocket propulsion . . . the menacing flood of Nipponese conquests after Pearl Harbor in 1941 . . . the US Navy's carrier-borne operations in the Pacific . . . the Battles of the Coral Sea

Left: RAF Tornado – Desert Storm

and Midway . . . and the United States' delivery of the atomic *coup de grâce* at Hiroshima and Nagasaki.

Some of the more localized struggles which succeeded World War II and Korea also find their expression in this collection – Vietnam, the Falklands and the Gulf – contests which took air warfare into the sophisticated realm of high technology and electronic guided weaponry, into a previously unknown world of ground-to-air, air-to-ground and air-to-air missiles. The astonishing latter-day developments reached their recent peak in Iraq where, at extreme distances, F-111s of the United States Air Force were 'locking onto' Saddam Hussein's armour at night and, closing with their laser-guided 'smart'

bombs, were then blowing his tanks out of the desert unseen by the naked eye.

All the principal powers – Britain and the United States, the old Soviet Union, Germany and Japan – have their place in this work. And so, too, do the airmen – naval and military, American and British, Commonwealth, South African, Allied and former enemy – all men whose deeds have embellished the annals of war.

In this collection, outstanding operational missions have been selected, in sequence, to characterize the twentieth century's almost unbelievable progress in military aviation and science. The authority of the text is undoubted. The illustrations and graphics colour its sweep.

Albert Ball – World War One flying ace

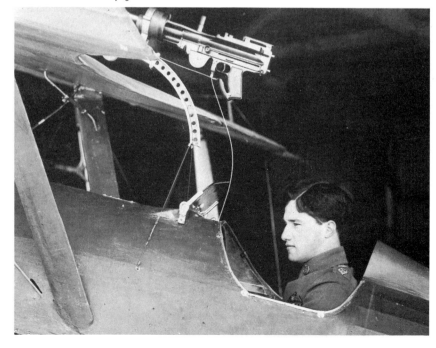

PANORAMA: THE STORY OF AIR WARFARE FROM THE SOMME TO DESERT STORM

Fighting in the air began in 1914, when four Royal Flying Corps (RFC) squadrons flew to France and scouted for the British Expeditionary Force. The slow two-seater machines were unarmed, but pilots and observers usually carried rifles or revolvers to defend themselves should they be forced down. Sometimes they saw German aeroplanes also making reconnaissances, and there began a crude form of duelling in the air when speeds did not exceed 70 m.p.h. and heights not more than 4,000 feet. In these early clashes there was a sense of sharing the same sport, which made a man hesitate to shoot down a crippled opponent; but later this affinity between opposing airmen disappeared.

The next step was to arm the two-seaters with machine guns, but as the air fighting intensified it was apparent that fast, single-seat scouts with forward-firing guns were required to carry out patrols and so obtain 'elbow room' (later referred to as air superiority) for the bombing and reconnaissance two-seaters. The French were first in this field. Their scout was armed with a machine gun that was fired through the propeller which carried steel wedges to deflect striking bullets, but it was Anthony Fokker who gave Germany a tremendous lead with his flying gun. Although France produced some experimental scouts armed with cannon, the machine gun was the standard armament on all fighting aeroplanes throughout this war.

It was Oswald Boelcke who evolved the preliminary tactics for the first flying gun, and who helped win for Germany her first period of supremacy in the air. To counter the Fokker superiority Brigadier General H. M. Trenchard, commander of the RFC, introduced formation flying and formed special fighting squadrons. On the Somme the *jagdstaffeln* won another phase of the air struggle and showed that good machines were more important than mere numbers.

So the air fighters began to fly and fight together. For defensive purposes the British thought a pair of scouts to be the ideal tactical unit, but when flying over enemy territory more strength was required, and flight commanders led small formations of between three and six machines. The vulnerable two-seaters had to be protected, and scouts provided the close escort and the above guard so that Trenchard could maintain his offensive. Later, offensive patrols were flown in squadron strength of about a dozen machines. Eventually squadrons were built into wings to counter Manfred von Richthofen's Circus, when sometimes fifty highly painted scouts flew together. Except for a few individuals such as Ball and Bishop, team fighting replaced lone-wolf tactics. As air fighting speeded up, aerobatics became less important, for slow speeds near the point of stall made aeroplanes easy targets. Duelling in the air vanished, and as the combats became less personal a pilot could not pause to consider the plight of his adversary, because in doing so he might himself be shot down. Courtesy and good manners vanished when pilots shot to kill.

The Zeppelin and the Gotha raids showed that Britain was open to bombing, especially at night, and drew attention to the need for a proper system of air defence, including specialized aeroplanes; for the single-seat scout was gravely handicapped at night.

Lieutenant W. Leefe Robinson caught the imagination of the country when, during the early hours of 3 September 1916, he won the Victoria Cross by shooting down a Zepplin, illuminated by searchlights, which subsequently burned on the ground for nearly two hours. Later, *Kapitanleutnant* Heinrich Mathy, the greatest airship commander of the war, fell at Potters Bar; another was sent down in flames at Billericay, and a fourth had to land in Essex. After that the airships turned from the strong London defences to raiding the north and the midlands. More were brought down, and the Germans, realizing that they were losing the contest, turned to aeroplane raids, and in November 1916 London suffered its first bomber attack. It was made by one machine, a two-seater having a 225-horse-power Mercedes engine, and the first that was known of its presence was when small bombs began to fall near Victoria Station at midday; the German observer took some photographs of military camps and airfields, but these fell into RFC hands when the pilot landed near Boulogne with engine trouble.

The first big daylight raid against London was in June 1917, when fourteen twin-engined Gotha bombers attacked the East End, killing 162 people. All the bombers returned safely despite the intervention of ninety-two British machines which went up to attack. As a result, Trenchard, acting on the premise that the only proper defence is offence, formed bomber squadrons which attacked ordnance depots, railways, and, indeed, targets in Germany.

Scout pilots were the defenders of the people, and their exploits were widely followed, not only for their dramatic quality but also because they took people's minds off the horror on the ground. When Georges Guynemer, fifty-four victories, failed to return from a patrol the children of France made him an immortal when they said he flew so high he could not come down again.

During the Kaiser's War the soldiers soon found that the airmen could help them by bombing and strafing enemy targets and Army commanders asked for the bombing of bridges, viaducts, and towns to isolate the battlefield and to stop the enemy from reinforcing it. There were so many requests for close air support and harassing operations that the Germans formed their *schlachstaffeln*, while the RFC fitted scouts with bomb racks and ordered a ground-attack aeroplane.

The soldiers wanted plenty of reconnaissance, and when the scouts began to strafe and bomb, the pilots were encouraged to report on enemy ground activities. Tactical reconnaissance by scouts increased that already supplied by the two-seaters, and by the end of the First War the scout was used for four main purposes – for day fighting (and occasionally for night fighting), for bombing, for strafing and for fighter reconnaissance.

Between the wars both sides forgot a lot of tactical lore, but the Spanish Civil War served to remind the Luftwaffe of the old lessons, and German fighter pilots were therefore far better prepared than their Royal Air Force contemporaries for the 1939–45 contest, when inept peacetime training cost the RAF dear. The rigid fighter attacks curbed initiative, and may be compared to the Royal Navy's equally foolish fighting instructions, which from Cromwell's time until almost the close of the eighteenth century severely restricted a commander's freedom of manoeuvre at sea. Just as Rodney's defeat of the French in the Caribbean in 1782 discredited the

fighting instructions, so the defeat of the Luftwaffe in 1940 discredited the fighter attacks, which, unlamented, have faded into oblivion.

Blitzkrieg (Lightning War) devised in Spain and rehearsed in Poland, was brought to near perfection on 10 May 1940. Then the mighty land force of the Wehrmacht, with its ten armoured divisions, and its formidable air component, the Luftwaffe, blasted, dive-bombed and stormed its way through France, brushing aside all opposition, which surrendered after six weeks. The bulk of the British Army was however allowed to escape at Dunkirk.

In the Battle of Britain Douglas Bader's wing was not unlike Mannock's, except that the Hurricanes and Spitfires flew higher and faster than the SEs. Radar and good communications gave Keith Park, AOC, 11 Group, centralized control over his squadrons, but this control was not applied too rigidly, and our fighter leaders were aided rather than controlled by the men on the ground. Without radar and radio the bravery of the fighter pilot would have been of little account.

This great battle was fought and won over the Channel, over the fields of Kent and Sussex, over the wolds of Hampshire and Dorset, over the flat marshes of Essex and the sprawling mass of London. Unlike the previous battles of destiny – Waterloo, Trafalgar and the terrible roar and devastation of the Somme bombardments – there was little sound or fury. People on the ground went about their business with little idea of what was taking place high in the sky. They saw a pattern of white vapour trails slowly changing form and shape. Sometimes they saw the contestants as a number of tiny specks scintillating like diamonds in the sunlight of those cloudless days. The skilful parries of the defence continued throughout those long days of the late summer. Had they not done so London would have suffered the fate of Warsaw and Rotterdam.

Göring's faulty judgement materially helped to win the battle. The

integrity of any commander is a precious thing, for men must know and respect their leaders. But the German airmen had little regard for Göring, and were frequently dismayed and baffled by his ever-changing orders. On the other hand, Dowding's qualities of leadership produced high morale throughout Fighter Command, which was the most important single factor in winning that contest.

Apart from its military significance, the Battle of Britain provides the moral lesson that Providence is not always on the side of the big battalions, a lesson we might remember in this divided world of warring camps. We might also remember that during this ordeal not all fighter pilots were British. The Poles, many of whom still live in Britain, made up one-eighth of the numbers.

Having won the day battle, the Blitz was upon us, and much bombing had to be endured before Fighter Command could offer some protection at night. As in the previous war, single-seaters were of little use on dark nights. Also, we had arrived at the stage when it no longer sufficed to design an aeroplane for one job and expect it to cope with another by sticking on a few extra bits and pieces. The era of the weapons system had arrived.

Germany's attack on Russia took the pressure off Fighter Command, and the well-proved defensive fighters, Spitfires and Hurricanes, began to fight offensively over France. Thanks primarily to those two experienced wing leaders, Douglas Bader and 'Sailor' Malan, the Royal Air Force had, at long last, got its fighting tactics right, and the finger-four formation, the Luftwaffe's *schwarme*, was flown operationally for many years. Fortunately Britain was not beguiled by her defensive victory, and bombers struck at Germany in ever-increasing numbers. Sometimes a few bombers were escorted on day missions over France, but, like the Luftwaffe during the previous year, too many escorting fighters were tied to the bombers and did not provide enough freelancing fighter sweeps.

The air fighting over France, in 1941, was often very strenuous, but it did not achieve much of military significance. RAF losses were greater than the Luftwaffe's, and even after the majority of enemy fighters were transferred to the East, for the attack on Russia, a comparatively small number of Messerschmitt 109s and excellent Focke-Wulf 190s reduced British penetrations over France and showed, once again, that good aeroplanes are more important than superiority in numbers.

The operations of Bomber Command began at three minutes after noon on 3 September 1939 and ended on the night of 2/3 May 1945. No other force in our long history has fought such a long and bloody campaign, assisted in honourable partnership by the daylight bombing of the US Army Air Corps.

When 'Mary' Coningham arrived in the Western Desert in 1941 there was little organization for air–ground operations, and it was the New Zealander who pioneered tactical air power and gained the Army's confidence. His successor, Harry Broadhurst, gave the Desert Air Force more flexibility by turning his fighters into fighter-bombers. In the North African and Italian campaigns tactical air power was significant. In Normandy and North-West Europe it was decisive.

Stalingrad was the most crucial, the most vicious and the longest drawn-out battle of the Second War. For the Germans it marked the beginning of the decline of the Luftwaffe which, eventually, was caught unawares by the strength and mobility of the Soviet counter-offensive. For the Russians it was the turning point for their Air Force which, at the end of 1942, had recovered from the crippling blows of the previous year and was modernized and strengthened by its own production resources and much help from the United States and the UK with aeroplanes ferried by way of the Arctic, Alaskan and Persian supply routes.

On 16 September 1943 forty-five Flying Fortresses were lost attacking Schweinfurt, and on 14 October of that year a further sixty were lost against the same target. There can be no doubt that the American daylight bombing would have been stopped had not the most significant fighter of the Second World War – the P-51D Mustang – made its dramatic appearance with the range to escort the bombers to Berlin and back.

Unlike Fighter Command during the Battle of Britain, when radar warning was short, the Germans had ample notice of the approach of raids across the North Sea and were able to reinforce the threatened area and organize a strong and concentrated air defence. The American fighter pilots had to overcome this defensive barrier, which included jets, and the air battles were the greatest and longest of the Second War. Thanks to good aeroplanes and aggressive leaders, such as Don Blakeslee, Hub Zemke and Gabby Gabreski, the Americans won a great victory.

The United States showed how its air power could shrink the globe when, in June 1944, their bombers, escorted by fighters led by Blakeslee, flew from England to Poltava in Russia. The second leg was flown to bases in Italy and on the third targets were attacked in eastern France on the way back.

The American and British combined bomber offensive exposed the heart of Germany to round-the-clock bombing and, together with the shorter ranged tactical air forces, won almost complete air superiority from Normandy to the Baltic. Hilary St George Saunders wrote:

Those who held the controls of a bomber in their firm young hands truly deserve a crown of bays. Night after night in darkness bathed in silver or veiled with cloud, undeterred by *the fury of guns and the new inventions of death* they rode the skies above Germany and paid without flinching the terrible price which war demands. Of a total of 70,253 officers, non-commissioned officers and airmen of the Royal Air Force killed or missing on operations between 3 September 1939 and 14 August 1945, 47,293 lost their lives or disappeared in operations carried out by Bomber Command.*

In his moving tribute, John Terraine wrote:

And what of the aircrew, the flyers, the ones who left their burnt bones scattered over all of Europe. In those young men we may discern the many faces of courage, the constitution of heroes: in lonely cockpits at dizzy altitudes, quartering the treacherous and limitless sea, searching the Desert's hostile glare, brushing the peaks of high mountains, in the ferocity of low-level attack or the long, tense haul of a bombing mission, in fog, in deadly cold, in storm . . . on fire . . . in a prison camp . . . in a skin grafting hospital . . . My title shows what I think of them: there is no prouder place, none deserving more honour, than the right of the line.†

On the other side of the world the Americans got off to an appalling start at Pearl Harbor when the Japanese knocked out the Pacific Fleet but not, as they later found out to their great cost, the United States; by the spring of 1942 the Japanese were masters of a large part of Asia, dominated the Western Pacific and controlled Indonesia. American strategy was to hold the line until sufficient strength had been gathered for amphibious attacks but in May 1942 the Japanese struck the US Fleet in the Coral Sea where all the fighting was by carrier-based aeroplanes, the surface ships not firing a shot – an indication of the trend of future battles in the Pacific. Then came Midway, the decisive battle that turned the Pacific War, where the brilliant flying by Navy and Marine pilots set new standards in carrier-borne warfare.

During 1945 the Americans fought their way to within bombing distance of Japan herself, whose military leaders would not consider surrender until the atomic bomb was used on Hiroshima and Nagaski and ended the Second War.

However, peace in the Far East was short-lived. In 1950 the South Koreans fell back in disarray and together with the 24th (US) Division were driven

* Hilary St George Saunders, *Royal Air Force, 1939-1945*: vol. III, *The Fight Is Won* (HMSO, London, 1954).
† John Terraine, *The Right of the Line* (Hodder & Stoughton, London, 1985).

back to the bottom of the peninsula where they set up a defensive perimeter base on the port of Pusan. As the North Koreans extended their supply lines, US fighter-bombers, already in complete control of the air, began to take a heavy toll of enemy forces and supplies. The fighter-bombers saved the day and gave the Allied army time to reinforce and break out.

At the end of the Korean War the versatile and flexible single-seat jet fighter was used for six purposes – for offensive and defensive day fighting, for visual and photographic reconnaissance, and for bombing and strafing. Because there were few strategic targets the fighter-bomber became the work-horse of Korea.

In Vietnam the heavy American fighter-bombers, designed to carry big loads over long distances, were at a disadvantage when close fighting the much lighter Russian-built MiGs, designed as pure interceptors, but Robin Olds, Randy Cunningham and others showed that experienced Phantom pilots could dog-fight and destroy them. Improved missiles had ranges of several miles and with his on-board electronics a pilot could, for the first time in our story of air fighting, destroy an enemy aeroplane without physically seeing it.

The destruction of the Dragon's Jaw Bridge in three days with 'smart' bombs, after years of effort with old iron weapons, was an important step in the development of fighter-bomber operations; the night-time bombing offensive of Christmas 1972 which continued for twelve nights against targets in Vietnam was of an intensity unprecedented in the annals of air warfare.

The morale of all air crews was raised by the knowledge that if they were brought down in the jungles, mountains or seas of South-east Asia, the men of the Air Sea Rescue would take great risks to get them out. Many gallant missions were flown by helicopter pilots and during this long war they rescued several thousand US and Allied fighting men, mostly in South Vietnam. However, the Jolly Green Giants were vulnerable to ground fire and therefore paid a high price.

Although the United States failed to achieve her aims in South-east Asia, her airmen, often with one hand tied behind their backs, fought well and steadfastly as their fathers had done over Europe and the Pacific. They developed and proved the technology of the new weapons which will influence all future wars. The war was not lost in the skies above Vietnam. Indeed, in 1973, the war in the air was won. But the war as a whole was lost in the hearts and minds of the American people. It was their decision.

The Yom Kippur War of 1973 showed that the Arabs had made much progress with their air defence systems, and the Israeli Air Force was only able to force a draw because of lavish aid from America. This was the first conflict in which the battlefields were regularly monitored by reconnaissance satellites.

Prior to the air fighting over the Falklands Britain gravely underestimated the qualities of the Argentine fighter pilots, forgetting, as our old friend Air Vice-Marshal Mike LeBas (himself born in the Argentine) pointed out, that a country which could produce racing drivers like Juan Manuel Fangio, and world-class soccer and tennis players, could surely produce first-class fighter pilots.

Because we were not well prepared to deal with limited wars of the Falklands type, the contest in Antarctica was fought with a mixture of high technology weapons and obsolete material such as Vulcan bombers; because of severe limitations on both sides the war in the air was a marginal affair.

During the air fighting over the Lebanon in 1982 American air superiority fighters, F-15 Eagles and F-16 Fighting Falcons, armed with the latest Sidewinder missiles and flown by Israeli pilots, proved superior to the Soviet-built MiG-21s and MiG-23s flown by Arab pilots. Heeding the fearful missile lesson of the Yom Kippur War the Syrian SAM missile batteries were demolished at a stroke by a combination of fighters, missiles and electronic systems.

Desert Storm introduced a new era of high technological warfare. Not long ago it would have been impossible to identify and destroy small targets in built-up areas leaving the surrounding buildings relatively untouched. The accuracy of the Tomahawk Cruise missiles, launched from battleships, submarines and B-52s, the suppression of SAM sites, the jamming of radars, the success of the new Patriot missile against the Iraqi Scuds, and the tremendous and varied Allied arsenal of weapons, all demonstrated the high quality of modern war technology.

The greatest achievement of Desert Storm, however, was by General Charles Horner's command and control organization from his Tactical Air Control Centre. Working through the patrolling AWACS (Airborne Warning and Control System) to his strike aeroplanes, this unit planned and co-ordinated the missions of five different Air Forces which often flew 2,000 missions in twenty-four hours. For the first time in the history of US air power, instead of the usual bickering between the Services about command and control – as in Vietnam – Horner controlled all Air Force, Navy, Marine and Army units. As the General dryly remarked, 'We all sang from the same sheet of music.'

PART I
THE FIRST WORLD
WAR

Tactical genius – Oswald Boelcke

1 · OSWALD BOELCKE, TACTICIAN

During the retreat from Mons in late 1914, as the squadrons of the Royal Flying Corps (RFC) fell back from airfield to airfield, so the combat units of the German Air Service advanced, following hard on the heels of their victorious armies. One of their pilots, Oswald Boelcke, was a keen, determined officer who proved to be an outstanding leader and was one of the first 'aces' to emerge from the air clashes over Flanders. He was also a tactician of rare quality and his teachings were followed by his countrymen long after his death.

Boelcke began his air fighting career in an unarmed two-seater and the duties of him and his observer were to scout for the German Army, to pinpoint the positions of Allied artillery, and to direct the fire of their own guns by a system of coloured lights fired from the air. The rifles and revolvers each carried were to defend themselves with should they be forced down, but whenever they saw Allied aeroplanes Boelcke tried to manoeuvre alongside so that his observer, Lieutenant von Wühlisch, could take a 'whack' at them. Thus a crude form of duelling in the air began. Speeds did not exceed 70 m.p.h. and heights were not more than 4,000 feet. In these early clashes there was a sense of sport that made a man hesitate to shoot down a crippled opponent; but later this affinity between opposing airmen disappeared.

The next step in the development of air fighting was the arming of two-seaters and here the British pinned their hopes on the Lewis gun, which was of simple design and had a useful rate of fire. The first problem was where to mount the gun so that it could be used to good purpose in the air, since if it was mounted in the ideal position along the line of flight (so that the pilot simply aimed his machine at his opponent) the bullets would strike the blades of the propeller. The solution was to fix it on the top mainplane, sufficiently high to clear the blades, and aim it with a simple sight. The drawback was that the gunner had to stand to aim and fire, or to clear one of the frequent stoppages in the mechanism – neither of which was a simple matter in a gale of 50 or 60 m.p.h.

In the spring and summer of 1915 duelling in the air intensified as both sides sought to reconnoitre enemy positions. It soon became apparent that there was a strong requirement for a properly armed single-seater 'scout' machine to carry out fighting patrols and so obtain 'elbow room' (air superiority) for the two-seaters. The French were first in this field with a scout whose machine gun was fired through the propeller, which carried steel wedges to deflect striking bullets, but they were soon overtaken by the Germans thanks to the genius of Anthony Fokker, who gave them a tremendous lead with his flying gun.

Unfortunately for the Allies, a French scout fitted with the new device made a forced landing in the German lines and was captured before the pilot, Roland Garros, an aviator of pre-war fame, could carry out his orders and destroy his machine. The machine was taken to Berlin where it was given to a brilliant Dutch aeroplane designer, Anthony Fokker, who was instructed to adapt the French idea to the German Parabellum machine gun. Fokker, who was then twenty-four, had designed, built and flown his own sporting planes, and had already secured a contract to build planes for the Germans and to train some of their pilots. The French invention and the Parabellum gun were given to him on a Tuesday evening and by Friday he had developed the first interrupter gear fitted to an aeroplane and returned to Berlin.

The Dutchman thought the French system of steel wedges mounted on a wooden propeller dangerous and crude. The deflectors reduced the efficiency of the wooden blades, bullets could still shatter them and there was some risk from ricochets. He determined to do better. His problem was how to get a bullet between the two blades of the propeller when it was spinning at slightly more than a thousand revolutions per minute; Fokker likened his problem to that of a child trying to throw stones through the revolving blades of a windmill.

With a speed that is a tribute to his genius he completed his design work, installed the gun and its interrupter gear on one of his monoplanes, lashed the tail of the machine to his touring car and drove through the night to a military airfield at Berlin. There he demonstrated his gun, which, unlike the Lewis gun, was belt-fed, to a group of staff officers who doubted whether it would work in the air because the propeller did not have steel wedges like the captured French machine. The Dutchman agreed to fire at a ground target from the air, and scattered the gathered staff officers when his stream of bullets ricocheted from the hard ground. Although Fokker riddled the target, they were still not fully convinced and said that the gun ought to be tested in actual combat. So the Dutch designer, a civilian and a foreigner in Germany, was bundled off to the front with his aeroplane with orders to demonstrate the superiority of his system and the machine gun by killing an Allied aviator.

The Flying Dutchman, masquerading in German field grey uniform as Lieutenant Anthony Fokker, flew to Boelcke's airfield at Douai, his Fokker E1 monoplane fitted with the machine gun that was to revolutionize air warfare. After a few uneventful patrols he came across a sitting duck in the form of an Allied two-seater cruising below him. Fokker began his attack in a long dive, but when the Allied plane was filling his sights and completely at his mercy he became nauseated with the whole affair and never fired a shot. He flew back to Douai, where he declared he was finished with fighting and was returning to his factory.

The question now arose as to which pilot should be entrusted with assessing the new gun in combat. Boelcke, impressed by the radical, clean lines of the monoplane, flew it without permission. Fortunately for him, the commanding officer at Douai was not too displeased by this breach of flying discipline and he was officially selected to appraise both machine and gun. Before leaving the hazards of the combat zone Fokker found time to explain both his aeroplane and the mechanism of the gun to Boelcke.

Boelcke was delighted with the Fokker, whose 80 horsepower rotary engine gave it a speed of about 80 m.p.h. at 5,000 feet. Compared with the clumsy two-seater Albatros, it was like riding a thoroughbred after a hack. He soon found that the single-seater gave him far more initiative and freedom of action than the Albatros. Now he combined the roles of pilot, navigator and gunner, whereas in the Albatros he was simply the driver. His only regret was having to part company with Wühlisch, for they had found the indefinable affinity of those who fly and fight together.

He found that the best tactics for his speedy Fokker, with its high rate of climb and good manoeuvrability, was to prowl on the German side of the front lines, taking full advantage of any concealment offered by the glare of the sun, clouds and their shadows cast on the earth. He carefully studied captured Allied aeroplanes so that he knew the type of gun each carried and its field of fire; thus he found the blind spots of British and French machines and fashioned his attacks accord-

ingly. He could climb his Fokker to 5,000 feet, and at this height he found that most Allied aeroplanes flew below him. Unless there was plenty of cloud cover it was against orders to cross the front lines, and he usually hunted on the German side of the lines, where lay the advantage of the prevailing wind. In the event of a forced landing he was on friendly territory, whereas Allied aircrews in the same predicament were almost invariably captured.

Having seen an opponent, Boelcke had the patience to hide and stalk in the correct up-sun position before attacking. Like a swooping hawk he fastened on his victim from a long slanting dive, closing to short range and firing accurate, short bursts from his gun, which he aimed with a simple ring and bead sight. Having dispatched his opponent from a final range of a few yards he climbed back to his cruising height and resumed his quest.

Aiming from astern was easy and seemed natural, because the Fokker monoplane was simply a gun which he flew at an opponent. The secret of success lay in closing to a good killing range, aiming, and then holding the gun platform steady when firing. Fighting in the Fokker seemed simple and straightforward after the intricate manoeuvres required in the Albatros so that Wühlisch could bring his gun to bear. Enemy machines could be shot down much quicker than before. The flying gun changed the conception of air fighting.

The German anti-aircraft gunners knew about the solitary Fokker pilot and recognized his machine. When they thought he was in danger of being attacked they fired a few warning rounds ahead of his monoplane, and they also provided covering fire when he evaded an opponent by diving towards the ground.

Another pilot of 62 section found out how a Fokker could easily regain its height after a diving attack. This was Max Immelmann, a serious youth, whose famous manoeuvre, known for long afterwards as 'the Immelmann turn', began with a dive

upon his enemy. After building up his speed in the dive he pulled the Fokker into a climb and opened fire from behind and below. After firing he continued climbing as if he were going to loop, but when his Fokker was vertical he kicked on hard rudder, turned sideways and dived on his opponent from above. The tactic was sound so long as the Fokker was superior to all other machines on the Western Front, and it was successful because the aggressor could attack in the same way again and again. But later, when more powerful engines became available, it was a dangerous move, for the lower pilot could climb after the Fokker and attack when it hung almost motionless in the vertical position, not under full control, and presenting an easy shot.

Boelcke's victory total mounted slowly. Owing to the 'Fokker scare' the French adopted a defensive policy, confining their *escadrilles* to short-range spotting and reconnaissance duties, while the RFC were forced to escort bombing and reconnaissance aeroplanes with the new Vickers Fighter, a two-seater pusher with a speed of some 80 m.p.h. and a ceiling of 10,000 feet. Irked by the lack of combat, Boelcke began to leave the sanctuary of the German lines and extend his patrols over Allied territory. Like countless other scout pilots, he found the sky's horizons too vast – and too dangerous – for one man to search and cover the whole time. He found that when he had spotted an Allied aeroplane three or four miles away, and most of his concentration was on the stalk and the gaining of an up-sun position for his attack, other hostile aeroplanes had a disconcerting habit of appearing within a hundred yards, and eventually this could only have one ending.

He reasonably concluded that in order to fly his Fokker, navigate to his patrol line, quarter the sky for hostile machines, dodge anti-aircraft shells and guard himself from surprise attack he needed another pair of eyes. And he especially needed this assistance when focusing on a parti-

Cockpit of Boelcke's Fokker E III

cular segment of the sky, because he often searched for twenty or thirty seconds before picking out a plane, plenty of time for some Allied fighter to creep up and attack him.

If an enemy approached unseen to within the lethal firing range of about 200 yards . . .

If that other pairs of eyes could be positioned alongside his Fokker, on his flank, then those eyes could protect him from a surprise attack while he searched and led. And who better than Max Immelmann to provide the other pair of eyes, especially as he was gaining experience on the monoplane and could usually land it without bending it! They worked out a method of wing waggling to signal to each other so that Immelmann, on the flank, would know when Boelcke, the leader, intended to attack or break off a combat.

Thus Boelcke and Immelmann began to fly and fight together. They guarded and protected each other, Boelcke with the gun and Immelmann with his eyes. They became the first *pair* of air fighters, which is still, nearly eighty years on, the basic formation of fighter squadrons throughout the world.

Soon better Fokker scouts, with bigger engines giving a speed of about 90 m.p.h., were introduced and with them the German Air Service made, in 1916, its first real bid for air supremacy over the Western Front. They were so superior to Allied aeroplanes that the average RFC pilot lasted only a few weeks and questions were asked in Parliament about 'Fokker Fodder' and 'The Fokker Scourge'. However, although Boelcke and his contemporaries had a better scout they seemed content to

fight defensively on their side of the lines and to lie in wait for the inferior British machines which were forever on the offensive.

To understand why RFC crews sallied forth in their vulnerable aeroplanes two or three times a day, day after day, and always on the offensive, we must glance briefly at the broad strategy which ruled the activities of the squadrons. At this time the RFC was commanded by Brigadier General H. M. Trenchard. This great leader realized that his job of supporting the Army could only be done by fighting over enemy territory. The Army wanted two-seaters above and beyond the front lines to bomb, photograph, reconnoitre and report the fall of artillery shells, and aircraft like these could not survive unless his scouts went further afield to try and hold the Fokkers. Thus Trenchard, the 'Father of the Royal Air Force' and the world's first air strategist, determined that air power could only be exploited through offensive rather than defensive action, and even when his casualties were very high, and much pressure was borne upon him to change his policy, he still followed his offensive strategy.

Trenchard replied to the Fokkers by introducing formation flying, by breaking up the miscellaneous collection of aeroplanes in each squadron and providing them with one type of machine and organizing the squadrons for specialized roles. The spring of 1916 saw a steady flow of new aeroplanes to France. The de Havilland Scout, capable of about 90 m.p.h., could climb to 10,000 feet in twenty-four minutes and was reported by the pilots to be superior in some respects to the latest Fokker. But the best scout of this period was produced by the French. Their Nieuport Scout had a Lewis gun mounted on the top-plane and could climb to 10,000 feet in nine minutes. It was ordered for the RFC because it was the first Allied scout to exceed 100 m.p.h. in level flight.

Meanwhile, the Germans were also grouping their scouts together and Boelcke was ordered to form his own *staffel* (squadron) of six machines. Both his and Immelmann's victories mounted at about the same rate. Immelmann was killed when his machine fell apart in the air, at which time his score stood at fifteen.

Trenchard's formation flying and specialized squadrons were beginning to pay such dividends that the first period of enemy air supremacy was ending. The Germans replied by raising permanent *jagdstaffeln* of fourteen scouts and Oswald Boelcke, now regarded as Germany's leading scout pilot and their foremost tactician, was selected to command one of these units. He was given a free hand in the selection of his pilots and one day, whilst visiting his brother, who was also in the German Air Service, he was introduced to a young lieutenant, Baron Manfred von Richthofen, who was eager to become a scout pilot. Soon afterwards Richthofen joined the new 'Hunting Pack'.

Boelcke's unit received a new scout – the formidably armed Albatros D-11. It carried twin Spandau machine guns that fired through the propeller and its 100-horsepower Mercedes engine gave a speed of about 110 m.p.h. and a ceiling of 17,000 feet. In early September 1916 he celebrated the beginning of his third year of air fighting with his twentieth victory. Soon some of the new Albatroses were serviceable and on 17 September Boelcke decided that the *jagdstaffeln* would fight together for the first time and led another four scouts on patrol. They destroyed five British machines without loss and by the end of the month had accounted for twenty-five aeroplanes for the loss of three pilots. Other *jagdstaffeln* were formed and once again the RFC were seriously challenged. Their casualties increased and Trenchard became concerned about the superiority of the enemy aeroplanes and their skilful pilots. He was obliged to curtail his long-distance fighting and although he still held to his offensive policy he knew that unless the RFC was provided with better aeroplanes it would be driven from the sky.

At the end of October, Oswald Boelcke, now with forty victories, was killed when his Albatros collided with another as they were both diving on an Allied machine. He was the first practical airman to study the development of air fighting and to develop the correct tactics. When he began to fly against the Allies, fighting was regarded as something of a sporting joust between gentlemen and not highly dangerous, but, by the time of his death, team fighting was here to stay. His unit was renamed *Jagdstaffel* Boelcke and the RFC dropped a wreath over his airfield on which was written: *To the memory of Captain Boelcke, our brave and chivalrous opponent.*

2 · DOG-FIGHT OVER POLYGON WOOD

During 'bloody April' 1917 German air power was again superior and the RFC passed through its greatest ordeal of the war. For example, on 5 April six Bristol Fighters led by Captain W. Leefe Robinson vc were set upon by Richthofen at the head of five Albatros Scouts of his *Jagdstaffel* 2. Two of the Bristols fell to Richthofen and two to his pilots, and in his subsequent report the German leader said that his own 'aeroplane was unquestionably superior to the Bristol Fighter both in speed and climbing powers'.*

To the pilots who encountered them, Richthofen and his men seemed to be everywhere at once. Richthofen's all-scarlet Albatros stood out in the sky for all to see. His British opponents dubbed him 'The Red Knight' and the French *Le Petit Rouge*. He allowed his pilots to paint their own scouts in whatever way they liked with the reservation that his was

Richthofen's Circus of Fokker Triplanes, 1918

the only all-red machine. Thus his brother Lothar, in *Jagdstaffel* 2, flew a red scout with yellow control surfaces, while another pilot favoured the same colour with black controls. Other German squadrons were quick to follow Richthofen's lead and soon the most vivid colour schemes were seen in the air.

On 13 April 1917, 'The Red Knight', again leading six Albatros Scouts, came across six unescorted RE-8s (known to those who had the misfortune to fly them as 'Harry Tates').† The unequal fight was soon over, all the RFC machines being brought down and all the pilots and observers, except two, killed. By the end of April his score had increased to fifty-two, and his victims, all British, numbered fifty-five dead, including Major L.G. Hawker vc, and twenty-six wounded or prisoners of war.

The end of April marked a change in German fighter tactics. Twenty

scouts were seen sweeping the battle area and were promply named 'Richthofen's Circus' because the red aeroplanes of *Jagdstaffel* 2 were present. These early sweeps were but temporary groupings of various units, but the German Air Service were soon convinced that they were tactically correct and formed the first *Jagdgeschwader*‡ of scouts. Manfred von Richthofen was recalled from leave to command and lead it.

Big dog-fights resulted from the assembly of many small formations. James McCudden, one of the RFC's exceptional leaders, was involved in one such scrap. He liked to cruise his own little band well over 'Hunland' and then, hoping for surprise, head

* H. A. Jones, *The War in the Air* (Clarendon Press, Oxford, 1931), vol. III.
† Harry Tate was a famous comedian of the day.
‡ JGI comprised *Jagdstaffeln* 4, 6, 10 and 11.

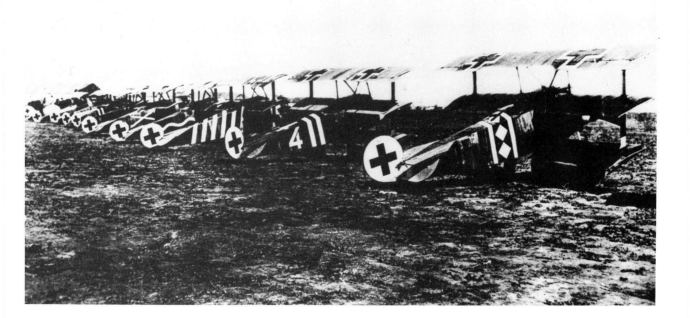

towards the Ypres Salient, where the British lines thrust towards the enemy. Once, from afar, well silhouetted against a golden band of evening sky, McCudden saw bunches of black specks moving slowly across the horizon, and when he got nearer he found about fifty aeroplanes fighting it out between 12,000 and 18,000 feet and many more below. This particular air battle, typical of those fought over Polygon Wood at this time, seemed to have a base five or six miles across where the fighting seemed fiercest, then to taper away to a narrow apex where it burst open, like the anvil head of a thunder cloud,

Left: James McCudden, outstanding air fighter

Below: Squadron line-up – Sopwith Camels

as eighteen or twenty scouts jockeyed for height. Like a cumulus cloud the air battle drifted slowly across the countryside, its shape ever changing as sections climbed and dived, joined and separated, fought and broke away.

The highest scouts looked like the new Fokker Triplanes, seven or eight of them painted red but each bearing small distinguishing marks – a white tail, a blue rudder, green ailerons – to set them apart from their master, whose crimson machine could not be seen. They all seemed very experienced from the way they threw their mounts around the sky. The Triplanes had a fabulous climb but an ugly reputation for falling to pieces when heavily stressed.

McCudden worked his way round the fringes of the battle. He wanted to bring off one of those rarities, a formation attack on four of the new Pfalz scouts, but his flight was jumped and badly split up by four or five Triplanes, and McCudden had to resort to a long spin to get out of serious trouble. He recovered at 7,000 feet, where the milling, turning machines looked like a swarm of bees, cleared his tail and slipped away, for caution was his watchword and he never allowed bloodthirstiness to cloud his better judgement.

These massive dog-fights were very dangerous to a pilot separated from his section, as Richthofen discovered when eight of his Albatroses attacked six slow FEs. The RFC two-seaters adopted a defensive circle, a cunning move because most of their blind spots were covered either by the aeroplane ahead or the one behind. As usual, the circling machines attracted others; more German patrols arrived and some Sopwith Triplanes came to help the two-seaters. Two FEs and four German scouts had already gone down when Richthofen, manoeuvring to get on the tail of an FE, was himself hit by a bullet which ripped open his skull and splintered the bone. He was temporarily blinded and paralysed and his red Albatros spun down out of control. Fortunately he regained his senses and was able to crash-land before he fainted again. Within a few weeks he was fighting again.

3 · THE RED KNIGHT FELLED

On 21 April 1918 the German Air Service lost its great scout pilot and leader, and the manner of this death illustrates the state of air fighting as the First War drew to an end.

On that spring morning von Richthofen left his airfield with only six machines, but he was joined in the air by one of his squadrons. At 12,000 feet he led his mixed formation of Fokker Triplanes and Albatroses westwards over the Somme Valley until they were over the front lines. Normally he patrolled farther back over his own territory but another German ground offensive was imminent and he had to prevent British two-seaters from photographing the preparations. Before they took off he had warned his pilots to keep a special look-out for the two-seaters, and to watch the stiff easterly wind which drifted them towards the enemy.

Much cloud and poor visibility made navigation difficult, but occasionally he caught a glimpse of the Somme and was able to pinpoint his position. Suddenly four Triplanes broke away and dived steeply on a pair of RFC two-seaters. Richthofen circled and watched the fight well below. The two-seaters were well handled and gave a good account of themselves. British anti-aircraft fire soon attracted eight Camels to the scene, and Richthofen turned his fifteen multi-coloured scouts to engage the Camels.

As usual, there was a hard core of stern fighting and manoeuvring, with some skirmishing on the flanks. Confident in his own ability to turn inside any adversary, he pirouetted his all-red Fokker through the jumble of twisting, turning aeroplanes. A side-slip here, a steep turn there, a dive and a zoom, he watched the ever-changing pattern of the fight and waited for a good opportunity, which

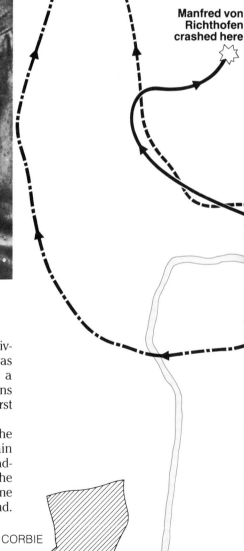

Baron Manfred von Richthofen

he seized when he saw a Camel diving away from the dog-fight. It was flown by Lieutenant W.R. May, a beginner, whose two machine guns had jammed. He was taking the first opportunity to make for home.

Richthofen went after May, but the latter's flight commander, Captain A.R. Brown, a Canadian of 209 Squadron, saw the Triplane on the tail of the Camel and gave chase. By this time both machines were near the ground.

May was aware of his danger and tried to throw off the red Triplane, but Richthofen, oblivious of the other Camel behind, stuck to his tail and calmly waited, as he had so many times before, to get May in his sights at the decisive range. Brown fired a burst from his twin machine guns and the Fokker crash-landed some two miles inside the British lines. When Richthofen was lifted from the cockpit he was dead. His opponents regretted that he did not survive the war.

Manfred von Richthofen crashed here

CORBIE

THE RED KNIGHT FELLED

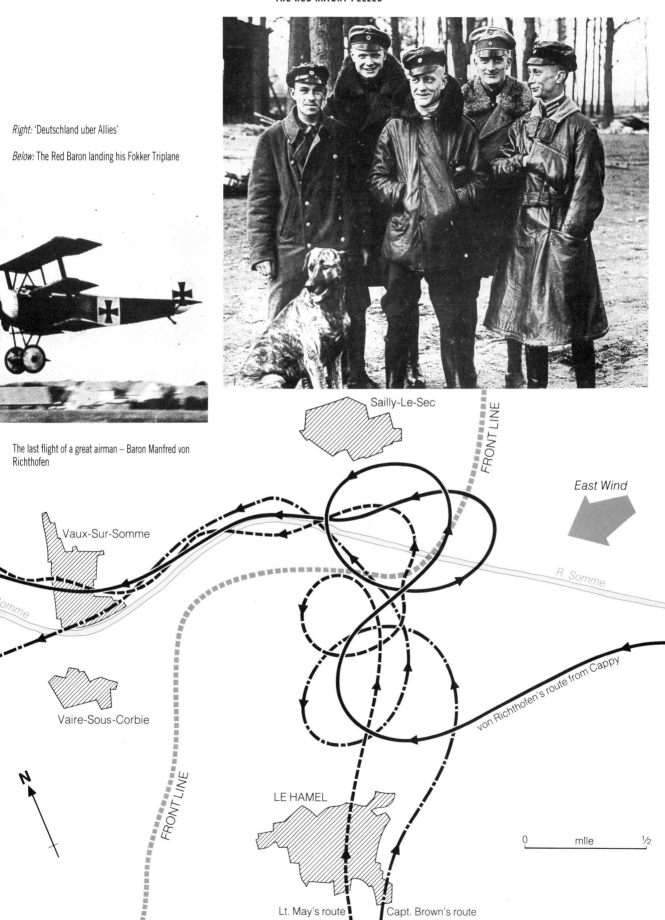

Right: 'Deutschland uber Allies'

Below: The Red Baron landing his Fokker Triplane

The last flight of a great airman – Baron Manfred von Richthofen

Sailly-Le-Sec

FRONT LINE

East Wind

Vaux-Sur-Somme

R. Somme

Somme

von Richthofen's route from Cappy

Vaire-Sous-Corbie

N

FRONT LINE

LE HAMEL

0 mlle ½

Lt. May's route   Capt. Brown's route

4 · THE LEADING ACES

During the early morning of 1 July 1916 when the shelling reached its climax the British infantry rose from their trenches and advanced towards the German positions. Machine guns (which had forced both sides to adopt trench warfare), began their hammering and the slowly advancing lines of khaki were moved down. Other groups and lines of men took their places and they too were slaughtered; then the reserves, company after company, battalion after battalion until there were no more and the chattering ceased. For this was the first day of the Battle of the Somme when Britain and her Empire lost 60,000 dead, the flower of her youth and manhood. The soldier-poet Wilfred Owen was moved to write:

What passing-bells for these who die as cattle?
– Only the monstrous anger of the guns.
Only the stuttering rifles' rapid rattle
Can patter out their hasty orisons*

For the airmen it was different. And how happily different is perhaps best described by John Magee, an Anglo-American airman-poet of a later war against the same foe, who wrote:

Sunward I've climbed and joined the tumbling mirth
Of sun-split clouds – and done a hundred things
You have not dreamed of – wheeled and soared and swung
High in the sunlit silence.†

The title 'Ace' originated in France and was given to any pilot who scored five or more confirmed victories in aerial combat. To earn a similar title in Germany a pilot had to shoot down ten aeroplanes, but in the Second War five became the accepted number. During the Battle of Britain

* Wilfred Owen, 'Anthem for Doomed Youth'.
† John Magee, 'High Flight'.

German Air Force's Ernst Udet *(right)* and his French counterpart René Fonck, in his Spad *(below)*

fighter pilots with five confirmed victories were considered for the award of the Distinguished Flying Cross.

The French grouped their stars together in a system of ace units, the

France's Georges Guynemer

dramatic quality, but because they took people's minds off the horrors of the ground war.

France and Germany chose to give great publicity to the deeds of their fighting pilots and to make them national heroes; in their own lands René Fonck, Georges Guynemer and Charles Nungesser of France, and Richthofen, Udet, Voss and Boelcke of Germany were idolized. When they died, as many did, they were mourned by their nations.

The leading aces fell into two categories: they were either leaders or loners. Albert Ball of Britain, forty-four victories, Georges Guynemer of France, fifty-four, and Billy Bishop of Canada, seventy-two, were all lone wolves who would rather hunt alone than with the pack. They did not possess the temperament to lead. They fought emotionally, from the heart, seldom weighing the odds against them, and depending on flying skills and marksmanship to destroy their enemies. They usually waited in the sun until a formation appeared below and then, exploiting speed and surprise to the full, swooped, hawk-like, on their opponents. Such tactics could be used only by individuals, because even a small formation of scouts could never stay together in such fast manoeuvres. They would have found their styles seriously handicapped had they flown as patrol leaders. Because they fought individually they never developed leadership qualities.

The great fighter leader, on the other hand, had a high sense of duty, was unselfish about his personal claims, and during the fight his pilots knew he would watch over them and bring them home. He studied the ever-changing developments in his craft and took great pains to pass on his knowledge to others. If he was allowed authority and freedom of action he made the most of it to plan and lead his squadron or wing on offensive patrols, and thus his character and ability influenced the pattern of air fighting. Both by precept and example the greater fighter leader inspired his pilots.

The lion-hearted Albert Ball

By shooting down eight aeroplanes in six days Ball's score climbed at about the same rate as that of the frail Guynemer, and there was a certain rivalry between these two great pilots that became more intense as their scores neared the half-century mark. Both men were excellent marksmen and contemptuous of heavy odds, but Guynemer took more risks than Ball and several times only a kindly providence saved him from destruction. His famous Spad, *Le Vieux Chartes*, was sometimes riddled with bullets, but such was his hatred of the Germans that he took scant notice of his comrades' advice for more caution. When, inevitably, he was reported

most celebrated of which were the five *escadrilles* of the *Cigognes* group, so named because each unit had a stork painted on the fuselage, the details of which varied between the units. It was indeed an honour to be posted to one of these *Cigognes* squadrons, but the British considered that the 'non-Ace' squadrons would have lower morale than the elite units and did not transfer such pilots to special units.

The aces were 'real fighting men' whom people identified and discussed. They were seen as the defenders of the people and, as the war progressed, their exploits were widely followed, not only for their missing no trace was ever found of Guynemer or his Spad, and later the Germans stated that both his grave and the wrecked Spad had been obliterated by British shelling. The children of France turned his death into a fairy story when they said he flew so high he could not come down again.

Unlike the other contestants, the British did not publicize the deeds of their outstanding airmen (during the Battle of Britain Douglas Bader was referred to as 'a legless airman'), but citations and decorations gave some indication of pilots' achievements and when Ball received considerable publicity in French newspapers it was immediately copied by the British press. Thus, Albert Ball was the first British scout pilot to become well known. He was brought down in the late spring of 1917 by a machine gun mounted on the tower of a church.

Billy Bishop was awarded the Victoria Cross for his action on 2 June 1917, when single-handed he attacked a German airfield at dawn

Canada's Billy Bishop in his Nieuport 17 Scout

just as the aeroplanes were being wheeled out. He destroyed three German machines which took off to attack him, strafed others on the ground and brought his bullet-scarred Nieuport Scout safely back to his own airfield. Later Bishop commanded 85 Squadron in France, but he always preferred to fly alone and in one period of twelve days shot down no less than twenty-five German aeroplanes.

The RFC's two outstanding air fighters were James McCudden and Mick Mannock. McCudden scored fifty-seven victories and Mannock seventy-three, and there can be little doubt that Mannock was the more gifted patrol leader and teacher. Mannock's fine score was slightly bettered by the great French air fighter René Fonck's seventy-five victories. He fought for the last two years of the war and was only once hit by an enemy bullet. If one is trying to decide which of the two was the greater, one must remember that from the first Battle of the Somme, in 1916, the Germans realized that Britain and not France was the power they must defeat in the air, and that for the remainder of the

war their crack squadrons were deployed against the RFC, so it was their squadrons who saw the most severe fighting. Richthofen's eighty victories were achieved against British aviators. It is for this reason that I consider Mannock a greater air fighter than René Fonck.

The first units of the American Air Service were not in action until the spring of 1918, although a great number of American volunteers had for long served with Allied squadrons, notably the famous *Escadrille Lafayette*. No US scout pilot's record compared with those of Mannock or Fonck, and their top scorer was Captain Eddie Rickenbacker, who shot down twenty-six aeroplanes during the last eight months of the war.

The modest Oswald Boelcke was one of the greatest air fighters. He set a fine example, and his practices were followed long after his death. Boelcke was killed, however, before the zenith of air fighting, and his achievements were eventually overshadowed by those of Richthofen.

Who was the greater air fighter: Richthofen, respected by his pilots, or Mannock, revered by his pilots? Their

Eddie Rickenbacker of the United States in his Spad

the faster scouts. But Richthofen did not regard fighting in the air as a sport; it was a very serious affair, where a calculating leader tried to destroy the enemy's reconnaissance aeroplanes, which did far more damage than the scouts. There can be no doubt that the tactics fashioned by the wily and highly elusive Richthofen were perfectly suited to the conditions under which he fought. When a few weeks after his death another leader, Hermann Göring, adopted more aggressive tactics, JGI was fought to such destruction that it was temporarily withdrawn from the battle. In my opinion, Richthofen's great achievements over a long period of operational service rank him as the greatest air fighter of the First War.

Mick Mannock – gifted patrol leader

personal scores were separated by only a small margin. Both men were good scout pilots and proved leaders. Mannock's two tours in France lasted some thirteen months, while Richthofen fought first as an observer and then for more than two years as a pilot with hardly a break, suffering a head wound from which he had not fully recovered when he was killed. For a long time Richthofen's Circus was the fighting spearhead of the German Air Force.

Mannock invariably patrolled over enemy territory, while Richthofen usually fought over his own ground. Here were two different air fighting roles, the one offensive, the other defensive. Mannock's tactics were to flush, stalk and kill his opponents, and since in his heyday the RFC outnumbered the German Air Service the odds were that he would not be surprised continually by superior enemy forces. By patrolling and fighting offensively he could exploit the inherent qualities of his scouts, speed and surprise, to the full. However, a single bullet in a vulnerable part of his

machine would mean, at best, a prison camp until the end of the war.

Because most of his victims fell on the German side of the lines, some of Richthofen's critics have asserted that he was a cautious fighter and not in Mannock's class. We must remember, however, that for the greater part of the war on the Western Front the German Army was on the defensive, and those units of the German Air Service deployed behind that Army were employed in an ancillary and similar defensive role. Richthofen did not govern the strategy of the war; on the contrary, he was a junior officer whose duty, because of the very nature of the air war and the fact that the German Air Service was heavily outnumbered by the Allies, was to inflict the maximum number of casualties on the Allies with the minimum risk and losses to his own units. In this he succeeded admirably.

Some writers have belittled Richthofen's deeds because he shot down a considerable number of our two-seaters when in their opinion it would have been far more sporting to attack

PART II
BETWEEN THE WARS

5 · SPAIN: THE PROVING GROUND

The Spanish Civil War began in the summer of 1936, and, although the Great Powers had agreed to a policy of non-intervention, Italy and Germany soon supported Franco. Air support for the Republicans was provided almost exclusively by Russian units under the command of Russian officers. Realizing that such a limited conflict would provide an ideal proving ground for his Luftwaffe, Göring ordered some Junkers 52 bomber-transports and a handful of Heinkel 51 biplane fighters to be flown to Spain

Left: The Messerschmitt was blooded in Spain in 1938

Below: Menace of ground targets: the accurate Ju 87 dive bomber

by volunteer pilots. This assistance was soon increased by the formation of a tactical air force, known as the Condor Legion, which consisted of bomber, fighter, ground-attack and reconnaissance squadrons, together with supporting anti-aircraft, communications, medical and supply units, all of which were highly mobile and could be moved rapidly from airfield to airfield. Wolfram von Richthofen, a relative of 'The Red Knight', was the Legion's chief of staff, and the driving force behind some of its highly successful operations.

As the war progressed better aeroplanes arrived from Germany, including the famous Junkers 87 ('Stuka') dive-bomber, whose screaming stoop terrorized all and sundry until

its successful operational life was cut short by Fighter Command a few years later. The secret of this two-seater was plain. Its dive-brakes allowed it to dive steeply at a steady speed of about 350 m.p.h., the two 500-kilo, or four 250-kilo, bombs being released so accurately, some 3,000 feet above the target, that a good pilot could get them within twenty or thirty yards of the aiming point. The Stuka carried two fixed forward guns and one free gun firing to the rear. Navigation and target identification were easier than in a single-seater because there were two pairs of eyes. Characteristic Teutonic thoroughness specified that the Stuka should carry a siren which delivered an ear-piercing shriek during the

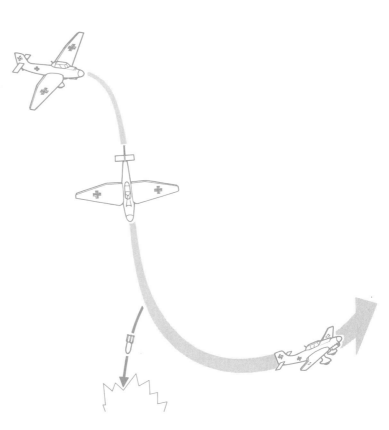

steep dive. Whenever there was little air opposition it was a formidable and precise weapon.

Richthofen, promoted to command the Condor Legion, made sure that the efforts of his airmen were closely integrated with infantry attacks. Some few minutes before an infantry attack went in a dozen twin-engined Heinkel 111 bombers attacked enemy ground positions while some twenty fighters circled overhead. Each 'vic' of three bombers made three separate attacks, while two squadrons of dive-bombers, flying in a loose echelon formation, cruised serenely on the flanks of the battle waiting for the smoke and debris to clear. The Stukas peeled off in rapid succession, plunged from the sky, released their bombs, pulled out and climbed and circled in line astern to repeat the treatment, except that on the next attack they strafed with machine guns. So, in less than half an hour, the long line of Stukas rose and fell a dozen times and, appropriately, the Spaniards called them *La Cadena* (the chain).

Immediately after this softening-up process the tanks and infantry began

their advance, supported by a few loose formations of fighter-bombers, which flew a few hundred feet above the battlefield and pounced on such items of enemy hardware that had survived the previous bombing. Whenever any pockets of enemy resistance were reported to Richthofen's control post more fighter-bombers, or Stukas, were ordered to the scene to quell the opposition, while overhead the fighters continued their protective patrols. And so it was until the day was won, and the standard of Nationalist Spain hoisted over the field of battle.

Sometimes German bombers attacked Spanish harbours to prevent the landing of supplies, and important bridges to hinder transports and troops. One of these bridges was near the small town of Guernica and on 10 April 1937 the bombers tried to take out the bridge. Unfortunately the leading bombers, with inexperienced crews and primitive bomb sights, missed the bridge and hit the town, which, being market day, was full of people. Other bombers dropped their loads on the burning, smoking wooden buildings, and when the

attack was over the bridge was left untouched, the town destroyed and more than a thousand Basques were killed.

Within hours of the attack several press correspondents arrived in Guernica and soon the world's newspapers carried banner headlines: 'Terror Bombing', 'Open Town Guernica Destroyed by Boche Planes' and 'German Brutality and Barbarism'; and Picasso, then in Paris and previously unpolitical, began his famous painting about the brutality of war. It was at this time that the young Adolf Galland joined the Condor Legion and began his distinguished fighting career that would take him to the top of the German Fighter Arm and admit him to the councils and confidences of Göring and Adolf Hitler. 'Dolfo', whom the authors have known for a long time and who is a truthful man, told us that Guernica had been bombed in error, 'a mistake', but pointed out that similar bombing mistakes were made several times by both sides in the Second War.

In little more than a year the future 'General of Fighters' flew some 300 ground attack missions in Heinkel 51 biplanes and although his aeroplane was shot-up on several occasions by ground fire, he saw little air combat, because Republican fighters were engaged farther afield by the formidable Messerschmitt 109B, superior to all else in Spanish skies and the forerunner of a long series of great fighters from the same stable. This angular German fighter made its debut a few weeks before the British Hawker Hurricane, and some months before its great Second War antagonist, the Supermarine Spitfire. These three cabin-monoplanes marked the end of the long reign of the biplane fighter.

Galland's tour of duty in Spain ended in the summer of 1938, just as the squadron he commanded was about to receive Messerschmitt 109s. He was sorry to leave Spain, for he hoped to stay and see some real fighting in his new Messerschmitt. Like Manfred von Richthofen, Galland was a keen hunter, and he regarded the strafing and bombing of ground tar-

Gentlemen of the Condor Legion

Close support in Spain

gets as a sort of poaching process where his weapons were not decently and cleanly used: he longed to be a fighter pilot where the true hunter could express his skill and judgement. Regretfully he handed over to the slim, immaculate and keenly intelligent Werner Mölders, twenty-five years old and a devout Catholic, who, fully exploiting the superiority of his Messerschmitt, destroyed fourteen Republican aeroplanes in the few remaining months of the Civil War and so became the Condor Legion's top scorer in Spain.

One of the most important lessons from the air fighting of the Kaiser's War was that the best formation for combat was the open, abreast style, with a spacing of fifty or sixty yards between each scout, so that pilots could keep station with each other, fly near their leader without risk of collision, and search the surrounding sky against the possibility of surprise attack. This formula, which was learned by both British and German pilots under the constant and unforgiving hammer of battle, was recorded in a thousand memoirs and memoranda; but was seemingly lost with the cease-fire, for when the Messerschmitts began to fight in Spain they flew in a close wing-tip to wing-tip formation totally unsuited for combat because of the lack of manoeuvring space and the absence of cross-cover.

Messerschmitt 109 pilots, soon realizing that their close formations were too vulnerable, quickly adopted a far better style of fighting, and their perfect fighter formation – for it has survived into the jet age – was based upon the *rotte*, which has the element of two fighters. Some 200 yards separated a pair of fighters, and the chief responsibility of number two, or wingman, was to guard his leader from attack; meanwhile the leader navigated and covered his wingman. The *schwarme* of four fighters simply consisted of two pairs and was exactly the same abreast pattern as that devised by Oswald Boelcke long ago, except that the spacing between aeroplanes was increased from about sixty yards, the turning radius of Boelcke's Albatros, to some 200 yards, the turning radius of a Messerschmitt 109.

Flying in three *schwarme* a Messerschmitt squadron stretched some one and a half miles across the sky, and each *schwarme* flew at varying heights, so that the starboard group, deployed down-sun from the leader, could search into the sun and guard the rest from surprise attack. These

Product of Werner Mölders fertile mind: a *Schwarme* of Messerschmitts.

staggered heights gave cross-cover in all directions, and also made the fighters far less conspicuous in the sky.

The Messerschmitts carried radio telephones and, for the first time, fighter pilots could receive and transmit clear and distinct speech. When he manoeuvred before attacking, Mölders could keep his team fully in the picture – a tremendous improvement over the previous methods when a leader signalled his intentions by rocking his wings or firing coloured lights. Up until then air fighting had been inarticulate. In Spain it became articulate. This made for better teamwork in the air, and closer control from the ground. For the air fighters it was a big step forward.

Victory for Franco ended the Spanish Civil War, and the Condor Legion returned to Germany where the lessons it had learned were carefully studied. In Spain, for the first time in history, an army and an air force had fought to a joint air–ground plan, where centralized control gave

the Condor Legion such flexibility that it was able to concentrate its striking power and paralyse the opposing ground forces. Richthofen, the driving force, had fashioned his command into a highly successful tactical air force and, once back in Berlin, he argued his case for more tactical air forces to fight, not in air battles, but jointly with the ground forces in air–ground operations. He was opposed by those high-ranking officers of the Luftwaffe who foresaw that more tactical air forces would inevitably mean less resources for the strategic bomber force, but Richthofen so won the day that *Luftflotten* were formed, consisting of bomber, reconnaissance, fighter and ground-attack squadrons. Strategic bombing came to be regarded as a short-term and often short-range affair.

For, influenced by their successes in Spain, the German concept of modern war was for their bombers to attack enemy airfields and industrial centres as the immediate prelude to air–ground operation, which would consist of great masses of armour rolling deeply into enemy territory,

supported by fighters to cope with the remnants of an opposing air force. More fighters would scout ahead of, and on the flanks of, the armoured columns. Dive-bombers would reduce the ground opposition and attack all road and rail communications while terrorizing the civilian population. Fighter-bombers would quarter and harass the surrounding countryside, taking out practically anything that dared to move, while paratroops would secure the flanks. And all these violent, irresistible thrusts would be actively supported by quislings and a fifth column. This was the new type of mechanized war, and it was known by a new and appropriate name – *Blitzkrieg* or Lightning War.

Blitzkrieg, that terrible combination of tactical air power and thrusting panzer columns, was soon to blast into Poland, and, a few months later, in the spring of 1940, to conquer Europe. In the following year it was to take the Germans to the gates of Moscow.

We in the West had nothing to stand up against it.

6 · FIGHTER COMMAND'S TEXTBOOK ATTACKS

While the enemy's Fighter Arm was getting its act together in Spain the Royal Air Force's fighter squadrons flew in tight vics of three, wing-tip to wing-tip. This disgraceful lack of modern fighter tactics cost many young lives as Hugh Dundas relates:

In eight days, 616 Squadron lost five pilots killed or missing and five others wounded and in hospital. About 50 per cent of the pilots who had flown down from Leconfield had gone. But still the remnants fought on, greatly inspired by the courage and leadership of Denis Gillam, who now showed the fiery and utterly fearless

1940 formation! The Royal Air Force soon learnt the hard way

character which was to make him one of the most distinguished RAF officers of the war. But on 2 September he too was shot down and injured. It was the final, knock-out blow. Without him the squadron was incapable of continuing the fight. And so, exactly fourteen days after our carefree and confident departure from Leconfield, 616 Squadron – what was left of it – was taken out of the line to re-form at Coltishall, near Norwich. To set against its losses, the squadron claimed sixteen enemy aircraft definitely destroyed, six probably destroyed, fifteen damaged. Of these Gillam had personally destroyed seven and damaged three.*

I [Johnnie Johnson] joined 616 Squadron at Coltishall, but we soon moved to Kirton-in-Lindsey, a few miles north of Lincoln. Here Billy Burton, a regular officer and a Cranwell Sword of Honour man, set about getting a demoralized outfit into shape.

One crisp autumn morning Burton called us together and said that in a few minutes we would take off in vics of three, line abreast, climb in sections line astern to 30,000 feet, dive to

*Hugh Dundas, *Flying Start* (Stanley Paul, London, 1988).

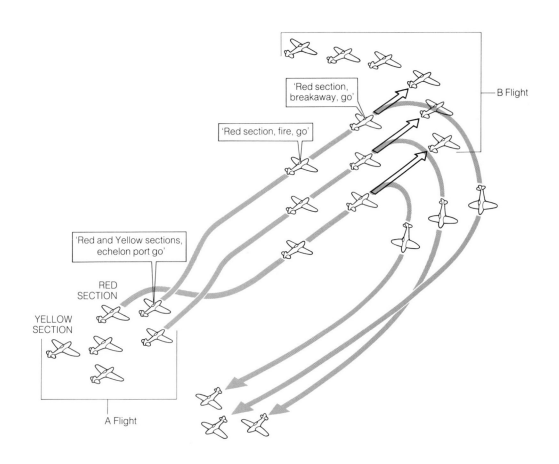

20,000 feet where A Flight would practise 'Fighter Command Attack Number Five' against B Flight, and then the roles would be reversed with B Flight attacking the fake bombers of A Flight.

Someone asked about other Fighter Command Attacks, and the CO explained there were six, published in the spring of 1939, all based on close vics of Spitfires attacking enemy bomber formations. Somewhere, he said, there was an official manual with diagrams and he would try and get a copy for the Squadron.

For the formation take-off Burton did not use full throttle – so that the rest of us had some power in hand and it seemed to me that we barely cleared the boundary hedge. After we had retracted our undercarriages and reduced revs Burton said, 'Sections line astern, go,' and we fell into our tight climbing formation and arced towards the east coast. The climb on that sunny morning was uneventful except for the odd command from a section leader exhorting a wingman to 'get in closer!' I was flying Yellow Two to Ken Holden and my wing-tip

Peacetime training – vic of three Spitfires

was inside and slightly behind his wing-tip. All my attention was concentrated on keeping this immaculate station; I could not look behind or to my starboard side even for a second.

At 30,000 feet B Flight, representing the bombers, broke away and dived to 20,000 feet and flew in a neat vic formation while the six Spitfires of A Flight manoeuvred into a position about half a mile behind. The CO ordered, 'Red and Yellow Sections, echelon port, go,' and still flying close together we gradually overtook the bombers. Burton said he would attack the third bomber from the port flank leaving Red Two and Red Three to engage their opposite numbers. The manual said that all three Spitfires were to open fire together and were to continue to fire until the leader ordered the breakaway, so Burton obeyed the book and at a range of 400 yards or so said, 'Red Section, fire, go.' Shortly afterwards, at about 220 yards, he said, 'Red Section, breakaway, go', and down they went to reform and attack again; then we of Yellow Section made our attack and, in theory, would have been followed by Blue and Green Sections.

This squadron practice took place

on the morning of 15 September 1940 at about the same time as a big force of German bombers, supported by some 700 fighters, attacked London. They were opposed by twenty-three squadrons of Fighter Command most of which flew in the tight vics of three – sitting ducks for the lively, roaming Messerschmitts in their excellent finger-fours. Even the forward-thinking Douglas Bader still flew wing-tip to wing-tip in his 'Big Wing' on this fateful day, but his wingman, Denis Crowley-Milling, told me that Bader completely ignored the textbook attacks and simply dived straight into the midst of the enemy formations.

Fortunately, some able leaders, especially 'Sailor' Malan, took matters into their own hands and began to fly in a new line astern pattern, the last man in each section being responsible for 'weaving' – swerving from side to side – so as to keep a good look-out to the rear. The 'weavers' were usually the first to go.

It was not until the spring of the following year, 1941, that we caught up tactically with the Luftwaffe when we copied their loose finger-fours. It had taken Fighter Command a long and expensive time to re-learn the lessons of Oswald Boelcke.

PART III
THE SECOND WORLD WAR

7 · THE NORWEGIAN CAMPAIGN: THE SINKING OF *GLORIOUS*

In early 1940 Flight Lieutenant P.G. 'Jamie' Jameson (Air Commodore P. G. Jameson), a tough, wiry New Zealander, was a flight commander on 46 Squadron and here is his account of the loss of *Glorious*.

In February 1939 we were re-equipped with Hawker Hurricanes and although we were sad to see our lovely Gloucester Gauntlet biplanes go, we knew that war against Germany was inevitable and it was a great relief to get the much more business-like Hurricanes with their greater speed, increased fire-power and a vast improvement in the blind flying instruments.

We were based at Digby, Lincolnshire, and our main role was defence of the shipping convoys moving along our east coast. During this time Squadron Leader 'Bing' Cross (Air Chief Marshal Sir Kenneth Cross) took over command of the squadron and I was one of his two flight commanders. Bing was conscientious, enthusiastic and a keen sportsman, playing rugby for the Harlequins and the Royal Air Force.

In April 1940, when the Germans had invaded and captured the southern half of Norway, it was decided to send our squadron and 263 (Gladiator) Squadron to the Narvik area in the north of that country. The distance was beyond the range of our fighters and we were to be taken there in the aircraft carrier HMS *Glorious*.

Our wooden propellers were replaced by three-bladed, metal, variable pitch ones so we had plenty of acceleration from the short (262 yards) flight-deck of *Glorious*; but they were much heavier than the

wooden propellers, which made our Hurricanes so nose heavy that we could not apply full brake when landing.

When all was ready we flew to Abbotsinch, an airfield near Glasgow, and taxied our Hurricanes across fields and lanes until we arrived at a jetty on the Clyde, where they were loaded on to barges for the twenty-mile journey to *Glorious*. The barges stopped alongside the carrier, the wings were removed and the whole Hurricane hoisted aboard. Later at sea we found that the wing bolts which fasten the wings to the fuselage were not on board which meant that our Hurricanes could not be flown. However, when the ship's engineers heard about this disaster they told us not to worry because if we sent a sample to their workshops they would make new ones – which they did.

Bing Cross knew very little about the Royal Navy except for inter-Service rugby games at Twickenham.

My immediate boss was J. B. Heath, Commander (Flying) of *Glorious*, who welcomed me on board and said come and meet the Captain. D'Oyly-Hughes was a very formidable man. We got no welcome from him. He looked at me and nodded. He never asked to meet the other pilots so I thought, well, this is the way they go on in the Navy.*

None of us was aware (at this time) of the unhappy relationship between the Commander (Flying) and his unstable bellicose Captain which was to bring about an immense tragedy in all our lives.

We steamed northwards, parallel with the Norwegian coast and crossed the Arctic Circle into the 'Land of the Midnight Sun'. An airfield was being built specially for us at a place called Skaanland, about

seventy miles north of Narvik and not far from Tromso. Unfortunately, because of heavy rain and melting ice, the runway was not firm enough and as *Glorious* was getting short of fuel we had to steam all the way back to Scapa Flow in the Orkneys to refuel.

On our return to the Arctic we heard that the airfield was ready to accept us. There was great excitement. *Glorious*, flat out, was making 30 knots! So far as I knew, no modern high-speed fighter had ever taken off from the deck of an aircraft carrier. The squadron commander was first off. I couldn't help wondering how he felt when he was running his engine up on the brakes, and then accelerating along the tiny deck. Would he get flying speed in time? On leaving the front end of the flight-deck his Hurricane sank momentarily, but then climbed away merrily, and I could breathe again.

The runway at Skaanland consisted of 700 yards of steel-meshed *Sommerfelt* tracking laid on bare earth. Bing came into land, but the ground was too soft. The wheels sank into the mud in spite of the steel mesh and the aircraft tipped over on to its nose. The next two landed perfectly but Flight Lieutenant Stewart's also tipped on its nose. Bing sprang back into his Hurricane, which had a serviceable radio, and instructed me to take the remaining Hurricanes to Bardufoss, an airfield about twenty-five miles away. This airfield had a very short, solid earth runway. We all got down safely, except for one pilot who overshot the end of the runway and ran a few yards into the heather-like scrub. However, when the aircraft had been towed out

* John Winton, *Carrier Glorious* (Leo Cooper in association with Secker & Warburg, London, 1986), p. 133.

and inspected it was found to be fully operational. Our main role at this stage was the air defence of the whole area – the Allied headquarters at Harstad, the airfield, the supply ships and the Royal Navy, and the ground troops during their coming assault on Narvik, which was held by the Germans.

On 28 May 1940 I was told that German transport aircraft were unloading troops in one of the fjords to the south of Narvik. I took off and led my section up several fjords to the south but did not sight the transports. Then we investigated Rombaks Fjord which runs inland from Narvik along the railway line to Sweden. We spotted two enormous six-engined flying boats hidden in a small cove and protected by high cliffs on three sides of the cove. To strafe the flying boats we had to dive steeply down the side of one cliff, firing as we went, and then make a steep turn along the fjord to avoid the cliff on the other side. We carried out four attacks, experiencing some ineffective anti-aircraft fire. When we left, at about six in the evening, both flying boats were blazing merrily and sinking.

Six hours later I took off with Pilot Officer Drummond, my number two, to patrol Narvik where he spotted three bombers. I could not see them so I told him to lead and soon I saw the enemy aircraft, two Heinkel 111s and one Junkers 88, flying in open line astern. Drummond gradually moved away to my left, apparently heading for the leading aircraft. I ordered him into line astern, but evidently he did not hear me. I attacked the rearmost bomber by climbing up under his tail and opening fire. There was a bright flash and my windscreen became obscured by oil. On breaking away I could see black smoke coming from his starboard engine. I approached again from the rear, and he jettisoned his bombs. There was no return fire so I assumed I had knocked out the rear gunner during the previous attack. I fired another burst and the starboard engine began to burn, the fire gradually spreading to the fuselage. Just before the

machine crashed on the cliff of Skjiron Fjord some of the crew jumped by parachute and landed in the fjord. Drummond also shot his target down, but unfortunately his Hurricane was hit by return fire and he had to bail out, and was picked up by the destroyer *Firedrake*.

The German invasion of France and the Low Countries knocked the bottom out of our mission and we were ordered to destroy our Hurricanes and get out of Norway. Sometime before we left the UK a combined team from the Fleet Air Arm and the Royal Air Force had carried out trials to see if Hurricanes could land on an aircraft carrier and had concluded that they could not. Hence the order to destroy our Hurricanes.

Bing thought we should try and save our precious fighters, which we knew were desperately needed in the UK, and flew in a Walrus to the two carriers, *Glorious* and *Ark Royal*. The latter's lifts were too small for Hurricanes so arrangements were made with D'Oyly-Hughes who said *Glorious* would work up to full speed to receive them.

We agreed that I would lead the first section of three Hurricanes back to the carrier. Somehow we had to get rid of the nose heaviness caused by the metal propeller so that we could slam on full brake. I carried out some trials at Bardufoss and found that a fourteen pound sandbag strapped in the fuselage, right down at the tail end, allowed the use of full brake.

We took off in the twilight of the Arctic night and were navigated out to the carriers by a Swordfish from *Glorious*. They were about 150 miles out from the Norwegian coast and looked quite impressive with their four escorting destroyers fussing round them. D'Oyly-Hughes had kept his word, and the old ship probably had not gone as fast since her speed trials when she was launched in 1916.

Despite the ships' size their flight-decks looked pathetically small. Lilliputian was the description that sprang to mind. *Glorious*'s grey deck reminded me of the back of an elephant, particularly as the flight-deck

had a round-down at the stern which was moving up and down like a cantering elephant's backside! We had to touch down as near the top of the heaving rump as possible to minimize the chance of over-shooting and crashing on to the fo'castle. (The flight-deck did not go right up to the bow of the ship.) There was quite a swell on and *Glorious* was at full tilt – about 30 knots – which meant that the landing spot was moving up and down at an alarming rate! Before taking off from Bardufoss I had decided that the only way to find out if it was possible to land on *Glorious* was to commit myself completely to the landing. If I got three-quarters of the way along the deck and then realized that I was not going to stop in time, it would be too late to take off again anyway!

While we were waiting for the signal to land Sergeant Taylor said his engine was running very rough and that he would have to land immediately. He made a perfect landing.

I came in on the approach at just above stalling speed, feeling my way because the sandbag away down in the tail was affecting the flying characteristic of the aeroplane. Suddenly, as I was getting near the touchdown point, the Hurricane dropped rapidly and it seemed she was trying to land on the quarterdeck below the flight-deck! I slammed on full throttle and that beautiful, lovely Rolls-Royce Merlin engine never faltered. It dragged us up on to the flight-deck and the Hurricane and I stopped about a quarter of the way along it. When the wind flowing along the deck gets to the run-down it follows the down-turn of the deck and causes a terrific down-draught. If you get too low on the approach and are caught in it you are pushed down, and if you have not got mighty engine power and quick reactions – that's it. Of course, the Fleet Air Arm pilots were trained to cope with this by doing a

End of a mission: sinking of HMS *Glorious* off Norway 1940

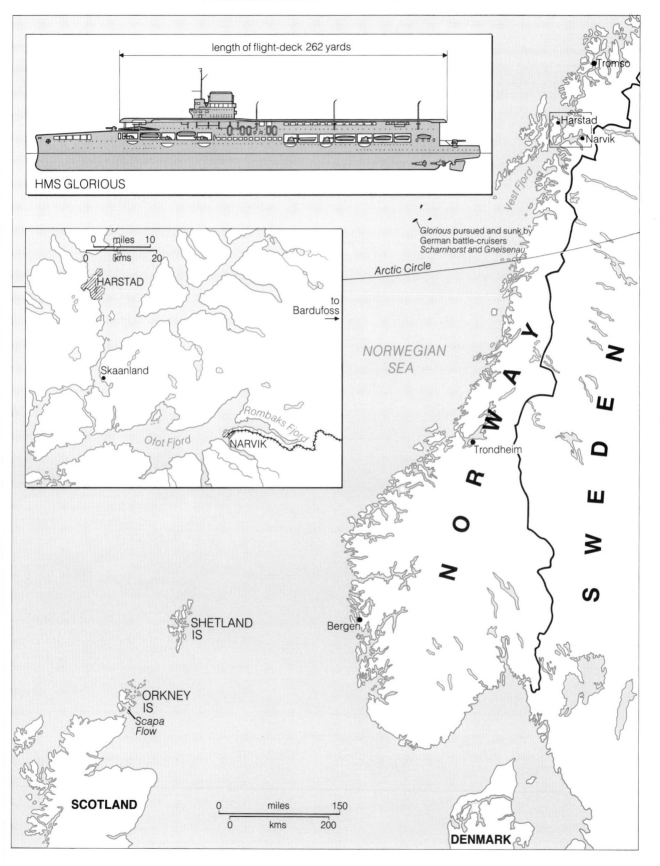

length of flight-deck 262 yards

HMS GLORIOUS

0   miles   10

0   kms   20

HARSTAD

to
Bardufoss →

Skaanland

Rombaks Fjord

Ofot Fjord

NARVIK

Tromso

Vest Fjord

Harstad

Narvik

Glorious pursued and sunk by
German battle-cruisers
Scharnhorst and *Gneisenau*

Arctic Circle

NORWEGIAN
SEA

Trondheim

N
O
R
W
A
Y

S
W
E
D
E
N

SHETLAND
IS

Bergen

ORKNEY
IS

*Scapa
Flow*

SCOTLAND

0   miles   150

0   kms   200

DENMARK

fairly steep approach, thereby keeping above the down-draught. Anyway all three of us managed to get down all right and no one used more than three-quarters of the deck.

When our Hurricanes were snugly stowed away in the hangar below, I went up to the radio cabin and asked the radio officer to send a signal to Bing at Bardufoss to let him know we had landed safely and giving him advice on the approach etc. As I was writing out the message the Captain strode in and I thought he was going to congratulate us for being the first modern fighters to land on a carrier. Instead, he snarled that we had 'landed before his ship was ready'. I apologized and explained about Taylor's engine, but he made no reply and left the cabin. For some reason or other Bing never received my message; perhaps the Captain insisted on radio silence in case the transmissions were picked up by the enemy, so giving away the position of the ships.

Whilst in the radio cabin I was handed a message from the Admiral, which had been flashed from *Ark Royal* by signalling lamp He congratulated us and added something to the effect that it was a great day for the Royal Navy. I think he felt that our efforts might help to speed up the re-equipment of Fleet Air Arm with more

The last Gladiator of 263 Squadron

modern aircraft. Early the next morning ten Gladiators of 'Baldy' Donaldson's 263 Squadron, followed by Bing Cross leading seven Hurricanes, all landed safely on *Glorious*. Squadron Leader Cross reported to the mercurial D'Oyly-Hughes who, true to form, complained that the RAF fighters had taken a long time to get down! We noticed the absence of J. B. Heath the Commander (Flying) and was told, 'The Captain has put him ashore!'*

The Hurricane pilots were very tired and after a breakfast of bacon and eggs and cocoa both Cross and Jameson found berths and fell asleep. However, unbeknown to the airmen, and for that matter most of the ship's company, at about 2.25 a.m. Commander Le Geyt in *Diana* noticed a signalling lamp in *Glorious* calling up *Ark Royal* . . . It was a request from *Glorious*, as Le Geyt recalled, 'for permission to part company and proceed ahead to Scapa Flow for the purpose of making preparations for impending courts-martial. The request was approved!'*

Thus *Glorious*, escorted by two destroyers, *Acasta* and *Ardent*, left the protection of *Ark Royal* and her screen of destroyers so that her Captain's persecution mania against his Commander (Flying) could be assuaged.

Bing Cross woke up before his flight commander and visited the chart room where he found they were about 200 miles from the Norwegian coast. He was told their chief danger was from submarines but that no sub could harm them at their present speed of 17 knots. On their previous crossing to Norway the carrier's own Swordfish had patrolled ahead and on the flanks of *Glorious*. Now, on this return journey there were no such flights and the flight-deck was deserted. Jamie's narrative continues:

My rest was rudely interrupted by a cacophony of sound outside the cabin door. I opened the door and saw heavy shells being winched to the quarterdeck. I said to a rating, 'What's going on? Is it another practice?'

'No sir. We're being chased by two German battle-cruisers, *Scharnhorst* and *Gneisenau*.'

This, I thought, is very bad news. I made my way to the quarterdeck and saw the two enemy battle cruisers astern, one either side, six or seven miles away, and at an angle to *Glorious* of about forty-five degrees. Swordfish amphibians were on board and I wondered why reconnaissance

flights had not been flown to spot the battle-cruisers miles away and so prevent this ghastly encounter.

I saw the flashes of the first salvo fired at the doomed *Glorious* whose guns did not have the range to fire back. Perhaps three minutes elapsed before this salvo hit the sea about twenty yards away. The second salvo hit the flight-deck setting fire to the Swordfish. I saw Bing at his abandon ship station on the quarterdeck. He later told me that he had realized he was watching a full-scale naval action and, with future staff college exercises in mind, thought it would be good experience if he watched the conduct of the battle from the bridge!

Bing walked to the flight-deck and another salvo hit the carrier on the starboard side, destroying the very stairs from which he had just stepped. A single round fell a few yards ahead of him. Fortunately, it didn't explode, but merely left a large hole with a raised lip through which came a wisp of smoke. Soon the German cruisers seemed to be hitting *Glorious* with about two salvoes out of every three.

The noise when the shells struck home was quite different from anything I had heard before. It was like the noise of tearing calico, but magnified a thousand times. A Fleet Air Arm pilot who had just come up from the hangar said: 'That last salvo set fire to your Hurricanes. But don't worry. We'll soon have it out.'

Glorious was burning and listing. The discipline was magnificent. I saw frantic efforts by officers and men of the Fleet Air Arm to raise their Swordfish to the flight-deck and get them armed with torpedoes. These efforts were of no avail, and about half an hour after the attack began the ship's intercommunication failed. Then the 'abandon ship' order was passed from man to man and someone said that the bridge had received a direct hit and the Captain was dead.

The abandon ship order was cancelled, but soon the original command was heard again. *Glorious* was still moving and there was a trail of

* Winton, *Carrier Glorious*.

rafts, wreckage and bodies in the wake of the ship. Bing said to a young lieutenant: 'What's the best way to get on a raft?'

'Wait till they drop a Carley float, sir. Then jump after it bloody quickly or else you'll have a long swim!'

One of the two escorting destroyers, *Ardent* and *Acasta*, put a smokescreen round *Glorious* and the firing ceased. The other destroyer attempted a torpedo attack against one of the battle-cruisers and was blown out of the water by the accurate German gunners. *Glorious* was still making way, at about 10 knots, and on board sailors were throwing water barrels and emergency rations overboard which, they hoped, would be collected by the survivors in life-boats and rafts.

I helped some sailors launch a dinghy. I was drenched by the spray, getting cold, and knew that it was a matter of minutes before the great ship went down. I made my way to the hangar to get my Mae-West which was on the tail-plane of my Hurricane. However, the water-tight doors were closed and I returned to the quarterdeck.

The smokescreen had disappeared and the battle-cruisers closed in for the kill. *Glorious* was listing badly. One side of the quarterdeck was awash. The other side was some fifteen feet above the sea and the angle was increasing all the time. On board the discipline was unbelievable, and I was greatly impressed by the excellent bearing of the sailors. There was not the slightest hint of panic. I thought the Royal Marine officers were tremendous.

By this time most of the crew had jumped overboard. I saw a small Marine about to jump into the sea and shouted to him to watch a raft tied to railings near the quarterdeck. The Marine jumped and the raft struck him on his head.

I decided it was time to go. I saw a Carley float with people in it about a mile away and decided to make for it. I took off my flying boots but, strangely, forgot to remove my tight-fitting tunic. I had a last look at the stricken ship. I think I was the last man on board. It was only half an hour since the first salvo struck.

I am a fairly strong swimmer and I headed for the Carley float, a contraption of large copper tubes with a trellis-type decking lashed to them. Bing saw me making good time with what he called my 'impeccable Pacific crawl'. When I reached the raft I thought there were already a lot of survivors on it and I asked Bing if I could come aboard.

I saw the small Marine drifting by with a large gash on his head. He was almost spent, so I slipped over the side, grabbed my Marine, a Geordie, and with help from other willing hands got him on board.

We watched the death of *Acasta*. Geyser spouts of water leaped up around her. Bursts of orange and scarlet glowed on her decks as shells hammered home. Soon she began to settle in the water, firing until her gun crews were swamped.

I did not see *Glorious* actually sink as I was sitting with my back to her. One moment she was there and the next the sea was empty except for rafts and a thousand pieces of wreckage.

The German battle-cruisers steamed by quite near to the float. Bing thought we might be picked up by the enemy so he took the squadron records from inside his Irvine jacket and threw them into the sea. But the German ships turned away and soon disappeared over the horizon. It was bitterly cold, the wind rose and waves continuously broke over the float.

We took stock of our situation. We were about a hundred miles inside the Arctic Circle and had neither food nor water. In these latitudes it was light all the time and we could only tell night because it was colder than day. It was very cold. Quietly, Bing asked me how long I thought we could survive. I said about six days and Bing thought this was a bit of an over-statement.

They were cheerful for some time. Bing and I encouraged them to sing popular songs of the day like 'Roll out the Barrel'. Our legs were in the water and soon the cold began to bite. Some men from the engine team wore only singlets and cotton slacks. Some of them began to look dazed. A small chubby cook slipped into the middle of the float and lay there, helplessly, while some of his mates tried to hold his head above water. He soon died of exposure.

Survivors of the *Glorious*: P.G. (Jamie) Jameson . . .

... and K.B.B. (Bing) Cross

During the long night nineteen men died. Shivering men removed their clothing, handed it to the lightly clad and slipped the dead into the water. I rescued one sailor who, asleep, fell over the side of the float. Another fell into the sea. I was about to go after him but Bing stopped me.

After midday the wind dropped and the sun broke through, drying and warming we survivors and instilling new life and hope. I saw an oar drifting by, retrieved it, and with some discarded shirts rigged a rough squaresail. Then from a button on my tunic I produced a tiny 'escape' compass and spirits rose when I told them I was setting course for the Faroes.

Throughout the second long night we were cold and miserable. The following morning Bing said we should use the trellis-like floor in the centre of the float as a platform. If we could cut it free it could be placed at right angles to the oval-shaped float and some men could lie on it and keep their legs out of the water. We began to unravel the many ropes that held the flooring in position. I produced my small 'escape' knife, but even so it took six hours to release the flooring. We took turns at stretching out on this makeshift platform, snatched a little sleep. We had gone nearly forty-eight hours without food or water. Our thirst was worse than our hunger. Once a seagull floated near the float and I tried to capture it, but it flew away unharmed.

We two officers were cross-examined about our position by the sailors. We knew that we were drifting down the Norwegian coast, but we told the men that we would reach the Shetlands or the Orkneys probably by tomorrow. This had the desired effect, spirits rose and bets were laid on the time of landfall.

There were some bitter disappointments. Once, three warships were seen and aeroplanes took off and circled the ships. We shouted and waved, but the aeroplanes landed alongside their parent ships, were hoisted on board and the ships steamed away. Other aeroplanes, both Royal Air Force and enemy, flew overhead but did not heed our lonely float.

We faced our third night on the float. I dozed, fitfully, and heard a splash as a man fell overboard. Willing hands stretched out to grasp his but he panicked, thrashed the water and drifted away to die. There were now only seven left on the raft.

At about three in the morning of the third day one of the sailors shouted when he spotted a small ship about three miles away. We all yelled and waved the shirt and jersey hastily ripped from the oar. Our great hopes turned to despair when we saw the ship turn away, but spirits rose again when we saw other survivors being rescued. Then it headed for the float and we wondered was it friend or foe? After our long ordeal did we face long years in prisoner of war camps?

Somebody saw the Norwegian flag fluttering from the mast. We all shouted and cheered. We were saved and amongst friends. Gentle hands lifted we seven survivors from the Carley float. Carefully we were carried below decks to the warmth of the boiler room, for none could walk, our legs being frostbitten from knees to toes. We were given mugs of steaming tea laced with whisky from the Norwegians' last half-bottle.

Our Norwegian friends took us to the Faroe Islands. One of our number died during the journey and another died on arrival, leaving five survivors out of the twenty-nine originally on the float. Altogether there were only thirty-nine survivors from the carrier and the two destroyers out of a total complement of more than 1,500. Bing and I felt very lucky.

8 · 'THE CUT OF THE SICKLE'

Blitzkrieg, Lightning War, was the basis of the aptly named 'Operation Sichelschmitt' ('The Cut of the Sickle'). It was drafted and re-drafted by a brilliant, yet unorthodox, young German general, Erich von Manstein, who proposed to drive great panzer wedges through the 'untankable' Ardennes, thrusting to the Channel and cutting the Allied forces in half. Hitler agreed von Manstein's plan and on 10 May 1940 ten panzer divisions, supported in the approved fashion by masses of fighters and dive-bombers and with medium bombers blasting targets further afield, drove westwards, thus beginning a brilliant fast-moving campaign never equalled in military history. It defeated Holland in two days, Belgium in eighteen, drove the British Army into the sea within three weeks and took another three weeks to defeat the long-famed French Army.

As the panzers rolled to the west the French and British armies moved to their battle stations in Belgium – hitherto neutral – and manned a long front line from Antwerp to the south, but there was a gap between the northern end of the heavily fortified Maginot Line and the beginning of the Allied front on the Franco-Belgium border. The elderly and out-dated French generals thought this gap, in the Ardennes, impassable for modern armies and paid scant attention to it. Thus the Allies relied on an obsolete First War strategy of holding a long meandering front, including the 'impregnable' Maginot Line manned by more than 400,000 troops.

Unlike the Germans we had only paid lip-service to Army–Air Force co-operation in the field because the Air Staff awarded the highest priorities to our offensive capability, Bomber Command, and to the defence of our industrial base, Fighter Command. Thus, direct Royal Air Force assist-ance to the BEF in France consisted of a few slow, two-seater Lysanders whose crews took photographs of enemy dispositions and plotted the fall of shells for the gunners.

Likewise there was little joint train-ing, as Gerald Strickland (Major General E.V.M. Strickland), a young cavalry officer saw it at the time:

When we got to France there was no Army–Air Force training. We were briefed about the German fighters and were told that the Royal Air Force would help us in the land battle, but they would also be en-gaged in something called the 'air battle'! This was the first time I, a regular officer, realized that something else could claim the attention of our fighters.

One morning I awoke to find the village in which my unit was billeted littered with scraps of paper. On examination, these turned out to be leaflets dropped by the enemy air force. Our morale dropped because the leaflets told us accurately of our location and strength and warned us of the bombing to come. Our morale was raised two days later when we became spectators of an aerial battle over the city of Arras when two Hurricanes shot down a German bomber. What a glorious sight and how it cheered us in the dreary round of tank maintenance and trench digging.

In May, the BEF was rushed out of its prepared positions (a hastily constructed earth and sandbag extension of the French Maginot Line) and into Belgium. Suddenly, somewhere just south of Brus-sels it all began when the air became filled with aeroplanes and they were all attacking us. We were bombed by Hein-kels, dive-bombed by Stukas, machine gunned by Messerschmitts, and during those few hectic days the only aeroplanes we saw with Royal Air Force roundels were low-flying Lysanders. Usually, these aircraft were hedge-hopping and being chased by enemy fighters. What they were supposed to be doing was and still re-mains a mystery. But now and then there was the noise of fighting high up in the sky and as we fought our rear-guard action back into France we passed crashed enemy bombers and fighters. We assumed that somewhere up above us the Royal Air Force was fighting this thing termed the 'air battle' and not allowing the Germans to have it their own way, but, as far as we were concerned, each and every day was a day of constant attack and harassment by enemy aircraft.*

So the mighty battle opened, and over the Ardennes a Luftwaffe pilot re-ported:

. . . the spectacle of a lifetime. Nose to bumper was the greatest combination of tanks – between 1,200 and 1,500 of them – yet seen in the war. Kleist's massive Armoured Group was moving forward in three blocks, one densely closed up behind the other . . . Uneasily, the panzer commanders aware of what a superb tar-get the dense, crawling columns pre-sented, gazed up to the skies; but there they saw only the reassuring black crosses of the Luftwaffe.†

Two days later von Kleist's panzers reached the Meuse and his leading elements crossed that night. The next day, 13 May, the panzers forced the river at Sedan – that ominous name which has figured in three wars be-tween France and Germany – and the shattering, devastating and demora-lizing impact of the screaming Stukas is well described by a sergeant of the 1st Panzer Division:

Three, six, nine, oh, behind them still more, and further to the right aircraft, a quick look in the binoculars – Stukas! And what we are about to see during the next twenty minutes is one of the most power-ful impressions of the war. Squadron upon squadron rise to a great height, break into line ahead and there the first machines hurtle perpendicularly down, followed by the second, third – ten, twelve

* Johnson Papers.
† A. Horne, *To Lose a Battle: France 1940* (Macmillan, London, 1969).

German armour slicing through the Low Countries and into France: May 1940

'THE CUT OF THE SICKLE'

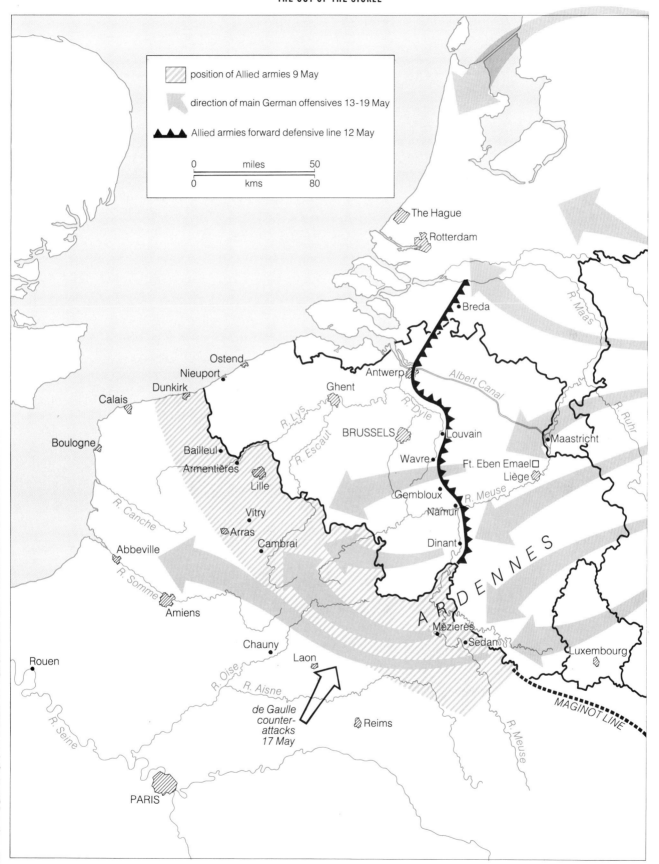

position of Allied armies 9 May

direction of main German offensives 13-19 May

Allied armies forward defensive line 12 May

| 0 | miles | 50 |
| 0 | kms | 80 |

The Hague

Rotterdam

R. Maas

Breda

Ostend

Nieuport

Dunkirk

Calais

Boulogne

Antwerp

Albert Canal

R. Maas

Ghent

R. Lys

R. Escaut

R. Dyle

BRUSSELS

Louvain

Maastricht

R. Ruhr

Bailleul

Armentières

Lille

Wavre

Ft. Eben Emael

Liège

Vitry

Arras

Cambrai

Gembloux

Namur

R. Meuse

R. Canche

Dinant

A R D E N N E S

Abbeville

R. Somme

Amiens

Mézières

Sedan

Luxembourg

Chauny

Laon

R. Oise

R. Aisne

de Gaulle counter-attacks 17 May

R. Meuse

MAGINOT LINE

Rouen

R. Seine

Reims

PARIS

The German advance, France 1940 – air-ground cooperation

aeroplanes are there. Simultaneously, like some bird of prey, they fall upon their victim and release their load of bombs on the target. We can see the bombs clearly. It becomes a regular rain of bombs, that whistle down on Sedan and the bunker positions. Each time the explosion is overwhelming, the noise deafening. Everything becomes blended together; along with the howling sirens of the Stukas in their dives, the bombs whistle and crack and burst. A huge blow of annihilation strikes the enemy, and still more squadrons arrive, rise to great height, and then come down on the same target. We stand and watch what is happening as if hypnotised.*

On the following day, 14 May, all Allied bombers were ordered to attack the enemy bridgehead, but some French formations fared so badly that their remaining missions were cancelled. Then came the turn of the advanced Air Striking Force. Seventy-one light bombers, in small formations of four aeroplanes, made concentrated attacks against five bridges and enemy columns near Sedan. Hurricanes were instructed to patrol the area, but these fought some distance from Sedan. When the light bombers made their approach they were set upon by hordes of Messerschmitts and many were destroyed. Others fell to the flak, and more were shot out of the sky on the way home; only thirty-one returned.

Five days of daylight operations had cost about half the Royal Air Force's bomber strength in France, and some squadrons had to be taken out of line.

As France disintegrated before the onslaught, Wing Commander Harry Broadhurst (well known before the war for his air-gunnery and aerobatic skills) arrived at Vitry, near Arras, to command 60 Wing (the previous incumbent having suffered a nervous breakdown) to find the airfield 'an absolute shambles'. He saw a burning Hurricane plunge to the ground with its pilot, Fred Rosier, a flight commander, parachuting safely

* Horne, *To Lose a Battle*.

down. The wrecked Hurricane of another flight commander lay in the back garden of the Officers' Mess, and more pranged fighters littered the airfield, pock-marked with bomb craters. He found that the sustained bombing had wrecked communications, isolated headquarters and had left his Hurricane pilots ignorant of the battle situation and the whereabouts of the nearest German armour. The obsolete Lysanders, used for 'Army co-operation' were finished – all shot out of the sky. He had, in fact, arrived as the all-important chain of command was collapsing – never to be re-established.

'Broady', as he was known, saw retreating and demoralized units of the French Army, and some were throwing away their arms and deserting. The local people, terrified by the Stukas, wanted peace. They were sometimes quite hostile and tried to block the grass airfield with tree trunks and carts.

Broadhurst heard that his friend, Wing Commander the Earl of Bandon, who was to become a legendary and deeply admired leader, had survived a disastrous mission when, on 17 May, he led twelve Blenheims of 82 Squadron against German columns near Gembloux. The bombers were set upon by a gaggle of Messerschmitt 109s and eleven were shot down, but 'Paddy' Bandon got back to England and within forty-eight hours was leading six Blenheims on another mission.

On 17 May Charles de Gaulle led one of the four French tank divisions against a panzer wedge at Laon, and later Erwin Rommel was momentarily halted by a small British counter-attack. But nothing could stop the superbly equipped panzers and their equally superbly equipped tactical air units, so that on 19 May the leading panzers had scythed their way to Abbeville, but a few miles from the coast, and other columns were thrusting towards Calais and Dunkirk severing all our communications and threatening to drive the retreating Allied armies into the sea.

Gerald Strickland recalls:

Once back in France we fought the battle of Arras. On that day I learned the lesson of air support. The Germans had little or no artillery and their tanks were few in number. But without pause from dawn to dusk we were pounded by German aircraft. Two squadrons of Heinkels, covered by fighters, broke up our forming-up drill and knocked out a number of our tanks; groups of Stukas dive-bombed us at our start line and during our advance to our objectives; and when we had entered the outskirts of Arras we saw for

the first time the pattern-bombing of a city. The German Army (and it happened to be Rommel's division on my part of the front) had little or nothing to do. A few of us got to our final objective only to hear that the BEF was fast making its way to Dunkirk. As we wended our tired way back, the German Army left us alone but the German Air Force gave us no respite. At intervals of about ten minutes on my way back to where I supposed our forces were, Stuka dive-bombers subjected us to terrifying bombardments. As a result,

Stukas with fighter escort

The Lysander – shot out of the skies

most of the eighty or so German prisoners I had were killed but, as luck would have it, my tank was not hit directly and the coming of night put an end to the performance. The interesting lesson here, and often forgotten, is that it was not the German armour that won this campaign in Europe but the German Air Force. Had the German Army followed up the air onslaught on horse or in omnibuses, the result would have been the same. Had the RAF been of sufficient strength, in those early days, to stem the German air assaults, the evacuation from, and subsequent fall of, France might have been avoided.*

Prime Minister Winston Churchill told the House of a 'tremendous battle . . . raging in France and Flanders' and later wrote:

The direction of the German thrust had now become more obvious. Armoured vehicles and mechanised divisions continued to pour through the gap towards Amiens and Arras, curling westward along the Somme towards the sea. On the night of the 20th, they entered Abbeville, having traversed and cut the whole communications of the Northern Armies. These hideous, fatal scythes encountered little or no resistance once the front had been broken. The German tanks – the dreaded 'chars allemands' – ranged freely through the open country, and aided and supplied by mechanised transport advanced thirty or forty miles a day. They

had passed through scores of towns and hundreds of villages without the slightest opposition, their officers looking out of the open cupolas and waving jauntily to the inhabitants. Eye-witnesses spoke of crowds of French prisoners marching along with them, many still carrying their rifles, which were from time to time collected and broken under the tanks. I was shocked by the utter failure to grapple with the German armour, which, with a few thousand vehicles, was compassing the entire destruction of mighty armies, and by the swift collapse of all French resistance once the fighting front had been pierced. The whole German movement was proceeding along the main roads, at no point on which did they seem to be blocked.†

The depleted Hurricane squadrons did their best and, lacking positive information about the ground battle, patrolled where the squadron commanders thought best. Whenever they encountered German bomber formations, escorted by their fighters, they were always outnumbered and many Hurricanes were shot down. Hurricane wings and squadrons, in full strength, should have opposed strong enemy formations, but their losses meant that each squadron could only put four or five fighters into the air. Every pilot was flying four or five missions a day and they were becoming very tired. Leading a few

Hurricanes on 21 May, Harry Broadhurst was patrolling the Lille–Arras area when they tangled with some Messerschmitt 109 fighters and he shot one down. Later that day he was ordered to withdraw 60 Wing to Merville and soon after to an airfield near Lille.

At Lille we were joined by another Hurricane wing, or rather what was left of it, led by Wing Commander Finch and it was here on 22 May that we received our orders to destroy everything, and go to Northolt. Finch was to take the airmen to Boulogne and I was able to take the Hurricanes back to England. I arranged for ground crews, two for each fighter, to see us off and they would be collected by transport aeroplanes of 24 Squadron later that day.

And so the airmen came home from a stricken France. For the soldiers, however, their situation was moving from bad to worse. On 22 May they had been driven within the 'Canal Line' round the port of Dunkirk, where Hitler, fearing the low-lying terrain, criss-crossed with canals and dykes, would bog down Guderian's panzers, issued a 'stop' order and stated that the Luftwaffe would 'finish off' the BEF. Meanwhile his panzers would re-group and drive south into the remaining French opposition.

From the German viewpoint, the campaign was of great significance because their faith in tactical air power had been justified beyond their wildest dreams. Under the constant protection of its fighter swarms, the dive-bombers had blasted away any opposition in the combat zone, and the Stuka, with its pin-point accuracy, emerged with a legendary reputation. Further afield, the medium bombers, again well protected by fighters, wrecked communications, halted the movement of reserves, and isolated the various Army/Air Force command posts so that they could not exercise any control.

* Johnson Papers.
† Winston S. Churchill, *The Second World War: Their Finest Hour* (Cassell, London, 1949).

9 · THE 'MIRACLE' OF DUNKIRK

On 22 May 1940 the BEF faced the prospect of being driven into the sea by Hitler's panzers, for they and some twenty French divisions were cornered within the 'Canal Line' round the Channel port of Dunkirk. To the south a French counter-attack had failed. The Dutch Army had already laid down its arms and the Belgian army was finished. All British Hurricane squadrons based in France had returned, or were returning, to the UK. Air cover was provided by Fighter Command.

On the evening of 23 May, General von Rundstedt, commanding Army Group A, did not think that there was any great urgency to breach the Canal Line. The Allies were trapped and it was only a matter of days before he drove them into the sea; meanwhile, his five armies were widely separated and he wanted time to consolidate their positions.

Consequently on that evening his Fourth Army was halted on the Canal Line. On the following day, Rundstedt's order was endorsed by Hitler who, on 27 May, instructed that the attack be resumed.

However, General von Kleist, commanding the 'Kleist Group' of panzers, decided to ignore the original order and

... pushed on across the canal. My armoured cars actually entered Hazebrouck, and cut across the British lines of retreat ... But then came a more emphatic order that I was to withdraw behind the canal.

After three days the ban was lifted and the advance was resumed – against stiffening opposition. It had just begun to make headway when it was interrupted by a fresh order from Hitler – that my force was to be withdrawn, and sent southward for the attack on the line that the remainder of the French Army had improvised along the Somme. It was left to the infantry forces which had come down from Belgium to complete the occupation of Dunkirk – after the British had gone.*

Dunkirk was an ideal target for the Luftwaffe for, unlike Warsaw, it lay on the coast and could be easily found when visibility was poor. Allied troops struggling into the town abandoned and burned many vehicles on the outskirts, and the smoke was another beacon for the bombers now gathering for the kill.

The enemy's daily programme usually opened with a few tactical reconnaissance aeroplanes searching for Allied positions, and there followed, shortly after dawn, a deluge of Stukas against shipping in the harbour. At breakfast-time some fifty Heinkels, with more escorting Messerschmitts, bombed the docks and, when the sun was at its zenith, more Heinkels attacked, followed by Stukas, which dive-bombed and then machine gunned the beaches, now filling with exhausted men. A great gaggle of Junkers bombers and twin-engined fighters worked over the town in the mid-afternoon, and the

Stukas were again hard at it for the last thirty minutes of daylight. German artillery was only four miles from Dunkirk, so that shelling and mortar fire filled the gaps left by the bombing; and the ground situation further worsened when the Belgians surrendered, leaving a gap in the defences. Little wonder that the first evacuation ship to leave Dunkirk was bombed, shelled and machine gunned before it reached Dover with many of its soldiers either wounded or dead.

Dunkirk is only a few miles across the English Channel, so that a Spitfire flying from Manston could spend some forty minutes over the town before returning with a safe margin of petrol. But the initiative lay with the Luftwaffe because no one could anticipate the timings of the attacks and enemy bombers could rapidly concentrate over the town. For all that,

* B. H. Liddell Hart, *The German Generals Talk* (Morrow Quill Paperbacks, New York, 1979).

Pea-shooters!

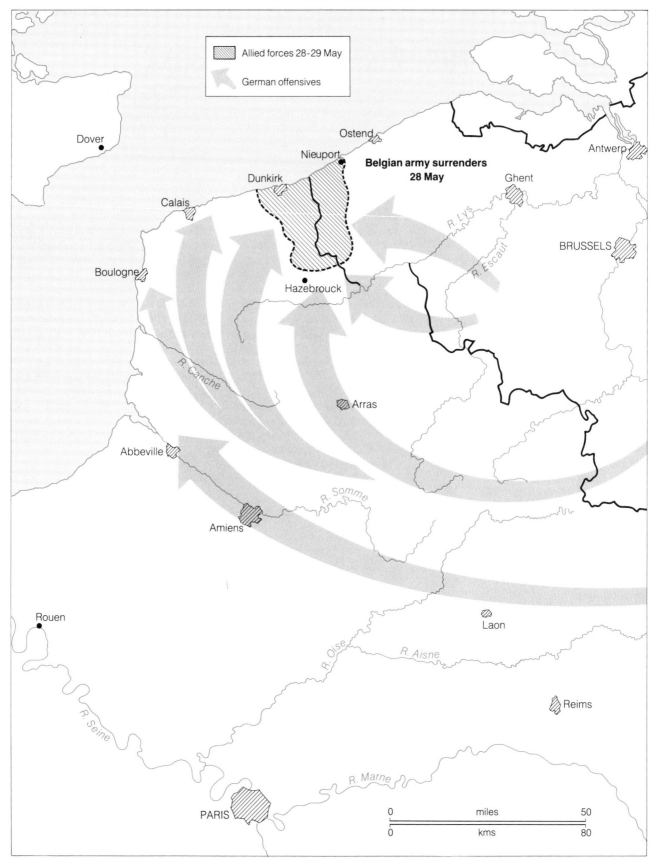

Allied forces 28-29 May

German offensives

Dover

Ostend

Nieuport

Antwerp

**Belgian army surrenders
28 May**

Dunkirk

Ghent

Calais

BRUSSELS

Boulogne

R. Lys

R. Escaut

Hazebrouck

R. Canche

Arras

Abbeville

R. Somme

Amiens

Rouen

Laon

R. Oise

R. Aisne

Reims

R. Seine

R. Marne

PARIS

| 0 | miles | 50 |
| 0 | kms | 80 |

Left: The deliverance of Dunkirk. *Above:* A feat of naval organization and execution that has no parallel

the radars in England constantly saw large gaggles, but Royal Air Force airfields in Kent were too far away for fighters to intercept from ground readiness; and when the bombers came in low there was no radar warning whatsoever. Accordingly, Air Vice-Marshal Keith Park, a tall lean New Zealander, thrice decorated for gallantry in the First War and now commanding 11 Group, had no option but to resort to the wasteful system of standing patrols, and each of his thirty-two fighter squadrons flew up and down the beaches at 16,000 feet or so for forty minutes and was then relieved.

Occasionally a squadron fought immediately it arrived near Dunkirk, and the pilots, having used all their ammunition, withdrew to re-arm. Sometimes Royal Air Force formation leaders attacked such large numbers that all a few Spitfires could hope for was one pass at the bombers before the 109s were upon them. Park therefore increased the strength of his patrols to two squadrons, and later to four squadrons, but this meant even longer periods when the men below were without fighter protection and had to suffer heavy bombing and a murderous hail of machine gun fire.

Sometimes the early morning mists of these dramatic June days cleared from Luftwaffe airfields in France before those in south-east England, and the Germans again had it all their own way. Sometimes cloud, or thick black smoke from burning oil tanks, hid the town and the drama below from Royal Air Force fighters. Whenever a Spitfire or Hurricane chased an opponent down to the sea every available Allied weapon opened up at both aeroplanes, for everything with wings was understandably regarded as hostile by the men on the beaches.

First light on 4 June saw the Germans only two miles from the beaches and the last ship to leave Dunkirk, and those on board testified to the fine bearing of the French troops who were left behind. The BEF and its Allies had fought and held off the enemy for nine days, and the Royal Navy, the Merchant Navy and a host of amateur yachtsmen had achieved the near-impossible by bringing home more than a third of a million men to fight again. Bomber, Coastal and Fighter Commands had upset the Luftwaffe to the extent that another Warsaw was prevented. Fighter Command could have done more had Dowding thought fit to use all his squadrons, but this would have left much of England wide open to air attack, and he was desperately aware that the air fighting had already cost him more than half his total strength.

There can be no doubt that Rundstedt's halt order on 23 May was a decisive factor in allowing the BEF to escape from France. Indeed, a few days after the evacuation, Kleist met Hitler on Cambrai airfield and ventured to comment that a great opportunity had been lost of driving the British into the sea. 'That may be so,' Hitler replied, 'but I did not want to send the tanks into the Flanders marshes, and the British won't come back in this war.'[*]

Much has been written about the 'miracle' of Dunkirk but as Winston Churchill remarked 'wars are not won by evacuations'. Indeed, the BEF escaped not by a miracle, but by the Royal Navy's overwhelming naval superiority, the splendid discipline of the British Army on the bombed and strafed beaches and the slender, but just adequate, fighter cover provided by the Royal Air Force.

The honours for this combined operation must go to the Royal Navy for a feat of naval organization and execution that has no parallel. 'At a few days notice 765 British ships of all sorts and sizes were assembled from diverse sources and devoted to a single end':[†] bringing back one third of a million men from a half destroyed harbour and a few miles of open beach in the face of the strongest army and air force in the world.

[*] Hart, *The German Generals Talk.*
[†] Major L. F. Ellis, *The War in France and Flanders, 1939-1940* (HMSO, London, 1953).

RAF Fighter Command

High-level radar station
Low-level radar station
● Fighter base
○ Sector station
■ Group Headquarters
□ Command Headquarters

Luftwaffe

● Bf 109 base
○ Bf 110 base
▲ Bomber base
△ Dive bomber base

LUFTFLOTTE 5
from Norway and Denmark

Grangemouth
Turnhouse
Drem
Cockburnspath
Drone Hill
Bamburgh
Acklington
Cresswell
Ottercops Moss
Newcastle
Shotton
Usworth
Danby Beacon
Catterick
Staxton Wold
Flamborough Head
Leconfield
Church Fenton
Easington
Kirton-in-Lindsey
Stenigot
Manchester
Ingoldmels
Digby
Watnall
West Beckham
Happisburg
Coltishall
Stoke Holy Cross
Nopton
Wittering
Dunwich
High Street
Martlesham
Bawdsey
Duxford
Debden
Bromley
Walton
North Weald
Stanmore
Hornchurch
Canewdon
Whitstable
Northolt
Southend
Foreness
Uxbridge
LONDON
Gravesend
Manston
Croydon
Dunkirk
Dover
Kenley
Lympne
Biggin Hill
Hawkinge
Thuleigh
Rye
Tangmere
Fairlight
Pevensey
Ventnor
Poling
Beachy Head
Worth

FIGHTER COMMAND 13 GROUP

FIGHTER COMMAND 12 GROUP

FIGHTER COMMAND 10 GROUP

FIGHTER COMMAND 11 GROUP

Strumble Head
St. Twnels
Pembrey
Filton
Box
Middle Wallop
Exeter
Hawkstor
St. Eval
Carnanton
Ramehead
W. Prawle
Drytree

ENGLISH CHANNEL

range of low-level radar

range of high-level radar

Cherbourg
Carquebut
Crepon
Caen
Plumetot
Le Havre
Beaumont-le-Roger
Eureux
St. André
Dreux
Chartres
Tours
Lennion
Brest
St. Malo
Dinard Dinan

LUFTFLOTTE 3

Rennes
Laval
Vannes
Angers

Amsterdam
Soesterburg
Rotterdam
Eindhoven
Antwerp
le Culot
St. Truiden
Ypres
Courtrai
Alost
Renaix
Marck
Guines
Tramecourt
Lille
St. Omer
Wissant
Arques
Marquise
Caffiers
Cambrai
Samer
Arras
Abbeville
LUFTFLOTTE 2
Amiens
Rosières-en-Santerre
Beauvais
Montdidier
Creil
PARIS
Orly
Melun
Étampes
Orléans
Audembert

0   miles   100
0   kms   160

10 · THE BATTLE OF BRITAIN: THE UNBROKEN SHIELD

ORDERS OF BATTLE

A fighter pilot flying at great height off the North Foreland during that fine high summer of 1940, when each day seemed full of blinding light and colour, saw the calm waters of the Channel splintered here and there by the wakes of a few tiny ships hugging the English coast. Before him the Pas de Calais stretched from the coast until it faded into a blue haze, and here lay the crack fighter squadrons of the Luftwaffe, some only thirty miles from Dover. Flying at a height of five miles he would not see the scores of airfields which dotted the landscape between Hamburg and Bordeaux and which housed two air fleets, *Luftflotte* 2 and *Luftflotte* 3, while *Luftflotte* 5 rested on Danish and Norwegian bases. This powerful air armada, containing some 2,800 combat aeroplanes, was thus disposed along a wide front so that air attacks could be delivered against Britain from many directions. The airfields were well stocked for the coming assault, while the refreshed and well-disciplined crews, flushed with victory, inspired by Nazi fanaticism and a blind faith in their Führer, listened to the loudspeakers blaring the martial strains of 'Bomben Auf Enge-land' (Bombs on England), and waited for Göring to give the signal.

When he turned westwards down the Channel he saw the flat lands of Kent, the chequered fields and chalk downs of Sussex gapped by tiny rivers and, on the far horizon, the rolling country of Hampshire and Dorset. He was too high to pick out the hamlets and villages crouching under down and wold, but he fleetingly remembered them and knew that all this splendour would soon be the backcloth of bloody combat. He remem-

Left: Spread of a great battle: Battle of Britain, September 1940

The Reichmarschall and the first General of Fighters – Göring and Mölders

The second General of Fighters – Adolf Galland – with friend

bered, too, other perilous times in the long history of his country, when other invaders had faced the narrow waters of the Channel; but this time it was different, because all would be won or lost in the air. And when he came down towards the crawling earth he saw the white cliffs at Beachy Head disentangle themselves from the haze, and a few seconds later he recognized his airfield lying at the foot of the downs and fitting into the landscape as easily as a thrush on her nest.

Dowding's squadrons were based throughout the land from Caithness to Cornwall, and their day-to-day operations were controlled by four fighter groups who were subordinate to Fighter Command. The groups were divided further into sectors, each a geographical area containing a sector station and satellite airfields. 11 Group, bounded by Lowestoft, Dover, Bournemouth, and Northampton, contained eighteen day-fighter squadrons and four night-fighter squadrons, while 12 Group's thirteen squadrons defended the Midlands and could, if need be, reinforce 11 Group. Farther north, twelve squadrons, including six equipped with obsolete Gladiators, guarded the industrial cities of the north-east and Scotland, while four squadrons were deployed in the west country. A further eight non-operational squadrons would take their place in the front line after more training.

30 AUGUST 1940

'On this day 242 Squadron had moved down to Duxford from Coltishall to be nearer the battle. Now it was being controlled from the local Operations Room and, in particular, by Wing Commander A. B. Woodhall, the

Top: 222 Squadron Spitfires take off from Hornchurch

Above: Douglas Bader at the helm of 242 (Canadian) Squadron

Left: 'Which serves it in the office of a wall, or as a moat . . .'

Station Commander. A well-tried First World War pilot, with a resourceful and tactical mind, Woodhall was to become a star among the RAF's wartime fighter controllers. Within two years he had transferred to the great air battle for Malta the lessons he was learning in the struggle for command of British and French skies. Profiting from his association with Bader, he was developing a genius for this exacting and responsible role.

As the squadron formed up round its leader, Woodhall's deep and measured voice spelt out the instructions. They were short and concise. Fly vector 190° for North Weald, height 15,000 feet – or, in the operational jargon of the hour, 'angels 15'. It appeared that 11 Group's important sector airfield, on the north-eastern periphery of London, was likely to be the target. The enemy, with some seventy-plus aircraft involved, looked bent on attacking in strength.'*

It took 242 Squadron fifteen minutes to get the height and be in the critical area. Positioning was now

On target – a raid near the Thames during the Battle of Britain

the key. No good, Bader knew, just to sit up over the top of North Weald at angels 15 – which was what 11 Group wanted – waiting for the onslaught. That was no way to defend a target. No matter what the theorists on the ground might say, no leader in his senses would try to protect, from directly above, a pocket handkerchief in a field 15,000 or 20,000 feet below.

Yet Bader was surprisingly charitable about the fallacy of such rigid, rule book thinking. 'We were learning . . . We were all learning. That was the point.' As he jockeyed for advantage, the catch-lines kept echoing in his mind:

He who has the height controls the
    battle
He who has the sun achieves surprise
He who gets in close shoots them down

Wasn't that, after all the enemy's concept? If North Weald was to be the target, thought Douglas, it was ten to one the attackers would make their run in from the west, with the sun at their back. He resolved, therefore, to make the instructions he was receiving from the ground his ally, not his master.

Working fifteen or twenty miles round to the west of the raiders, he climbed another 3,000 or 4,000 feet above the given altitude. He had enough time to do it.

The positioning was just right. As the gaggle of bombers, with its Messerschmitt 110 escort, turned into the target from the west, 242, with all the tactical advantage, came in out of the sun fast and hard, cutting into the attacking force before it had time to realize what had hit it. It was a classical 'bounce'. The interception that fighter leaders dream about. The sort of thing which occurs once in fifty sorties. Everyone got in among the Dorniers or 110s. Turner, Crowley-Milling, McKnight, Ball and Bader himself all registered kills; some collected more than one.

Douglas would have been entitled to give this matinée performance a rave notice in his log-book; but he

* Laddie Lucas, *Flying Colours* (Hutchinson, London, 1981).

Above: Too close for comfort – German bomber attacked by a Spitfire

Right: Victor of the day-to-day battle – Air Vice-Marshal Keith Park AOC 11 Group

played it cool, preferring to confine himself, with Sherlock Holmes and Dr Watson, 'rigidly to facts and figures'. The record could speak for itself: 'August 30 Hurricane D one hour, thirty minutes. Intercepted 100 E/A (enemy aircraft) with Squadron. Shot down twelve. Self two Me 110s.'

15 SEPTEMBER 1940

Except for the Duxford and Wittering Wings the squadrons of Fighter Command usually fought singly because there was no time to form them into wings. However in early September Göring ordered that his bombers be provided with stronger fighter escorts which took longer to assemble and gave Park more radar warning. Thus, he instructed his controller that when time permitted squadrons should be sent into the battle in pairs.

There was a crispness in the air on this fine Sunday morning of 15 September 1940, when the radars began to detect enemy formations gathering together over Calais. By 11.00 it was obvious that a massive attack was threatening and thirty minutes later the enemy vanguard crossed the coast of Kent.

The defensive arrangements, so carefully tended throughout the long weeks of fighting by Keith Park, worked so well that he had time to deploy seventeen fighter squadrons.

The 'Hole' – Operations Room, Fighter Command

Robert Standford-Tuck – Bob Tuck – of 267 Squadron, outstanding fighter pilot and leader

South African hero A.G. (Sailor) Malan, OC 74 Squadron

Ten of the eleven squadrons of his Group were sent off in pairs whilst the Duxford Wing of five squadrons headed south. Minutes later, as the Spitfire wing 'tallyhoed' over Canterbury, Park threw in his reserve of six squadrons.

The invaders were met, fought and harried by an outstanding and diverse gathering of fighting men – perhaps the most outstanding ever to defend these shores. They were led into the hostile legions by squadron, flight and section leaders some of whom, for the past few months, had fought continuously over France, Dunkirk, the Channel and southern England. Now they were seasoned air fighters who had the advantage of flying over their own country and defending their own homeland . . . Skilled air fighters from the Empire – South Africa, Rhodesia, Canada, Australia and New Zealand – defending the 'Old Country' which still had a very real meaning and significance for them . . . Veteran air fighters, not of our own kith and kin, but from Poland, Czechoslovakia, Norway, France, Holland and Belgium, some of whom had fought, since the autumn of 1939, in three air forces and had old and bitter scores to settle – and little to lose.

Because they had good and respected leaders, good aeroplanes and were fighting for a just cause against the evil Nazis, their morale, that 'precious pearl', was very high; and now that Göring had switched his bombers to London their battered airfields were recovering, the days were getting shorter and they scented that they could hold the ring until the weather closed in.

After a two-hour break, which gave the defending squadrons ample time to rearm and refuel, the aggressors returned in three heavily escorted bomber formations which crossed the coast on a twenty-mile front between Dover and Dungeness, within five minutes of each other. This time, the radar warning was shorter, but nine wings and several independent squadrons came into action over south London, where there was some

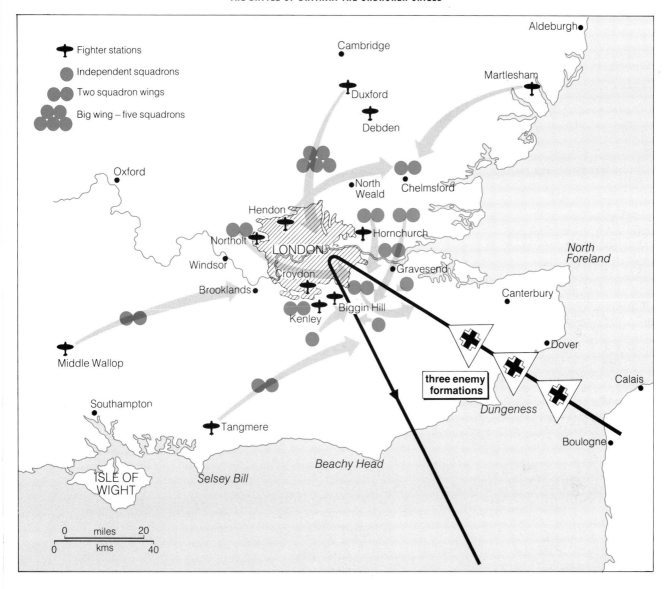

Climacteric! 15 September, 1940

stiff fighting. Once again, the defenders had the best of the exchange. There were fewer 109s than usual and these seemed less aggressive, so that some of the bombers were very roughly handled. Two formations were broken up near London – one retiring after a head-on attack by a lone Hurricane – and bombs were scattered over a wide area. The Germans were harried by more Spitfires and Hurricanes as they withdrew.

The fighting over London was at its height when about twenty Heinkels bombed Portland harbour. Only one squadron succeeded in intercepting,

and that after the bombing. The final daylight operation was an attempt by another twenty bombers to hit the Supermarine Works near Southampton, but the anti-aircraft gunners put up a heavy barrage and the factory was not damaged. At dark, the bombers returned to London and continued their work throughout the night.

The fighting on this day cost the Luftwaffe fifty-six aeroplanes against our twenty-six pilots. More bombers struggled back to France – on one engine, badly shot-up and with many crew members dead or injured. At the

briefings the bomber captains complained bitterly of incessant Hurricane and Spitfire attacks from squadrons that had long ceased to exist – if they could believe their own Intelligence and the Berlin radio.

The fighting on this day clinched the victory, for two days later, on Hitler's instructions, the German invasion fleet left the Channel ports for safer places, and Operation Sealion* was called off, never to be repeated.

* Operation Sealion – German codename for the invasion of Southern England.

11 · THE WESTERN DESERT, MEDITERRANEAN AND MALTA

TACTICAL AIR POWER

The principles of air support were thrashed out during the First War, and only their application had changed with the improvements in aeroplanes, weapons and communications. Fortunately, Royal Air Force leaders had stopped a determined attempt to make the Service adopt the dive-bomber as a primary weapon for air support, for the Army and Navy had been so impressed by the Stuka that they had fallen into the trap of believing that such an aeroplane was

itself a battle winner. In reality, it was capable of exploiting a battle that had already been won – the air battle. The legend of the Stuka was slow in dying, for the Germans used this dive-bomber in one way or another until almost the end of the Second War; but it was never successful in the face of strong fighter opposition.

The Royal Air Force knew that the fighter-bomber was the only suitable type of aeroplane for bombing and strafing whenever enemy fighters were about, and that the battlefield must be isolated to stop the enemy from moving into, and within, the

combat area. They also knew that the fighting men on the ground wanted close air support at the right time and the right place, and that the whole thing depended upon confidence between airman and soldier. However, up to this point in the Second War such confidence did not exist.

After Dunkirk the Army was very suspicious of both the Royal Air Force's intention and ability to provide tactical reconnaissance and air support. Although the so-called Army Co-operation Command had been formed, it had few teeth, for the Air Staff awarded the highest priorities to

Me 109 escorting Ju 87

offensive capability, Bomber Command, and to the defence of the industrial base, Fighter Command. In 1942 the hundred or so fighter squadrons in the UK spent all their operational flying time on fighter sweeps, bomber escorts and convoy patrols. Occasionally, perhaps once or twice each year, fighter-pilots fired cannon and machine guns at static targets before an Army audience. On one occasion the military's low opinion of the air–ground capability was not improved when some of their top brass were killed by a Polish Spitfire squadron. Nor was inter-Service confidence helped by the Dieppe fiasco when, throughout that long day, fighter leaders, including one of the authors, were unable to contact the headquarters ship for information about that bloody ground situation.

Since the Royal Air Force was equally suspicious of the Army's will to come to grips with Rommel's crack Afrika Korps and to get on with the ground fighting, inter-Service relations in the Middle East were at a low ebb especially when the Army called for the control of all air forces in the field including the specific allotment of aeroplanes down to divisional level. This was heresy to the air marshals who firmly believed that centralized control was the only method of achieving concentration and flexibility and dreaded the breakdown of the Royal Air Force into 'penny packets'. The situation worsened when the GOC, Western Desert Force, called for an 'air umbrella' for the defence of the ground forces during their approach to the battle area! Eventually, the Prime Minister thought it opportune to state that the Royal Air Force was an independent service and would remain so.

There was room for much improvement in Army–Air Force affairs as Air Chief Marshal Sir Kenneth Cross recalls:

When I started in the desert we had nothing. There was no understanding with the Army. No organization. No centralized control and no command structure. Nothing. We had so-called Army Co-operation squadrons but you know what happened to them in France. No one had any idea of Army–Air Force integration and because we did not have any command organization the Army told the Air Force what to do.

When Malcolm* won his Victoria Cross – the only one ever awarded to a pilot of the tactical air forces – leading his squadron of ancient Bisleys against a well-defended enemy airfield in Tunisia, the order to the wing headquarters was actually issued by two Army officers! Can you imagine that?†

Air Commodore Jimmy Fenton, another distinguished airman, said:

In the early days there was a complete lack of co-operation with the Army, and when we were retreating I would sometimes get a hundred Army officers calling at my wing headquarters asking if we knew what was going on, where were their headquarters, and so on. The British Army could fight all right but it was not centrally controlled as was the Afrika Korps under Rommel. It changed pretty radically after Alamein and that was one of Montgomery's major achievements.

When the New Zealander Mary Coningham took over the Desert Air Force in 1941, it was a semi-organized shambles and Mary sorted it out and got a bit of morale and decent administration into it. The New Zealander was one of the first practical Allied airmen to comprehend the ebb and flow of the land battle and to understand the soldiers' constant requirements for reconnaissance and air support.†

'Bing' Cross said:

The Army's scapegoat for all their failures was 'lack of air support'. Senior Army officers had repeatedly said: 'If you can keep the enemy air off our backs that's all we ask, we can cope with the rest!' So Coningham's job was to achieve air superiority so that the Army, hopefully, could get on with the ground battle – and in this he succeeded.

Coningham, like many of his contemporaries, was not a practical airman and had to rely on others for tactical advice. But he was a political airman and it was at his urging that the Desert Air Force and the Eighth Army formed a joint headquarters and the GOC, Neil Ritchie and Coningham, lived alongside each other, and for the first time we had an Army–Air Force organization jointly to process requests for air support. It was a big improvement.†

'We have,' said Winston Churchill, 'a very daring and skilful opponent against us, and, may I say across the havoc of war, a great general,'‡ who struck with such speed and vigour that on 21 June 1942 the British garrison at Tobruk surrendered, and three days later Rommel's panzers entered Egypt. As secret documents and staff papers were burned in Cairo, Auchinleck sacked his GOC, Eighth Army, and himself took over; he decided to make his stand on a narrow defence position between El Alamein and the impassable Quattara Depression.

The stoic nine-day defence of Bir Hacheim by General Koenig's 1st Free French Brigade drew the whole of the German dive-bomber force, plus long-range bombers flying from Crete. Coningham's Desert Air Force flew some 1,500 sorties in support of the fortress some of which could be seen by the defenders who signalled Coningham, 'Bravo! Merci pour la RAF,' and the AOC courteously replied: 'Bravo à vous! Merci pour le sport!'

Retreating along the narrow coastal road the vehicles of the Eighth Army were helplessly bunched together, nose to tail, for several days during the 400-mile withdrawal, and had the enemy fighter-bombers been active the retreat would undoubtedly have been turned into a rout. In the event only six British soldiers were killed by enemy strafing. There were two reasons for this incredible immunity. First, the Luftwaffe did not have the vehicles and the mobility (including the prepared landing grounds all the way back to Egypt) of the Desert Air Force, who only withdrew from their airfields when they could actually see our bombing some twenty miles distant. Second, Arthur Tedder, Air Officer Commanding-in-Chief, Middle East Air Force, saw his chance and threw the considerable

---

* Wing Commander H. G. Malcolm, Officer Commanding 18 Squadron.
† Johnson Papers.
‡ Speech, House of Commons, 27 January 1942.

weight of all his squadrons against Rommel's squadrons, his supply lines and airfields.

Tedder reinforced his subordinate, Coningham, with Spitfires from Malta and Hurricanes from training units in the Delta. At this desperate hour the lack of a joint headquarters was of little consequence since the simple requirement was to stop Rommel. In one crucial week the Desert Air Force flew more than 5,500 sorties, and at the same time Tedder attacked with anything that could fly and drop a bomb – obsolete Bisleys and naval Albacores, Beaufighters, Baltimores, Bostons, Hudsons, Mitchells and Halifaxes, as well as Liberators and Fortresses from the newly arrived USAAF squadrons. Towards the end of this first battle of Alamein, Tedder could muster no less than ninety-six Allied squadrons and formations. Shuttle bombing, both by night and day, was commonplace embracing big formations of up to 150 fighters and bombers.

The War Diary of the Afrika Korps shows what they thought of these air attacks:

... two bombing attacks on the 21st Panzers Division while the GOC is there

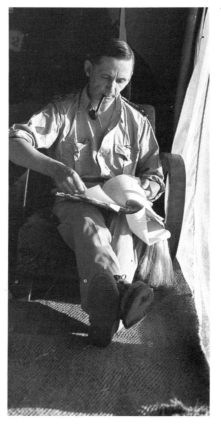

Left: Carpet bombing
Above: Tedder – the thinker
Below: Central Mediterranean ... 'nerve' area of World War Two, 1942-43

... enemy Air Force very active today but there is no sign of the Luftwaffe ... 15th Panzer Division reports that it is unable to continue its bombing attacks owing to lack of fuel ... bombing attacks are made every hour causing considerable losses. There is nothing to be seen of the Luftwaffe.

Indeed, there was nothing to be seen of the once flexible Luftwaffe which, thanks to constant air attacks against their supply routes across the Mediterranean, could not keep up with Rommel's rapid advance. This was just as well, for the ageing Hurricanes and American Tomahawks and Kittyhawks were no match for the angular Messerschmitt 109Fs. One squadron of Spitfire Vs had recently arrived whose pilots, fresh from their experience of fighting over France and Malta, firmly believed that height was all-important and didn't want to fly lower down where they would surely be jumped by the speedy 109s. Small wonder, therefore, that when they began flying well above the ground-attack pilots they were soon accused of failing to 'get stuck-in' and fighting a private war which had little influence on the real thing. Gradually both sides came to appreciate the other's view: the ground-attack pilot

The Honorary Air Commodore of 615 Squadron and General Montgomery

'Coningham, with Tedder's support, got the organization straight and goodness knows what we would have done without him. No one has any idea of what the airmen at the top went through in those days. Tedder and Coningham together were simply splendid. They broke Rommel's last thrust and saved the Eighth Army at Alamein.'[†]

In mid-August, 1942, Lieutenant-General Bernard Montgomery took over the Eighth Army at, for him, an opportune time since Rommel had been stopped and more tanks, aeroplanes – and Americans – were arriving in the Middle East. Monty, as he was soon known, was an able professional commander who knew the value of tactical air power and realized that the very weapon which the Germans had themselves invented – *Blitzkrieg* – could now be turned against them.

When, on 17 August, Ultra warned that Rommel would soon attack, Tedder and Coningham, with swelling numbers of aeroplanes, began their offensive while the Eighth Army remained in its defensive position. Thousands of sorties were flown against the Germans and the Italians, and the War Diary of the Afrika Korps reported that, apart from colossal material damage, the morale of both officers and men was severely shaken by the incessant bombing. On 3 September, Allied reconnaissance pilots saw the Axis forces in full retreat and thus began the long trek which took the Eighth Army out of the Middle East and into Tunisia. The second battle of El Alamein was not the victory of the Eighth Army alone. Nor was it the victory of the Eighth Army and Coningham's Western Desert Air Force. It was the victory of the Eighth Army and all Allied air forces in the Middle East – including the American squadrons. Rommel himself recorded what he thought: 'British air superiority threw to the winds all our tactical rules ... the strength of the Anglo-American Air Force was ... the deciding factor!'[‡]

that the presence of the high Spitfires was some insurance against the Messerschmitts – the fighter boys that failing to come down meant that the battle was sometimes over before they could engage. Later the Spitfires became fighter-bombers and carried bombs, and when things were quiet in the upper air they took an active part in strafing and bombing.

'During the retreat,' I[*] said to Bing Cross, 'Coningham was anxious about his forward airfields and withdrew them, and his headquarters, inside the Egyptian border. The joint headquarters was lost, but immediately Montgomery arrived on the scene Coningham went to see him and the general wholeheartedly agreed they must live alongside each other. How would you summarize "Mary" Coningham's stewardship in the desert?'

[*] Johnnie Johnson
[†] Johnson Papers.
[‡] Brigadier Desmond Young, *Rommel* (Collins, London, 1950).

The British people, hungry for success after years of humiliation and defeat, made much of the desert victory. At home the church bells were rung and Montgomery, hitherto largely unknown, suddenly became overnight a national hero, and Churchill later wrote: 'Before Alamein we never had a victory. After Alamein we never had a defeat.'*

THE 'CAB RANK'

The second Battle of El Alamein was the beginning of the counter-offensive which, eventually, was concluded in central Germany; but there was still some fighting to be done in North Africa, and with the swelling numbers of British and American squadrons, the air command structure was changed. Coningham, promoted to air marshal, took over the new North-West African Air Force whilst Broadhurst, promoted to air vice-marshal, assumed command of the Western Desert Air Force.

At thirty-seven Harry Broadhurst was the youngest air vice-marshal in the Royal Air Force and unlike our previous high-ranking commanders in the Fighter Arm (Leigh-Mallory, Park, Sholto Douglas and Coningham) he had fought in this contest and continued to fly operationally through the war. Later, it was held that a man could not properly command a group (the Army equivalent of a division) unless he had completed an operational tour: Don Bennett of the Pathfinder Force and Basil Embry of 2 Group were prime examples of this policy and because they and their pilots spoke the same language they did not have to rely on second-hand opinions.

The big difference between Coningham and Broadhurst was that the former always considered himself an 'equal' of the Army commander because they occupied a joint headquarters and took joint decisions, whereas Broadhurst thought that because the Army were doing the bulk of the fighting, and occupying the ground, they were the senior partner and the AOC's job was to provide the ground forces with the best possible tactical air support. Montgomery, of course, soon realized that in Broadhurst he had an able air commander and trusted him. Thus, despite the big difference in their ages (and their widely differing lifestyles) they got on well together and their close relationship had an excellent effect on Army–Air Force co-operation down to battalion–squadron level.

As Bing Cross recalls:

When Broady took over the Desert Air Force, it was more or less plain sailing for our American friends had invaded the other end of North Africa and the Luftwaffe, always good on priorities, left a few 109s facing the Eighth Army whilst the remainder, reinforced by Focke-Wulf 190s, turned to their main tasks of protecting their essential bases at Tunis and Bizerta.

Broady, always a practical airman, looked around for something to do with the Desert Air Force. The task of 'keeping the enemy off our backs' was being well looked after by the Americans so he decided to give his chaps a much better close support capability – and who better to do it than him?

* Winston S. Churchill, *The Second World War: The Hinge of Fate* (Cassell, London, 1951).

The desert team: *(left to right)* AV-M Harry Broadhurst, Sir Arthur Coningham, Sir Bernard Montgomery, Sir Harold Alexander, Sir Arthur Tedder and L.S. Kuter (of the USAAF)

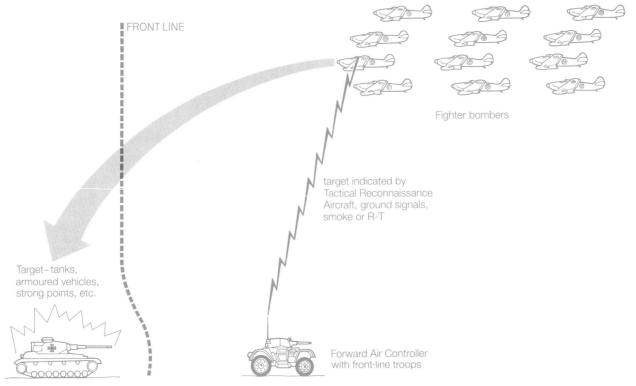

FRONT LINE

Fighter bombers

target indicated by
Tactical Reconnaissance
Aircraft, ground signals,
smoke or R-T

Target–tanks,
armoured vehicles,
strong points, etc.

Forward Air Controller
with front-line troops

Calling for support: Broadhurst's 'cab rank'

He wanted to give the soldiers closer and more positive support, for, at this time, we could not bomb or strafe within 500 yards of our own troops, largely because of identification problems. Also it took about one hour between the origin of a request for air support and the time the fighter-bomber required to get to the target including about twenty minutes flying time. Further, he was far from happy about the big disparity between our claims of enemy transports, gun and tanks destroyed and the actual number counted when we arrived on the battlefield.

One of the first things he did was to lay on a demonstration with about twenty fighter-bombers strafing an old truck and was not amused when no one hit it. The boys were all convinced that they would all get killed by the accurate German flak, but, by using his considerable experience in ordering difficult operations, he convinced the squadrons that ground attack was not necessarily synonymous with sudden death. Broady gave the Desert Air Force far more flexibility by turning his fighters into fighter-bombers so that they could both fight in the air and provide the soldiers with close support. He had the situation, the equipment and the time to do it, and I used to call him 'Cab Rank

Broadhurst'. He did it well, becoming Monty's friend, and the soldiers' friend. But 'Mary' Coningham did a great job with the Desert Air Force before Broady arrived.*

He was called 'Cab Rank Broadhurst' because, to cut down the time from Army request to time over target, his pilots, already in the air, were briefed by Royal Air Force controllers. These were located in armoured cars, called contact cars, situated with the forward troops and in radio contact with the fighter-bombers. Pilots and ground controllers used similar photographic maps, with a grid superimposed on it, and the controller gave targets to the waiting 'cab ranks' of fighter-bombers.

This 'Rover David' system, linking the fighter-bombers with the armoured cars, later proved very successful especially in Italy. 'Rover' patrols were decided upon the day before at a joint conference, and enemy targets, stationary or moving, were attacked within a few minutes of a request from those forward troops in contact with the enemy. Our

fighter-bombers were soon operating very close to our forward troops and on one occasion, in Italy, they attacked enemy troops holed up on the other side of a street from our own forward positions.

The advancing Eighth Army was halted at the Mareth Line which, years before, had been constructed by the French in the blind traditions of the Maginot Line. German troops were well dug-in and there was some stiff ground fighting. Montgomery planned a set-piece attack for 20 March 1943 and despite the poor weather forecast, which was likely to ground the Desert Air Force, he decided to go ahead. The opening stages of the frontal attack did not go well because well-sited anti-tank guns knocked out a lot of British armour, and two days later Montgomery had little option but to withdraw his troops and attempt a flanking left-hook across some very hilly and rough terrain.

* Johnson Papers.

74

The crucial obstacle before our troops was a high concentration of German armour deployed on a front of about four miles between two hills. Broadhurst, remembering the *Blitzkrieg* devastation in France, concentrated all his aeroplanes against the target to stun and paralyse the enemy – as the BEF had been stunned and paralysed some three years before.

After two nights of heavy bombing, three formations of bombers, escorted by fighters, made low-level flights to the combat area and achieved complete surprise. Immediately afterwards, Kittyhawk fighter-bombers were fed into the area at intervals of fifteen minutes, bombing and strafing at low heights, and Hurricane 'tank-busters' attacked and broke up enemy tank concentrations. Spitfires patrolled overhead to ward-off any 109s while other fighter-bombers attacked all known German airfields and landing grounds within a hundred miles. Thirty minutes after the first bomb fell our infantry advanced behind a heavy barrage slowly creeping forward at about one hundred feet per minute. Thus Broad-

Hurricane tank buster

hurst's pilots could see the bomb-line and shot-up any moving thing ahead of it.

The result of all this concentrated activity by the Western Desert Air Force was that, during the night, Eighth Army armour passed through the bottleneck as the Mareth Line was turned. 'The outstanding feature of the battle,' recorded Montgomery,

'was the air action in co-operation with the outflanking forces.'* What he did not record was that he never again went into a set-piece battle without the assured support of his airmen.

* Denis Richards and Hilary St George Saunders, *Royal Air Force, 1939-1945:* vol. 11, *The Fight Avails* (HMSO, London, 1954).

Royal Artillery at work: Mareth Line, February, 1943

VICTORY OVER THE GULF OF TUNIS

Before the curtain finally fell on the air fighting in North Africa, and activity moved across the Mediterranean to Sicily and Italy, a remarkable last scene was played out over the Gulf of Tunis. It provided the South African Air Force, in the form of 1 Squadron (Major D. D. Moodie), with its Spitfires and 7 Wing (Lieutenant-Colonel D. H. Loftus), composed of 2, 4 and 5 Squadrons, with their P-40 Kittyhawks, with one of the great aerial coups of the Mediterranean theatre.

Ultra had given exceptional advance warning of the enemy's intention to fly in troop reinforcements early in the morning of 22 April 1943. It was a last ditch attempt to aid the crumbling Axis forces in Tunisia.

Moodie took off with twelve Spitfires and six Polish Spitfires as top cover. Their task was to escort three Kittyhawk squadrons of the 79th Pursuit Group to the Gulf of Tunis which Ultra had warned that the enemy transports would be crossing from the north-west. Doug Moodie was to rendezvous with the Americans at Hergla at 07.55.

'Snowy' Loftus, leading 7 Wing, was airborne at the same time with orders to rendezvous with a Royal Air Force squadron and sweep the Gulf. But the Americans were late at the rendezvous and somehow or other the two South African formations joined together and set course to the north.

When still about eight miles from the island of Zembra, some great six-engined transport planes were seen flying south-west, low over the water. They were Messerschmitt 323s, each capable of carrying a hundred men, and were flying, according to Captain V. (Pops) Voss* 'in a great vic of fifteen with a smaller vic of five inside it'.† They were escorted by Messerschmitt 109s, Macchi 202s and RE 2001s.

At first the Kittyhawks did not see the great armada, so Doug Moodie ordered two of his sections to attack, while he stayed up with his section, and the Poles, to give top cover.

'A great slaughter now began,' wrote Voss, 'the Spitfires peeled off and went down in steep power-dives with cannons hammering to draw first blood. Almost simultaneously the Kittyhawks turned back.'†

It was a battle rare in the annals of air fighting ... thirty-six Kittyhawks and eighteen Spitfires in combat with the gunners of twenty huge transports and their dozen escorts.

Below them lay the opaque mirror of the Gulf broken by the splash of plunging, blazing machines, the air streaked with cannon fire and smoke trails as the shouting pilots gave the *coup de grâce*. 'Right, left and centre,' Voss continued, 'they were falling in great masses of red flame and black smoke into the sea.' The Italians, at the rear of the formation, abandoned their charges. As Lieutenant D. T. Gilson slashed down

Above: 'Snowy' Loftus and South African pilots

Left: Me 323

Right: Defeat in North Africa

* Professor Vivian Voss, the noted South African historian, was a pilot in the RFC in World War One, serving in 48 Squadron with Keith Park (Air Chief Marshal Sir Keith Park).

† J. Ambrose Brown, *Eagles Strike* (Purnell, Capetown, S. Africa).

towards the air fleet, four Macchis dropped their long-range tanks and dived away, leaving him to sweep over the gliders and down first one, then another in a great mass of flame.

Lt. G. T. van de Veen's report shows how swiftly the killing was done. Pouncing on a Me 323 already burning he sent it flaming into the water ... he switched to another which also hit the sea. When his cannons packed in he machine-gunned a third to destruction. Meanwhile Lt. M. E. Robinson had tangled with the German escort ... twice he selected the wingman of a fighting pair and though attacked many times held on with remorseless bursts of fire until they went down in flames. Then, out of fuel, harassed by a Messerschmitt and a Macchi he had to run for it and belly-flopped near Hergla.

Meanwhile 'Snowy' Loftus' Kittyhawks fell on the transports. The great six-engined aircraft loomed huge in the sights as Major J. E. Parsonson led 5 Squadron in a head-on attack. The leader set two alight, both burning furiously and breaking on impact with the sea. 'We hunted them like wolves,' he recalled. Lt. F. A. Weingartz had sent his first to destruction, the whole glider engulfed in fire, when he heard Major Parsonson calling the squadron to catch one trying to get away. Wein-

gartz attacked three times. First the engines caught fire, then the fuselage, then he saw one flap break away and just before crashing into the sea the great body broke in two just aft of the wing root. Lt. R. W. Humphrey saw his first burst enter a fuselage and rake the cockpit. Flying dead astern he saw large pieces of the mainplane breaking away before it crashed into the Gulf. His second victim went into the water nose first. An immense splash obliterated the entire machine as it rapidly sank. At the same time Major Human had taken a section of 5 Squadron down in a beam attack, himself getting one; five others claiming one each.

Lt. H. Marshall, 4 Squadron, closed in on his chosen victim, seeing the whole mainplane catch alight from the burning engines and the stricken giant plunge below the surface. His second Me 323 stopped the full blast of all his guns at 250 yards and with a tremendous flash disintegrated in the air. He shared a third with a persistent Kittyhawk flown by Lt. F. M. F. Green who also claimed two-and-a-half, both being seen to burn and break up on impact with the sea. Four other pilots of 4 Squadron claimed one each.

2 Squadron, fated to top-cover work, was represented in the final score when Lt. Moon tackled an Re 2001 which had

attempted to dive through to attack 4 and 5 Squadrons. Moon sent the Italian into the sea.*

The enemy fleet was first sighted at 08.30. By 08.50 the last of them had gone into the sea. There were no apparent survivors. Pilots circling the unruffled sea saw only patches of oil burning on the water, then, hearing their commanders calling, they set course for home. High above the South Africans, the Polish airmen were heard crying their characteristic 'Bravos!' They claimed to have shot down six of the escort. This classic twenty minutes cost the South Africans one Kittyhawk down in the sea, its pilot, Lt. R. A. Steel, escaping by dinghy. 239 Wing (RAF) lost three pilots but at what stage they joined the fight South African records do not show.

True to form the fighter pilots claimed more 323s than were actually sighted! But, whatever the true figures, this remarkable engagement put an end to all further daylight reinforcement flights.

* Brown, *Eagles Strike*.

ISLAND STRATEGY

Two signals sent by Winston Churchill to General Auchinleck, C-in-C, Middle East, at a crucial moment during the great battle for Malta in 1942, underscored the importance the Allies attached to holding the diminutive Mediterranean island. The first, dispatched on 8 May, ran as follows:

The Chiefs of Staff, the Defence Committee and the War Cabinet have all earnestly considered your telegram in relation to the whole war situation, having particular regard to Malta, the loss of which would be a disaster of first magnitude to the British Empire, and probably fatal in the long run to the defence of the Nile Valley.

2. We are agreed that in spite of the risks . . . you would be right to attack the enemy (in Cyrenaica) and fight a major battle, if possible in May, and the sooner the better. We are prepared to take full responsibility for these general directions, leaving you the necessary latitude for their execution. In this you will no doubt have regard to the fact that the enemy may himself be planning to attack you early in June.

The second followed two days later, on 10 May.

The Chiefs of Staff, the Defence Committee and the War Cabinet have again considered the whole position. We are determined that Malta shall not be allowed to fall without a major battle being fought by your whole army for its retention. The starving out of this fortress would involve the surrender of over 30,000 men, Army and Air Force, together with several hundred guns. Its possession would give the enemy a clear and sure bridge to Africa, with all the consequences flowing from that. Its loss would sever the air route upon which both you and India must depend . . . Besides this, it would compromise any offensive against Italy . . .

and [other] future plans . . . Compared with the certainty of these disasters, we consider the risks you have set out to the safety of Egypt are definitely less, and we accept them.

One other opinion, expressed with the full advantage of hindsight some forty years later, confirms the correctness of the stance which Churchill and the Chiefs of Staff had adopted towards the Mediterranean fortress. It is given by Lord James Douglas-Hamilton, lawyer, author, minister of the Crown and nephew of Squadron Leader Lord David Douglas-Hamilton, commander of 603 (City of Edinburgh) Squadron at Takali at the height of the battle, in his eminently readable book *The Air Battle for Malta.**

* Mainstream Publishing, Edinburgh, 1981 and Airlife, Shrewsbury, 1990.

Ju 88 pressing an attack on Grand Harbour

Based upon his uncle's wartime diary, Lord James refers in the course of the narrative to the Island's primary role as an offensive base. He points to the intrepid part played in the conflict by the crews of the Royal Air Force's bomber and torpedo-carrying aircraft, the Blenheims, the Wellingtons and the Marylands and, later, the Baltimores and the Beauforts (with their long-range escorting Beaufighters), and by those of the Fleet Air Arm with their Swordfish and Albacores, and the Royal Navy's submarines. This is what he says of them:

(They) had destroyed ships in the Axis convoys (crossing the Mediterranean to Libya) amounting to far more than 400,000 tons, with the result that Rommel and the Afrika Korps were starved of most necessary supplies. The war in North Africa had become a war of logistics and by the time El Alamein took place (in October 1942) the British 8th Army was attacking from a position of far greater strength . . .

As General Montgomery had acknowledged, the Battle of El Alamein could not have taken place if Malta had fallen earlier in 1942 . . . Supplies would have reached Rommel and the Afrika Korps for the most part unhindered: the Afrika Korps would rapidly have built up its strength and would probably have seized the Nile Delta. Certainly the war for North Africa and the Middle East would have taken a different course.

'PRESSED TO THE LAST GASP'

It is against this strategic background that the battle for this ancient island, with its 2,000-year-old history, must be seen.

What, then, was it like to live with a Royal Air Force squadron through those cataclysmic times which reached their nadir in the spring of 1942, of which Churchill was later to write in a graphic passage in his *History of the Second World War*: 'In March and April (1942) all the heat was turned on Malta and remorseless air attacks by day and night wore the Island down and pressed it to the last gasp . . .'*

To picture the intensity of the air battle and the imperishable contribution made by the squadrons' air and

Top: Bombers of the Regia Aeronautica leave their mark

Above: Bombs gone! Ju 87 dive bomber turns for home

groundcrews, it is necessary for the reader, first, to grasp the smallness of the Island. Seventeen miles long by nine wide and no more than roundly 150 square miles in total – a shade smaller than the Isle of Wight – it represented a tiny area to absorb the weight of the enemy's concentrated bombing onslaught. Moreover, there were broadly only four targets to attract the Axis powers' attention: Grand Harbour and the capital Valletta and their environs to the east, and the three airfields running in a line north-westwards from Halfar in

* Winston S. Churchill, *The Second World War: The Hinge of Fate* (Cassell, London, 1951).

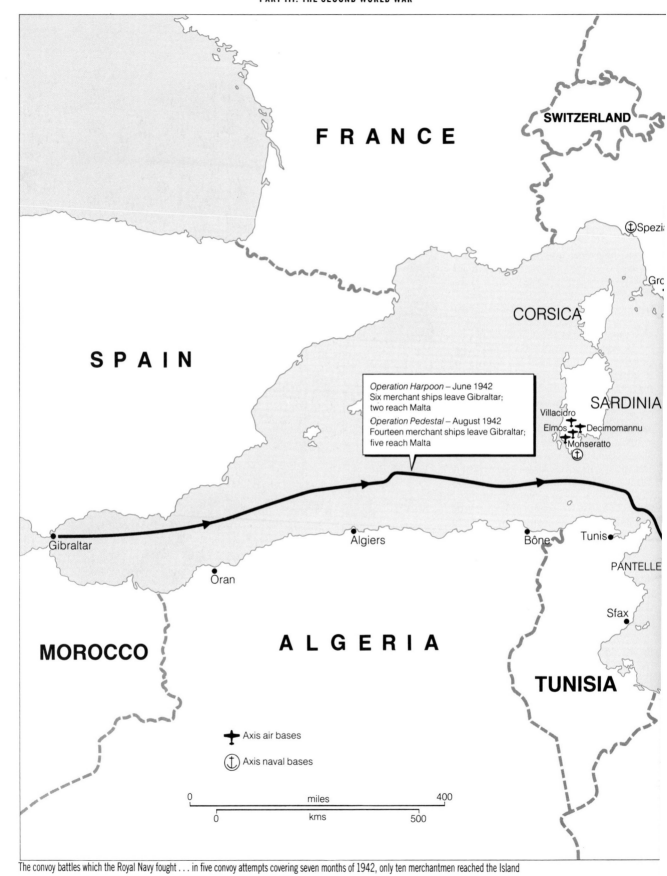

FRANCE

SWITZERLAND

Spezia

Gro

CORSICA

SPAIN

SARDINIA

Villacidro

Elmos Decimomannu

Monseratto

Operation Harpoon – June 1942
Six merchant ships leave Gibraltar;
two reach Malta

Operation Pedestal – August 1942
Fourteen merchant ships leave Gibraltar;
five reach Malta

Gibraltar

Algiers

Bône

Tunis

PANTELLE

Oran

Sfax

MOROCCO

ALGERIA

TUNISIA

Axis air bases

Axis naval bases

0	miles	400
0	kms	500

The convoy battles which the Royal Navy fought . . . in five convoy attempts covering seven months of 1942, only ten merchantmen reached the Island

0 miles 5

St. Pauls

MOSTA Naxxar

Mtarfa St. Julians

RABAT SLIEMA

Takali

VALLETTA

Sigiewi

Grand
Harbour

Luqa

Krendi

Safi

Halfar

MALTA

YUGOSLAVIA

ITALY

ALBANIA

Naples

Taranto

GREECE

Athens

ermo

Messina

SICILY Catania

etrano Gerbini

Comiso

Gozo MALTA

CRETE

Operation MF5 – February 1942
Three merchant ships from Alexandria are sunk

Operation MW10 – March 1942
Four merchant ships leave Alexandria; three
reach Malta but are destroyed whilst unloading

Operation Vigorous – June 1942
Eleven merchant ships forced to turn back

oli

Benghazi

Tobruk

Alexandria

El Alamein

TRIPOLITANIA

LIBYA

CYRENAICA

EGYPT

the south to Luqa, the main base, in the centre, and on to Takali, the fighter field, three or four miles beyond.

It was principally against these four easily identifiable bombing points that the Luftwaffe, with its 600 front-line aircraft, and the Regia Aeronautica, with its strength of some 350 in support, concentrated the weight of the attack.

In *two months*, March and April 1942, Malta actually withstood twice, repeat twice, the tonnage of bombs that had fallen on London during the worst *twelve months* of the Blitz. In one stretch, Malta had to endure 154 successive days of round-the-clock bombing. The longest continuous spell Londoners had to face at the peak of the Nazi attacks lasted for no more than a third of that time, fifty-four days, a hundred less than the small Mediterranean fortress.

Another comparison is worth noting. In the German Air Force's famous attack on Coventry in November 1940, 260 tons of bombs were dropped on the Midland city. Thirty times that weight fell on Malta's Grand Harbour in six weeks of March and April alone.

THE GREAT CONVOY BATTLES

All the Air Force squadrons watched with mounting concern the sustained plight of the seaborne convoys upon whose supplies the Island's ability to survive depended. Between February and August 1942, both months included, when the Axis controlled most of the southern and northern coasts of the Mediterranean, the Royal Navy and the Merchant Navy made five attempts to run the gauntlet to the beleaguered Island, with convoys sailing either from east or west or both together. They embraced, in total, thirty-eight merchantmen with their massive naval escorts.

Malta lay, quite isolated, some 800 miles from Gibraltar to the west and approximately 1,000 from Alexandria in the east. The passage of the eastern convoys through the celebrated Bomb Alley, formed by the enemy-held Benghazi blister to the south and Crete to the north, was as dangerous as that through the Narrows, and past the island of Pantelleria, from the west.

With the Italian fleet based at Taranto and other ports on the Italian mainland always ready to strike from the north, and with the Luftwaffe's land-based Junkers 88s and 87s in North Africa, Sardinia, Sicily and Crete ever at the ready, progress was a hazardous business. The losses were appalling.

The February convoy, code-named Operation MF 5, from Alexandria, with three merchantmen, never made it, two of the merchant ships being sunk and the third damaged. Its March successor of four cargo ships also run from the east – Operation MW 10 – delivered two merchantmen, *Talabot* and *Pampas*, to Grand Harbour after *Clan Campbell* had earlier been sunk. A fourth, *Breconshire*, hard hit, had to be towed the last miles to the Island, there to be beached in Marsaxlokk Bay. All three arrivals were then destroyed by air attack after no more than 5,000 tons of supplies had been unloaded.

The June effort from Alexandria – Operation Vigorous – under the command of Admiral Vian, run concurrently with another – Operation Harpoon – from the west, fared worse. It was forced by murderous air attack and the imminent intervention of the Italian fleet to turn back with heavy losses . . . a terrible reverse.

Its western counterpart, hammered mercilessly by air and sea for three tortuous days, could supply the Island with no more than two merchant vessels out of six, their 25,000 blessed tons of supplies prolonging its life by barely three more months.

The August attempt, made again from the west – Operation Pedestal – produced the fiercest air-sea battle of the lot with the Luftwaffe, the Regia Aeronautica and the Supermarino throwing in everything they had in what turned out to be a final attempt to grip Malta's jugular and strangle the fortress to death. Only five of the original fourteen merchantmen,

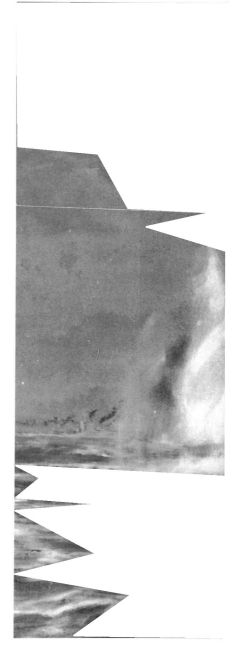

covered in the final stages by a maximum, do-or-die effort by the island-based Spitfires, struggled through the blitz to Grand Harbour. Included in this gallant number was the US tanker *Ohio*, carrying vital oil, kerosene and fuel. Its British crew, with the aid of three Royal Navy destroyers, *Bramham*, *Penn* and *Ledbury*, and the minesweeper *Rye*, in an astonishing act of seamanship, brought the oiler, with its decks awash, into Grand

Harbour to the cheers of the waving Maltese gathered along the bastions.

High up above the prize arrivals, UK, Commonwealth and US fighter pilots, with their new-found Spitfire strength, fought a spirited defensive battle while the Army gunners, standing resolutely to their posts amid the onslaught, raised a protective steel canopy over the ships. Here was yet another example of the closeness of the co-operation between the three Services and the Merchant Navy with arms linked in an all-out effort to sustain the Garrison and bring succour to the Island's indomitable people.

The cost of these blockade-busting operations was very high, and none suffered more heavily than the crews of the Merchant Navy. Out of the total of thirty-eight merchantmen setting forth on these five Malta-bound convoys, only ten ever reached their destination and of these three were then

HMS *Illustrious* under attack by the Luftwaffe

sunk after berthing or beaching – a fearful 'abort' and loss rate of almost 74 per cent.

If furious air battles were fought out over these convoys as they neared the Island, equally vigorous engagements were daily being joined for control of the daylight air high up over Malta. The work of the fighter squadrons, supported by the ground-crews, could fill a chapter of Royal Air Force history as 1941 merged with 1942. With their antiquated Hurricane IIs, outperformed and vastly outnumbered (but never outflown) by Field Marshal Kesselring's Messerschmitt 109Fs, based sixty miles away across the Straits in Sicily, the pilots achieved the impossible. For months before the arrival of the Spitfires, and for a while thereafter, it was the UK representatives who held the fort. Men of the calibre of Mortimer Rose, Don Stones, Bob Wells, 'Butch' Barton, James MacLachlin, Innes Westmacott, Jack Satchell, George Powell-Sheddon, 'Rags' Rabagliati, Philip Wigley, Sonny Ormrod and others, many of whom had already had a basinful in the Battle of Britain (and a few in the Battle of France), wrestled with the odds and made the enemy fight for every mile he crossed of the Island's air space. Often able to put up no more than half-a-dozen, cannibalized Hurricanes against the hordes of 109s, 87s and 88s, they held the line in a remarkable act of war. One or two of the irrepressible day pilots like Powell-Sheddon, Stones and 'Cass' Cassidy took the fight to the enemy at night.

AN EXCEPTIONAL COMMANDER

Presiding day and night over the air battle was an outstanding leader, Air Vice-Marshal Hugh Lloyd, Malta's imperturbable yet ruggedly astute Air Officer Commanding (AOC). Lloyd was at his best when things looked bleakest – when, for instance, the lowest point had been reached in the spring of 1942 and invasion (Operation Herkules) appeared to be imminent. He never regarded himself as being bound by Queensberry rules. His ringcraft was his own. Alarmed questions from the Air Ministry or HQ, Middle East, could always wait. He was his own man, the original aircraft hijacker, meeting shortages by collaring, for his own operational purpose, bomber and photographic reconnais-

Lloyd of Malta

sance aircraft as they touched down at Luqa *en route* for the Middle or Far East.

Air Marshal Sir Ivor Broom, then a 21-year-old sergeant pilot, tells how he and his crew, in their Blenheim, were held at Luqa by the AOC ('only for a day or two, Sergeant Broom') in September 1941 instead of flying on to India and the Far East as they had intended.

The next day the crew were astonished to find themselves 'on the detail' with 105 Squadron for one of those lethal low-level, daylight shipping strikes which, from Malta and the United Kingdom, caused just about the heaviest prolonged casualties of the war. It was one of four missions they were asked to fly in five days; and when 105, after being shot to pieces, had to return to East Anglia to reform, the sergeant pilot and his crew were then summarily transferred to 107 Squadron, 105's Blenheim counterpart, there to spend the next four gruelling months before being posted home with what re-

mained of the Squadron. They never did see the Far East!

Lloyd became a legend. There was the singular occasion later on, at the height of the bombing, when, in the Mess at M'dina, he was addressing a roomful of fighter pilots just arrived from England. A particularly heavy raid was building up with guns cracking and bombs falling as he reached his peroration. 'Get in close to the enemy,' he was saying, 'see the whites of his eyes before you shoot. If you don't get him, he'll get you . . . '

Just then a 2,000-pounder, shrieking and whistling, seemed as if it must hit the villa. Led by the Australians and New Zealanders the pilots made a headlong dive for the protection of the billiard table or any other cover they could find. A few moments later, dusting themselves down, they crept sheepishly from their hiding places to find the AOC, still standing erect, utterly impervious to the danger which had just passed. '. . . You will see, gentlemen, what I mean!'

He offered a final thought. 'Win this battle, gentlemen, achieve the victory and forever after you will be able to tell them of Malta and say with pride, 'I was there.' The Australians never let anyone forget it. Whenever some misfortune or accident befell a pilot, and he was feeling particularly low, there would be a sympathetic pat on the head and a rich Melbourne accent would cut through the gloom. 'Never mind, sport, you'll still be able to tell them of Malta and say with pride, "I was there"!'

REINFORCEMENT BY AIRCRAFT-CARRIER: THE ONLY WAY

What Lloyd of course, knew was that the day-fighter battle must be won – or at least contained – if the Island was to give cover to the seaborne convoys and maintain its governing role as an offensive base from which the Royal Air Force's and Fleet Air Arm's crews could strike at shipping and the port installations feeding Rommel and his Afrika Korps.

Spitfires and more Spitfires was the cry. And the only practical way in which these aeroplanes could be supplied to the Island was from the aircraft carriers operating from a fly-off point some fifty miles north of Algiers and roundly 650 miles west of Malta, just outside practical enemy bomber range.

It was a hazardous business with the fighters' overload, ninety-gallon drop tank slung under the fuselage, sharply increasing the all-up weight and making the short take-off run from the flight-deck a testing affair. The ever-present threat of submarine attack added to the unease.

For the Royal Navy, the aircraft carrier *Eagle*, which initially accommodated sixteen or seventeen aircraft (later to be increased, with better stacking, to thirty-two), and elements of the Mediterranean Fleet, bore the brunt of these operations. Inexperience and, alas, incompetence on the Royal Air Force's part, however, clouded and seriously delayed the early reinforcing operations. It

caused an exasperated Chief of the Air Staff, sitting at his desk in Whitehall, to write on a file, 'It's quicker by rail!' And when the limited flow of Spitfires did eventually begin to materialize, the wastage on the ground at Malta, in the face of the enemy's relentless bombing attacks, was disastrous.

Seldom, in March and April 1942, were the defenders able to muster more than a handful of aircraft to meet the increasing Axis attacks. Outnumbered often by ten, fifteen and twenty to one, the pilots, like their Hurricane predecessors, performed heroics; but much more was needed.

It was at this critical point in April, when the Island's fortunes hung by a frayed thread, that Churchill persuaded the President of the United States to allow the vast carrier *Wasp*, with its ability to house forty-eight Spitfires in addition to its own aircraft, to be brought into play.

Twice she made the run down the Mediterranean to the usual fly-off spot. The first, however, on 20 April, when forty-seven Spitfires of 601 and 602 Squadrons, led respectively by Lord David Douglas-Hamilton and John Bisdee, and with Wing Commander E. J. Gracie in the van, were successfully launched, ended in catastrophe. The Axis monitored the progress of the reinforcements and timed a series of strongly pressed bombing attacks against the Island's airfields while the aircraft were still on the ground waiting to be refuelled after arrival. No more than seven were flyable forty-eight hours later. It was a punch to the solar plexus.

The Prime Minister prevailed upon the President to permit the US Navy and *Wasp* to make another run on 9 May, this time in concert with *Eagle* to provide a tally of sixty-four aircraft. In Malta, elaborate and greatly improved plans were laid to receive and

Fly-off point for critical reinforcement of Spitfires from aircraft carriers HMS *Eagle* and USN *Wasp*, 20 April–18 May 1942

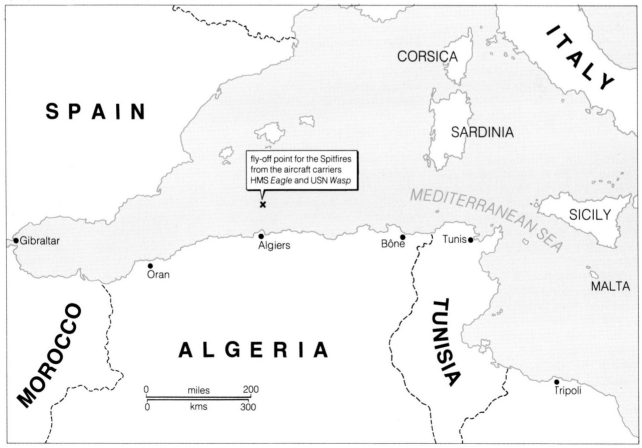

Royal Navy's carrier *Eagle* heading for fly-off point

immediately turn round the arrivals. Island-based pilots, with weeks of fighting behind them, were sent back to Gibraltar to lead in the reinforcements.

The scene was transformed. When the Luftwaffe attacked, it was hit by an altogether stronger and more concentrated defence. Badly mauled, Kesselring's marauders came back again and again with their customary courage, but their supremacy had passed. For them, it was 'Never glad confident morning again.' Nine days later, on 18 May, *Eagle* flew off a further sixteen Spitfires to swell still further the defender's new-found confidence. The battle had at last been turned.

The intervention of the US Navy with *Wasp*, and a brilliant combined operation with the Royal Navy, had tipped the precarious balance in the Allies' favour – but not before a somewhat bizarre incident had made history.

Jerrold Smith, a Canadian, whose brother Roderick was also to become a stalwart in the Island's defence and, subsequently, one of Canada's successful wartime fighter leaders, had lost his ninety-gallon overload fuel tank on take-off from *Wasp*. With no chance of reaching Malta without the additional fuel, Smith decided to go for broke and try for landing back on the American carrier's flight-deck without any arrester gear – the first time it had ever been attempted with a Spitfire. Astonishingly, he succeeded at his second attempt finishing up no more than a foot or two from disaster.

Douglas Fairbanks Jr, liaison officer on board *Wasp*, at once took Smith down to the wardroom of this supposedly totally 'dry' US warship. Pressing a very large Scotch and soda into the Canadian's hand, he looked furtively around the empty room. 'Here,' he said, 'drink this – quick.'

As *Wasp* steamed out of the Mediterranean and into the Atlantic, Churchill signalled congratulations to the ship's captain, 'Who said a *Wasp* couldn't sting twice?'

Four months later, the carrier was lost in the Pacific, sent to the bottom by a torpedo fired from a Japanese submarine. Mercifully, her splendid crew, who had brought relief to Malta, was saved.

THESE NAMES MADE NEWS

High drama, played out in the Mediterranean sun, inevitably created its *corps d'élite*. The names of a few pilots and leaders from the 1942 Spitfire class will forever have their place in the battle history. Gracie, Grant, McQueen, Nash, Ronnie West, Hurst and Daddo-Langlois from the UK; Brennan, Goldsmith, Boyd, Yarra and Yates from Australia; Hesslyn, Geoff West, Rae and Verrall from New Zealand; Plagis and Buchanan from Rhodesia; McNair, Connell, Beurling, Jones, McElroy, Linton, Middlemiss and de Nancrede from Canada; and from the US ex-Eagle Squadron contingent, Peck, McLeod, Tilley, Booth, McHan and Kelly . . . Here was a galaxy of talent mixed with solid, dependable worth.

At the top of the day-fighting list, however, stood Percival Stanley Turner, the Canadian wing commander in the Royal Air Force, who, by the time he reached Malta, had already fought through the Battles of France and Britain, and had taken his proper place in Douglas Bader's Tangmere Wing of all the talents in

the offensive sweeps over northern France in 1941.

Sent out in a Sunderland flying boat in February with the first batch of sixteen reinforcing pilots, Turner's remit was to take hold of the Island's flying and lead the Spitfires when they arrived. In the event, he stamped his mark on 249 Squadron and its other counterparts, scrapped the prehistoric vic formations and made pairs of aircraft, flying fast three or four hundred yards apart in wide-open, line abreast, the basis of the aerial defence.

Stan Turner had been told the Spitfires would be on the Island by the time he and his advance party arrived. The reality was otherwise. As he stepped from the tender on to the quayside at Kalafrana soon after dawn on a beautiful early spring morning, the air-raid sirens started wailing out their welcome.

Presently, five old Hurricane IIs, strung out in an antidiluvian vic formation, passed overhead, clambering, labouring to gain height. Eight or ten thousand feet above, a couple of *staffeln* of Messerschmitts raced across the sky, dominant in their loosely flown fours in extended line abreast, crossing over in the turns and sweeping in ahead of the incoming raid.

Turner looked up at this awesome sight and stood there askance. 'Good God!' he exclaimed, turned on his heel and made off towards the Mess.

When Turner came to leave the Island some six remarkable months later, his departure was as droll as his arrival. It was July and Group Captain A. B. Woodhall, in charge of Operations at Headquarters, came over to the Mess in M'dina one evening to tell us that he and the AOC would be leaving on the 14th of the month at the end of their exceptional tours of duty.

He broke the news that Hugh Pughe Lloyd would be followed on the 15th by Air Vice-Marshal Keith Park of Battle of Britain fame. Turner, always a pungent critic of things he considered wrong, had crossed swords once or twice with Park over tactics when he was flying with Bader's Duxford Wing during the Battle. Park heard of the Canadian's criticism and didn't much like it.

Woodhall's news of Keith Park's imminent arrival stunned the wing commander. He put his glass down on the bar counter and looked the group captain straight in the eye: 'The guy,' he said with a decisive finality, 'will have me off the Island inside of a month.' As things turned out, it took little more than a week!

CLASSIC CONTROLLING

If Turner had his place around the summit of Malta's elite, Group Captain Woodhall must be ranged with him and Hugh Pughe Lloyd as an architect of victory. In a phrase, Woodhall was the outstanding ground controller of the war with an ability at the art which set him apart. With his Battle of Britain and Fighter Command experience behind him, he turned the controlling process into something which approached genius.

A First World War pilot, he was well versed in tactics – the value of height, sun, speed, surprise and, with it, position . . . Position was his ultimate aim

Nucleus of 249 Squadron: *(left to right)* Flight Commanders Daddo-Langlois and Lee with Paul Brennan, Ray Hesslyn and CO Laddie Lucas

Malta marvel – Canada's Percival Stanley Turner

clarity of the spoken instructions were a passport to success. They spelt reassurance in an agitated pilot's mind. Such was their impression that, fifty years on, they still remain an unmistakable echo in a survivor's ear.

Backing Woodhall's brilliance were two facets of the Island's intelligence service. One, Ultra's secret unravelling of the German coded cyphers passing between HQ staffs and units, was known only to those at the pinnacle of Malta's military machine. The squadrons were totally unaware of the organization and its ability to anticipate many of the enemy's decisive moves. Thus it was that when the threat of invasion was at its height, the Chiefs of Staff in London were able to quell the local high command's fears by disclosing Ultra's knowledge of the movement of Luftwaffe units from Sicily to North Africa and the Eastern Front. These were quite incompatible with the ordering of Operation Herkules. Would that this super-secret information had been available to the Island's junior echelons! Sleep would have come more easily.

To supplement Ultra's disclosure of Axis intentions was the 'Y' Service, Malta's listening process which picked up the enemy's transmissions that flowed between base and aircraft in flight and ships at sea. Much was gained from these intercepted messages in the ebb and flow of battle and no praise is too high for the staffs who manned the intelligence networks, working daily underground in close and ill-ventilated conditions which no authority in peacetime would ever tolerate. Theirs was a selfless and devoted existence which contributed massively to survival and victory.

AFTER LLOYD, PARK

Hugh Lloyd's unparalleled tenure at the air command's apex ended on 14 July after fourteen months of unrelieved pressure. Woodhall left the Island at the same time. Both had become palpably exhausted by their

in handling a defensive interception. He was an opportunist who could read an incoming raid with uncanny prescience. He was seldom wrong in divining the enemy's purpose. It was this magical knack which, in the bleakest times, when the odds were stacked so heavily against a defending formation, allowed him to pit ten or a dozen Spitfires against an enemy plot of a hundred or hundred and twenty plus and come out of it with honours often much better than even. It was the confidence which he instilled from the Operations Room, deep in the bowels of Valletta, which compelled pilots faithfully to follow his word.

The line could never have been held in March and April 1942 without Woodhall's ability to translate the enemy's track, which he saw on the Ops table, into a scoring opportunity for the greatly outnumbered defence. His was a priceless skill.

But Woody (even a newly arrived sergeant pilot knew 'Woody' as his personal ground station, not the impersonal call sign of Gondar) was the first to recognize that his effectiveness would have been sharply reduced had he not had the advantage of the Island's advanced radar system to support his talents. It was far superior to the primitive device that the enemy had at his disposal in Sicily. Malta's radars, the first to be installed outside the United Kingdom, became the tools of Woodhall's hand. His artistry enabled him to exploit this gain to the full.

Again, his voice was a potent force in his armoury as a controller. Voice has always been a strong factor in a man's personality. Pick up the telephone and the voice at the other end conveys an instant impression of the caller. So it was with Woodhall in the rough times of 1942. Those deep, resonant, unhurried tones, and the endeavours, but each departed knowing that the corner had irrevocably been turned and that, despite all the continuing privations and worries, a truly decisive battle had been won.

Lloyd was followed on 15 July by the New Zealander, Air Vice-Marshal Keith Park, former AOC of 11 Group, Fighter Command, in the Battle of Britain, whose fertile, tactical brain had brought victory for his squadrons in the day-to-day fighting over southeast England and, under his C-in-C, Sir Hugh Dowding, salvation for the British people. His was an inspired choice.

Park, tall, spare and spruce, and always well groomed, assumed control when the Island's fighter strength had reached an unprecedented 130 serviceable Spitfires and the vital striking force of bombers and torpedo-carrying aircraft at Luqa was secure. The desperate days of spring and early summer were far behind.

The new AOC, with his positive and decisive mind, switched at once to the attack, sending elements of his fighter force north across the sixty miles of Straits to hit Kesselring's raiders on the nose as they built up over Sicily and began to head south. In effect, the Axis attackers now caught the sharp end of Park's tactics twice – once in the vicinity of their home ground and again when they approached Malta where the AOC had retained a telling defence.

It was a double thrust at the enemy's heart which found its maximum effect during the Luftwaffe's final and short-lived October blitz, plainly designed to aid Rommel and his fatally extended Afrika Korps ranged against General Montgomery's Eighth Army, now standing in strength on the Alamein Line with the convincing success of the battle of Alam Halfa nicely behind.

It has been widely canvassed that Park's policy of 'Forward Interception', effective though it undoubtedly was, 'won' the battle of Malta. This is not so as the Royal Air Force's historians, writing in retrospect with the benefit of the facts before them, are at pains to make clear.

This [policy] was only possible because of the increased fighter strength in Spitfires . . . It saved bombs and crashing aircraft from falling on the Island, but it is an exaggeration to claim that [it] 'saved' Malta. The battle for Malta had been won before Air Vice-Marshal Lloyd left the Island. After the enemy had called off the spring blitz in April 1942 and Rommel became deeply committed to his offensive (in Libya), the existence of Malta as an air and naval base was never seriously threatened by concentrated air attack.*

The truth of it is, of course, that the Malta battle was a victory for inter-Service co-operation in the face of daunting conditions – of the Royal Air Force with its UK, Commonwealth and US representation, and the magnificence of its groundcrews, working in concert with the Army and the Royal Navy, the Merchant Navy and, at two critical moments in April and May 1942, with the US Navy and its blessed carrier *Wasp*. And all this rested upon the steadfastness and resolve of the Maltese people to support the Garrison and see things through.

For the Axis, defeat was effectively sealed when Hitler funked invasion, setting Operation Herkules aside 'until further notice' against the best advice. Instead, he preferred to rely on the saturation bombing of Malta to remove the thorn from Rommel's side. His reliance proved to be misplaced as Field Marshal Kesselring made quite clear in his ultimate assessment.

The abandonment of this [invasion] was the first death blow to the whole undertaking in North Africa . . . Strategically, the one fatal blunder was the abandoning of the plan to invade Malta. When this happened, the subsequent course of events (the withdrawal from North Africa and the loss of Sicily and Italy) was almost inevitable.†

Incomparable controller – Group Captain A.B. Woodhall

* Air Historical Branch (RAF), Draft Narrative (Malta), unpublished.
† Field Marshal Albert Kesselring, *The War in the Mediterranean, Part I*, AHB6, Trans. No. VII/104.

12 · BOMBER OFFENSIVE AGAINST GERMANY

'ROUND THE CLOCK'

The round-the-clock offensive against the Third Reich, pressed to the limit by the Royal Air Force's Bomber Command and by the US Eighth Army Air Force was the key which unlocked the door to the victory of the Allied armies in Europe. Mounted in tandem from the autumn of 1943, against the strongest and most lethal fighter defence ever assembled, it tore the heart out of the Nazi regime, smashed their evil empire, heralded the Normandy invasion and the Allied march through France, Belgium and Holland, across the Rhine and into the home of the *Herrenvolk*.

The American bombing campaign was totally different from that of Bomber Command. Both began their offensives by bombing in daylight but the British suffered such high casualties that they were forced into attacking under cover of darkness. Night bombing, however, proved very in-

accurate, and when Air Chief Marshal Sir Arthur Harris arrived his policy was brutally simple. Since his force could not hit what it chose, it would hit what it could – large sprawling German cities. So began the much-publicized 'Thousand Bomber Raids', with devastating firestorms such as that which in 1945 destroyed Dresden.

The Americans were by no means ready to adopt the same policy because they believed in precision bombing. In the 1920s General 'Billy' Mitchell had infuriated the US Navy by demonstrating that aeroplanes could hit and sink battleships. By the late 1930s the Americans had produced the B-17 (Flying Fortress) bomber and the famous Norden bombsight which together, they boasted, could put a bomb into a 'pickle barrel' from 25,000 feet.

Their slogan was 'Victory through Air Power', and today I can still remember how the young American

aircrews threw themselves into the business of making daylight bombing work. When, in late 1942, Spitfires first escorted a few B-17s over France they lacked experience, got lost and missed their targets. Consequently, the British air marshals once more argued that the American effort should be incorporated into their own night offensive. But Churchill, who saw the wisdom of 'bombing the devils round the clock', supported the American doctrine and the eventual outcome was Operation Pointblank aimed at liberating Europe by a combined bomber offensive, with the two bomber forces complementing each other in sustaining night and day attacks.

Day after day, night after night, 'undeterred by the fury of the guns and the new inventions of death' they battled their way over Germany and paid a high price for the victory. Of the Royal Air Force's total of 70,253 aircrew killed or missing on operations, no less than 47,293 came from Bomber Command.

'All across Germany, Holland and France,' wrote a B-17 navigator, 'the terrible landscape of burning planes unrolled beneath us. It seemed that we were littering Europe with our dead.'* Indeed, our American cousins lost some 43,000 aircrews killed or missing from daylight operations over Europe.

BERLIN: FIRST DAYLIGHT ATTACK

The Australian 'Digger' Kyle (Air Chief Marshal Sir Wallace Kyle), one of Bomber Command's rugged wartime leaders, described the first daylight raid on the capital of the Third Reich:

Sir Arthur 'Bomber' Harris

* Elmer Bendiner, *The Fall of Fortresses*, (Putnam, New York, 1980).

'One of our aircraft failed to return'

At the beginning of 1943 I was Station Commander at Marham, Norfolk, with Mosquitos of 105 and 139 Squadrons. It was about 15.00 hours on 29 January when I received a telephone call from Group Captain S. C. (Sam) Elworthy, then Group Captain Operations at Bomber Command. I had just stood both squadrons down after a very heavy week. He told me that the C-in-C wanted Mosquitos to attack Berlin the following day at 11.00 hours precisely, when Göring was scheduled to speak at an open-air rally. What did I think?

This was, to put it mildly, rather a surprise, not so much because of the target (Berlin), but because of the timing which would restrict our tactical freedom of action. It meant that we would be exposed to fighter attack both during penetration and, again, on withdrawal when the advantage of surprise had gone. I said we would be lucky to get away without severe casualties. Elworthy, who knew the operational form well enough, agreed and offered to represent this to the C-in-C.

Before long, he came back to con- firm that we were to go. There followed a pause. 'You haven't heard all of it yet. We want you to attack again at 16.00 when Goebbels will be speaking at a similar rally.'

We decided to send three aircraft from 105 Squadron on the morning raid and three from 139 in the afternoon. The choice was made by tossing a coin. Squadron Leader Reynolds and Flying Officer Sismore led the first attack and Squadron Leader Darling and Flying Officer Wright the second.

We thought we would get away

with the penetration phase by staying at low level until the last moment before climbing to 25,000 feet for the bombing run. The route chosen was pretty well direct and we were able to stay under radar cover as far as Hanover. Withdrawal was to be by diving at maximum speed to low level, heading north to Norway, without too much regard for Swedish air space, and then directly back to base. This was about the limit of endurance for the Mk IV Mosquito in the low-high-low profile.

The morning attack went exactly to plan and bombs were dropped at precisely 11.00 hours. Even the heavens were on our side because, at the very last moment, after Sismore had told Reynolds it would have to be an ETA release, he spotted a hole in the otherwise complete cloud cover. It was plumb over Berlin and they could see the lakes and Spandau. The bombs hit the north-east area of the city. The tactics had worked and all aircraft returned safely. It was a superb piece of accurate flying and navigation. (We had no radar aids then.)

We were apprehensive about the afternoon attack because the defences had obviously been stirred

Experience on the staff: Air Commodore S.C. (Sam) Elworthy

up. We certainly didn't think we would follow the same penetration and withdrawal route. After a lot of discussion with the crews we decided on the simple solution of reversing the routes.

We calculated the run-in would have maximum surprise, especially using the fringe of Swedish air space; and, most of all, the withdrawal phase would be in dusk conditions over Germany and Holland at low levels.

Sure enough, we got away with the penetration, but the flak was more intense and Squadron Leader Darling was picked off after bombing.

In the bar that evening we had the satisfaction of listening to a tape recording of the air-raid alarm which accompanied the first raid, and the cancellation of Göring's speech by the announcer. As Goebbels's speech and rally were also disrupted by the second attack, we felt we could claim success.*

THE BATTLE OF HAMBURG: OPERATION GOMORRAH

Towards the end of July 1943 we achieved what I regard as the greatest victory of the war, land, sea or air. This victory was in the Battle of Hamburg . . . The result was absolutely staggering!†

Bomber Command, under the leadership of the 51-year-old Air Chief Marshal Sir Arthur Harris, fought three major strategic battles in World War Two – the Battles of the Ruhr, Hamburg and Berlin, in that order.

The Battle of the Ruhr, which opened in March 1943 and lasted until July, possessed one unquestioned advantage over the other two. The targets were all nicely within range of Oboe, the remarkably efficient blind-bombing device which the Germans were unable effectively to jam. A real plus for the Allies in the electronic 'war', it achieved a degree of accuracy which other comparable radar systems could not quite repeat in the two subsequent contests. However, the cost in aircraft and crews in the fiercely defended Ruhr Valley was relatively high with some 870 aircraft missing giving a loss rate of a shade over 4½ per cent. Aircraft could be replaced, but the loss of so many dedicated and experienced crews was quite another matter.

Digger Kyle and his aircrews

* Laddie Lucas, *Wings of War* (Hutchinson, London, 1983).
† Air Vice-Marshal C. C. T. Bennett, CB, CBE, DSO, *Pathfinder* (Frederick Muller, London, 1958).

A Halifax bomber over Germany

Nevertheless, the onslaught was an undoubted success and left Bomber Command with its collective tail well up as it faced the next stage in the strategic offensive.

The last battle of the three – that of Berlin – which embraced among other deep-penetration attacks sixteen long winter night raids on the capital, cost some 1,050 aircraft missing and, with them, upwards of 7,000 precious aircrew. It endured for five gruelling months from November 1943 until March 1944 at its height, a respite coming only in the period before D-Day and the Normandy landings when the Command's sting was being directed temporarily at short-range targets in enemy-occupied territory.

With Berlin lying well outside the range of Oboe, the attacking force relied primarily upon the device known as H2S for the marking and blind-bombing process. With the electronic sets carried in the aircraft, this aid was seen as a mixed blessing. While its operational benefit in the right conditions and circumstances was proved, it also had inherent disadvantages, one of which was to enable the enemy's radars to 'home' on to it, even at extreme distances.

Such was the increased strength and improved equipment of the Luftwaffe's night-fighter force that the results of this deep-ranging campaign to the heart of the Third Reich fell well short of Harris's declared expectations. Moreover, they were achieved

at a loss rate a little in excess of 5 per cent. Nevertheless the effort, in terms of human endeavour, represented a paragon of the aircrews' persistent courage and the enduring support they received from those on the ground whose job it was to keep the aircraft flying in the long winter days and nights.

Between these two protracted battles was sandwiched the short and supremely effective assault on the north German port of Hamburg, lying beside the River Elbe, seventy miles north-east of Bremen and 180 miles north-west of Berlin.

Hamburg, the country's second largest city, with a population approaching 1.8 million and an important shipbuilding and engineering capacity, was attacked four times in concentrated strength between 24 July and 3 August 1943 by Lancasters, Halifaxes, Stirlings and Wellingtons of Bomber Command's main force. Additionally, the old seaport, which for centuries had enjoyed close seafaring and trading links with England, was visited separately twice during this ten-day stretch by a small force of Mosquitos from Air Vice-Marshal Bennett's Pathfinder Force 'just to keep the Germans' nerves on edge'.*

For good measure, the challenge was also taken up twice during daylight, on 25 and 26 July, by the heavily armed B-17 Fortresses of General Ira C. Eaker's Eighth US Army Air Force which dispatched a total of 252 aircraft against Hamburg on these two days, unescorted for much of the route, for a loss of 17 bombers, each with a crew of ten, amounting to 6.7 per cent of the attacking force.

The brilliant P-51 Mustang fighter, product of the engineering genius of North American and Rolls-Royce had yet to come into operational service. In the hands of such exponents as Don Blakeslee, Hub Zemke, James Goodson, Francis 'Gabby' Gabreski, Don Gentile, Dave Schilling and others, it would transform the US Eighth Bomber Command's daylight offensive with its long-range escort capability. Till then, the B-17s fought on 'naked' against the Focke-Wulf 190s and the Messerschmitt 109s deep in German airspace, defended only by their plethora of 0.5 inch heavy-calibre machine guns and the guts of the men behind them.

For Harris, Hamburg stood out as a particularly attractive target. Densely populated, and therefore suitable for his aggressive Area Bombing policy, it also housed the yards of the celebrated Blöhm and Vos shipbuilding giant, which in peacetime had produced ocean-going liners and which, in war, had given the German Navy some of its most prized fighting ships, the cruiser *Admiral Hipper* and the largest and most powerful battleship afloat, *Bismarck*, among them.

Moreover, with the Battle of the

Don Bennett of the Pathfinders

Atlantic now at its peak, the city's production of U-boats represented a festering thorn in the Allies' side. Turning out these marauders at the rate of two a week, Hamburg's shipyards were well on their way to a wartime production total of some 400, a good enough reason for the 'maximum effort' which was now being planned for this target.

Hamburg had two other operational attractions for Bomber Command. Unlike Bremen, Hamburg was comparatively easy to locate. Situated in the 'throat' of the broad and fast-running Elbe, hard by the north German coastline, the areas of water within its periphery showed up with good definition on the bombers' H2S blind-marking screens, an important consideration with a target which was well outside normal Oboe range.

The timing of the battle was also specially propitious. Thanks to the scientists, the Royal Air Force had had for more than a year the means whereby the German *Wurzburg* and *Lichenstein* radars could be swamped, and their effectiveness as early warning devices significantly impaired.

This development, which was coded, somewhat teasingly, Window, consisted of thin strips of tinfoil – alu-

minium foil – stuck to a piece of quite stiff paper and done up into bundles of hundreds and then thousands. This counter-measure was designed to be released from aircraft in the bomber stream as they approached and entered enemy territory to saturate the defensive radars. It was intended to cause havoc for the ground controllers whose job it was to direct the night-fighters on to the track of an incoming raid.

There had been, however, almost a year's delay in bringing the invention into operation. The authorities were troubled lest the enemy would copy it and start using it in attacks against Britain. Those responsible for home defence, security and the safety of the approaches to our shores – Fighter Command, Anti-Aircraft Command, the civilian ministries and the Royal Navy – were alarmed by such a prospect. Harris argued forcibly for its early introduction in the offensive contending the risk was minimal with the steady decline in attacks on Britain.

Happily, clearance for the use of Window by Bomber Command was given by the War Cabinet and the Joint Chiefs of Staff just as the C-in-C was about to mount his concentrated assault on Germany's second city. In the event, the effect upon the enemy's radars both on the ground and in the air far exceeded the Allies' best hopes. For a time, the crews were on a winner . . .

To saturate the defences and the military and civilian services, and to maintain an unbearable pressure upon the population, Harris and his planners sent in the main force squadrons on the nights of 24/25, 27/28, 29/30 July and 2/3 August. The overall effect was cataclysmic. Nothing like it had been seen before. The final August mission, flown in appalling weather, was a failure and can be quickly described.

* Bennett, *Pathfinder*.

Right: 'The greatest victory of the war' – Pathfinder Force's Don Bennett, on the Battle of Hamburg

NORTH SEA

Kiel Canal

Kiel

Rostock

Cuxhaven

HAMBURG

night bombing raids
24/25, 27/28, 29/30 July
and 2/3 August

Bremerhaven

R. Elbe

Bremen

R. Aller

R. Ems

BERLIN

Hannover

Magdeburg

R. Elbe

ESSEN

GERMANY

R. Ruhr

Kassel

Leipzig

Cologne

Erfurt

Bonn

Koblenz

Frankfurt

Schweinfurt

CZECHOSLOVAKIA

R. Mosel

R. Main

miles	
0	50
kms	
0	80

Heavy cumulo-nimbus cloud, much of it ten-tenths, hung over northern Germany and the North Sea approaches giving violent electrical storms and dangerous icing conditions. It was a pig of a night which fouled up the operation almost from the start. Of the 737 aircraft which set out only some 425 were believed to have dropped their loads in the target area. Even some of the Command's most experienced and 'press-on' crews felt obliged to turn back in the face of such conditions. Thirty-three bombers – just under 4.5 per cent of the main force, and getting on for double the exceptionally low average of 2.4 per cent which obtained in the first three attacks – were lost during the night. Of the missing numbers, five – or 15 per cent of the loss – were thought to have succumbed to the storm rather than to the defences.

Set against the unparalleled success of the opening missions, this culminating raid was a failure with much of the bombing being widely scattered. Even so, after its three horrendous predecessors, it was a demoralizing last straw for the remaining inhabitants, who were now without water, light and even the most rudimentary services. Not surprising, then, that by the end of the fourth night of fear close to a million of the population – mostly women, children and the aged – had either evacuated themselves from the maelstrom or were now resolved to do so.

As for the initial three attacks, the first, mounted on 24/25 July in excellent weather conditions and light winds, fully lived up to the C-in-C's and his Group Commanders' most sanguine hopes. Right up to the opening of the battle the citizens of Hamburg had been enjoying a spell of agreeably warm days and sunshine, with temperatures staying consistently in the low eighties Fahrenheit. Everything was tinder-box dry.

In this raid, packed into fifty minutes with zero set at 01.00 hours, 792 heavy bombers – 348 Lancasters, 246 Halifaxes, 125 Stirlings and seventy-two Wellingtons, involving some 5,470 aircrew – dropped 1,454 tons of high explosives and 1,006 tons of incendiaries on the unprepared burghers of this proud city.

One of the first Pathfinders to set things in motion with his markers and bombs was a young pilot officer from 83 Squadron, A. C. Shipway. Despite recurrent trouble with the blind-flying instruments in his Lancaster – only the artificial horizon was working – Shipway pressed on with palpable courage to the target when he would have been fully justified in turning back. Five minutes early over the aiming point, he circled the area before releasing his target indicators and bombs precisely on time.

Although hit heavily by flak, Shipway nursed his aircraft home to complete his mission in true Pathfinder tradition. The subsequent award of the Distinguished Flying Cross was a just reward for a night of high endeavour.

Meanwhile, with Window turning the defending radars upside down and causing the maximum disruption to delicate electronic systems, the Luftwaffe's night-fighters and the anti-aircraft defences were thrown into utter confusion. Great was the glee of the staff manning the 'Y' Service listening post in south-east England* as they heard the German ground controllers metaphorically throwing up their hands, first in annoyance, then in disbelief and finally in resignation at the dislocation of the radars and their inability to pass any worthwhile information about the incoming raid to their night-fighters.

Lord Trenchard's memorable stricture about the need to keep the scientists *on tap*, not *on top*, was this time stood on its head. Here, with Window floating about the north German airspace, the boffins were undeniably on top, scoring a comprehensive triumph for the squadrons of Bomber Command.

Out of the 792 bombers dispatched in the mainstream, 741 crews claimed they had attacked the principal target after forty-six had aborted. And when the account was ruled off the next morning no more than a dozen air-craft were found to be missing for a minimal loss rate of 1.5 per cent.

As for Hamburg, when the all clear was sounded at one minute past 03.00, the inhabitants of that part of the city which had borne the brunt of the attack found the five fire brigades quite unable to cope with the fires now raging and the control system had totally broken down. The city had virtually surrendered to the attack.

When the Eighth Bomber Command of General Eaker's Eighth US Army Air Force attacked the same target in daylight a few hours later, fires and dense smoke were still enveloping the area. Leading the assault were Lieutenant-Colonel Maurice Preston, commander of the 379th Bombardment Group, and his counterpart with the 91st, Major David Alford. Each of these two leaders from Brigadier-General Frank Armstrong's First Bombardment Wing was able to report that while the pall still covering the city impaired the chances of precision bombing, the target areas as a whole had been hit 'right on the nose'.

No doubt about it, the Battle of Hamburg was off to a good start.

If the opening round of Operation Gomorrah had been a success, the second, fought out during the night of 27/28 July, immediately following the second daylight attack of the USAAF which Lieutenant-Colonel Leland G. Fiegel of the 381st Bombardment Group and Major William R. Calhoun of the 91st had led, literally set the city alight. This was to be Sir Arthur Harris's most spectacular raid of the war with his main force – a gala performance. It had, moreover, a rather special but little known human feature which greatly pleased the crews of 83 (PFF) Squadron and their CO, the redoubtable Wing Commander John Searby.

The recently appointed Commanding General of the US Eighth Bomber

---

* The 'Y' Service listened to the transmissions passing between enemy ground stations and airborne aircraft.

Command, the 37-year-old Brigadier General Frederick L. Anderson, slipped unobtrusively into the second pilot's seat of the Lancaster which was captained that night by the Squadron's Flight Lieutenant Ricky Garvey, a highly regarded Canadian, whose designated marking task in the middle of the assault ensured that the General would have a ringside view of the fighting.

This engaging young General, fresh from the Air Staff in Washington, had already flown with Bomber Command a couple of nights before in an attack on Essen in the Ruhr. Fred Anderson had said little about it, telling his Chief of Staff to keep quiet and get on with running the Command in his absence.

A favourite of Harris's, and one after his own heart, Anderson was normally always present at 'morning prayers', the C-in-C's so-called first conference at his High Wycombe Headquarters where the ensuing night's operation was initially discussed. Like others among his senior compatriots, this personable commander set an example in 'leading from the front'.

Nor was he alone in this second blow of Operation Gomorrah. As Martin Middlebrook points out in his characteristically well-researched book, *The Battle of Hamburg*,* five of Bomber Command's best-known station commanders had left their administrative duties behind to take part in the mission.

The five station commanders were Group Captains H. I. Edwards vc from Binbrook, S. C. Elworthy from Waddington, H. L. Patch from Coningsby, A. D. Ross from Middleton St George and A. H. Willets from Oakington. Two even more senior officers would fly in later raids of the Battle of Hamburg. They were Air Commodore W. A. D. Brooke, of 4 Group, and from 1 Group, Air Commodore A. M. Wray, a veteran Royal Air Force pilot known as 'Hoppin' Wray from a First War leg injury. All would return safely.*

The route for this second onslaught was much the same as the first (and also the third). Crossing the North Sea to the north of Heligoland, and flying

on eastwards to a point thirty miles or so south-east of Kiel, the bomber stream then turned sharply south, proceeding purposely over the Baltic port of Rostock before turning south-west again for the critical run-in to Hamburg.

In favourable weather, with no more than a light crosswind at 20,000 feet over the target, Bennett's Pathfinders set up the markers for the 735 heavy bombers of the main force (forty-one had aborted) to follow. For a second time, Window played its full part in swamping the air and ground defences, causing yet again extensive disruption to the radar control systems.

Allowing for the natural 'creep back'* inherent in these attacks, the weight of the massive high explosive and incendiary loads fell a mile or two short of the aiming point on the north side of the Elbe in the heavily populated districts of Billwarder Ausschlag, Borgfelde and Hamm, and at the end of the forty-five minute jam-packed attack, still shorter in the

* Martin Middlebrook, *The Battle of Hamburg* (Allen Lane, London, 1980).
* The understandable tendency of crews in the face of intense searchlight, ack-ack and night-fighter defence was to bomb short of the aiming point. This became known as the 'creep back'.

General Carl (Tooey) Spaatz, first commander of the US Eighth Air Force

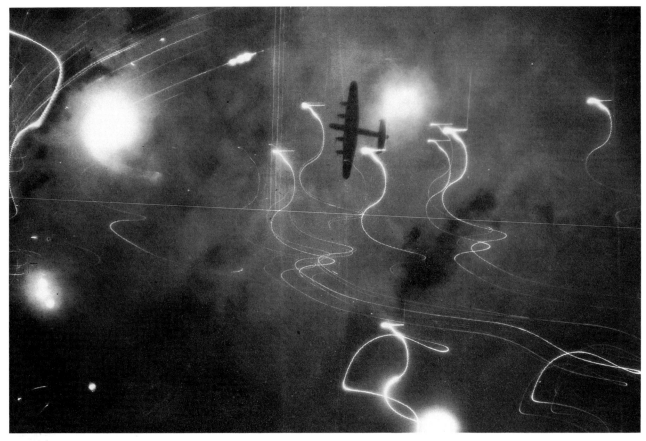

A Lancaster over Germany

equally well-populated neighbour-hoods of Wandsbek and Horn.

It was a first-class obliteration job covering a large region of the city with the U-boats yards absorbing their full share of the bombs.

After completing the task, the bomber stream continued on a south-westerly course away from the target, before turning some 90° to starboard on to a north-westerly heading to cross out between Bremerhaven and Cuxhaven and eventually onwards to leave Heligoland well to the right.

Throughout the assault, and as the bombers withdrew, the Luftwaffe's single-engine night-fighters, relying on a running commentary from ground control and guidance from searchlights and ack-ack, made a series of visual attacks on the bomber stream in what the German Air Force now called the *Wilde Sau* (Wild Boar) tactic. With Window throwing the radars into disarray, thus impairing the conventional work of the night-

fighter crews, the spirited introduc-tion of Major Hajo Hermann's newly created *Wilde Sau* force seemed like a worthwhile ploy.

But as the Royal Air Force had earlier established, single-seat fighters operating at night, without the aid of a radar operator to assist the chase, could only be of limited value. *Wilde Sau* was no substitute for the real thing, rather a hurriedly impro-vised palliative.

Bomber Command's loss of seven-teen bombers on this second con-centrated onslaught, for the happily low loss rate of 2.4 per cent again owed much to the new magic of Win-dow. But from now on the impact of this counter-measure would gradu-ally diminish as the enemy learned to live with it and introduced his own improved radar devices and arma-ment.

For the populace of Hamburg, the outcome of this second attack was

catastrophic. Quite apart from the destruction caused by the 1,500 tons of high explosives which had rained down, the effect of another 1,000 tons of incendiaries was to start a fire-storm raging over great areas of the city. As with the first raid, the fires quickly gathered strength until they were again beyond the fire services' control. But this time, as the fire raged ever more fiercely, the hot air above it began to rise at an increased rate and draw in cooler air to replace it, thus fanning the flames to greater fury. Very quickly the winds thus created mounted to speeds of 100–150 m.p.h. Temperatures rose to a fantastic 1,500° Fahrenheit (800° Centigrade). Hamburg was now gripped irretriev-ably by a mighty firestorm.

Inhabitants who had jammed the shelters during the actual bombing were now faced with a terrifying de-cision – run for it and risk being swept along on the wind and blown help-lessly into the flames or stay where they were under cover and face almost certain suffocation from carbon monoxide poisoning.

The height of the firestorm was reached between 03.00 and 03.30 when the bombers were well on their way back across the North Sea, heading for their Lincolnshire and Yorkshire bases. The fires burned on out of control into the dawn and beyond; but when day broke there was little light, for a great pall of smoke rising to a height of 20,000 feet enveloped the city.

The extent of the casualties was never accurately known, but estimates of 40,000 killed and a further 100,000 injured in this one raid were considered to be too low. By the end of the day – 28 July 1943 – Hamburg was a smouldering ghost city, almost deserted. For the local services and their officers, this was in fact a blessing. Had thousands remained instead of fleeing, there was no way the auxiliary services could have coped with all the people's needs.

Harris sent Bomber Command back the following night for its third attack in five days. Of the 777 aircraft which took part, 707 claimed to have bombed the smoking and scorched target area despite an altogether better-marshalled and organized defence. By the time the squadrons had completed their mission and were once more headed back across the North Sea, twenty-eight of their aircraft were missing. Another 1,000 inhabitants of Hamburg had been left for dead among the debris and the fires which were raging afresh.

This terrible trinity of raids had now devastated 6,200 acres of the most densely built-up areas of the city while all four of its shipbuilding yards lay severely damaged – a notable gain for the Allies now fighting a life-and-death battle in the Atlantic with the U-boats.

With the fourth attack of 2/3 August still to come, the contest for Germany's northern seaport and manufacturing centre had already been won by Harris's squadrons. A loss rate for the three attacks of no more than 2.4 per cent compared favourably with an average level of 6.0 per cent for all Bomber Command's previous raids on this lethally defended city. The low casualty rate owed much to Window.

Albert Speer, head of the German Armaments Ministry, made a significant statement about the Hamburg assault in his interrogation by the Allies after World War Two. It went some way towards vindicating Sir Arthur Harris's unshakeable but controversial belief in Area Bombing as a war-winning weapon.

We were of the opinion that a rapid repetition of this type of attack upon another six German towns would inevitably cripple the will to sustain armament manufacture and war production. It was I who first reported to the Führer that a continuation of these attacks might bring about a rapid end to the war.

Hamburg devastated

17 AUGUST 1943: SCHWEINFURT AND REGENSBURG

Here is Johnnie Johnson's account of this day's events:

On this day my Canadian Spitfire Wing took off from Kenley, Surrey, re-fuelled and again became airborne to rendezvous with the First Bombardment Wing which would attack the German ball-bearing factories at Schweinfurt. At the same time the Fourth Bombardment Wing would attack the Messerschmitt factories at Regensburg and land at airfields in North Africa, but the Schweinfurt bombers would return to England.

Just before noon the First Bombardment Wing set off from nine English airfields, circled and climbed

Target Regensburg: attacking B-17s of USAAF

over East Anglia and slowly assembled into two big formations, separated by five or six miles. In all there were 230 B-17 Flying Fortresses. We found them over the North Sea and took up our escort positions a few thousand feet higher and down-sun of the bombers, and flew with them to the Dutch border. Then because of our Spitfires' limited range, we had to leave them to be escorted only by a few squadrons of P-47 Thunderbolts. In a few minutes, they too would have to return to England, leaving the B-17s to make the two-hour flight to Schweinfurt alone – against the flak and the crack fighter squadrons of the Luftwaffe. They would have no difficulty in telling friend from foe because there would be no friends.

We fighter pilots knew that the Fortresses were in for a very rough time

as they fought to prove their long-held doctrine that self-defending bomber formations could get to their targets in daylight and return with reasonable losses. We knew that the air fighting would be tougher than three years previously in the Battle of Britain, because the enemy radars plotted the Fortress formations building up over East Anglia and their listening service intercepted many radio messages from US ground stations and formation leaders. Thus, German controllers had ample warning of these daylight raids and were able to gather fighter squadrons from distant bases to oppose the intruders.

We knew from our intelligence briefings that the Fighter General himself, 'Dolfo' Galland, planned the fighter defence of the Reich, and had arranged for long-endurance aero-

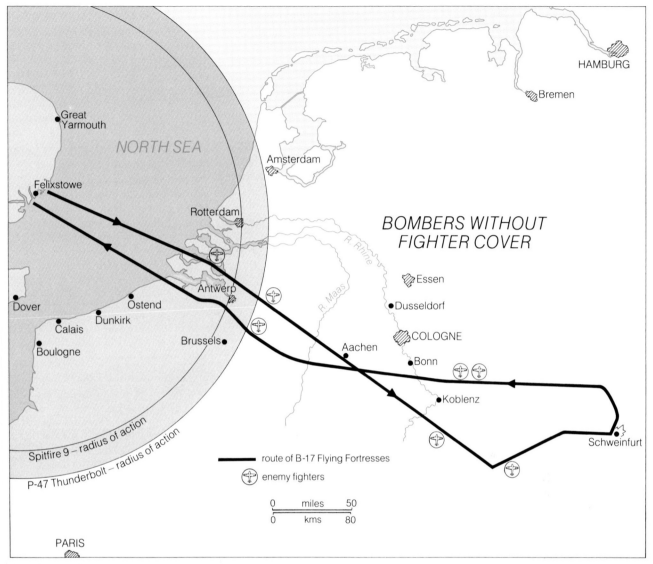

Schweinfurt. The US Eighth's historic attack: 17 August, 1943

planes to shadow the bomber formations and to report on their course and height, on the strength of their fighter escort and on the progress of his fighters. We knew, too, that the enemy had linked fighter airfields in western Germany, Holland, Belgium and northern France with their control and reporting system. These bases were pre-stacked with fuel, ammunition and spares so that German fighter pilots who had been separated from their squadrons could join together and, led by the senior pilot, could re-enter the fray.

To our regret the Spitfire was never a long-range fighter, and because of its poor radius of action we had to leave the bombers a few miles east of Antwerp. While we were with the bombers we did not see a single enemy fighter, but once the armada had left Aachen behind it was set upon by hundreds of German aeroplanes not all of which could be classified as fighters. The lean, agile Messerschmitts harried the intruders, *Sturm* (storm) squadrons of Focke-Wulf 190s made head-on attacks with their fixed guns and even some ageing Stukas hung above the bombers, waiting like falcons for the right moment to swoop down and release their bombs, fused to explode amidst the Fortresses. One navigator of a B-17 wrote:

I do not recall seeing a rocket actually hit a B-17. I remember only the fireworks and the gust of wind. The smell and sight of battle are still with me – the acrid gunpowder and the disordered plexiglass cabin – but I cannot recall a sound of battle except the clump and clatter of our own guns.

There was a running chronicle from the tail and the waist describing the fall of planes from the high group where six of the 379th had been assigned. 'Plane in flames, 'chutes opening'; 'Plane falling like a stone – no 'chutes.' So it went. We droned on. When I was not at the gun I was scribbling in the log the time, place and altitude of flak, of rocket bursts, of kills and fallen comrades, of headings and checkpoints . . .

. . . I do remember looking down somewhere after Eupen and counting the fitful yellow-orange flares I saw on the ground. At first – so dense am I – I did not understand them. Here were no cities burning. No haystack could make a fire visible in broad daylight 23,000 feet up. Then it came to me as it came to others – for I remember my headset crackling with the news – that these were B-17s blazing on the ground.

The afternoon was brilliant, but, as I remember it, the earth was somber, smudged, dark green and purple. In the gloom those orange-yellow fires curling black smoke upward were grotesque. I was as incredulous as I had been when first I saw a fuselage red with the blood of a gunner's head blasted along with his turret. As we followed that trail of torches it seemed unreal. I see it now as a funeral cortège with black-plumed horses and torches in the night.*

Direct hit

As the ragged, yet unbroken, formation made their bombing run up to Schweinfurt, the fighters backed off for now it was the turn of the 88-mm ground batteries whose accurate bursts stained the sky with evil black flowers.

The aerial column of the First Bombardment Wing stretched out for more than twenty miles over the German countryside as it fought its way towards Schweinfurt. The lead plane was *Oklahoma Okie*, flown by Lieutenant Colonel Clemens Wurzbach and navigated by Lieutenant David Williams, who was responsible for guiding the whole force to the target. Just behind, in *Lady Luck*, was Brigadier General 'Bob' Williams, the commanding general of the First.

The fighter attacks were concentrated and fierce as the German pilots defended their homeland. David Williams spent so much time at his twin guns that his navigator's log was 'sparse', and at times empty cartridge cases were stacked almost to his knees. The head-on attacks from formations of *Sturm* fighters loosened up the close bomber formations and Bob Williams several times had to order his force to tighten formation. Yet twenty-one B-17s were shot down before the Wing reached the target area.

The lead planes placed their bombs accurately within the factory area, raising a pall of smoke as a marker to the groups following. Bombing procedure required that each plane fly straight and level for the final minutes between the Initial Point – where the bombardier takes over control of the aeroplane – and the Aiming Point over the target, and then turns away towards the Rallying Point and so home . . .

The last B-17 cleared the Aiming Point at 15.16. Behind it Schweinfurt's ball-bearing factories were burning from eighty direct hits. It looked, pilots said, like a gigantic bed of coals!†

Then we banked sharply and streaked away to the west and north. The flak was reported as intense and accurate over Schweinfurt, though neither Bohn nor I remember it as being more horrendous than at many other targets we had seen. We both recalled the deadly persistence of the fighters after the target. Again and again they came at us, through us, from dead ahead, from either side, usually from below but sometimes from above. They darted like dolphins amid a formation of plodding tugs.

In England monitors heard the German pilots gathering from all over France and Germany to ambush our homeward flight. German control was pinpointing our painful progress to Bonn, Aachen, Cambrai, Brussels.‡

Back at Bradwell, in the middle of the afternoon, the controller telephoned to say that the Americans were in trouble and we were to take off immediately.

Over Belgium my Spitfire Wing was fanned out across the vault of the sky, scanning its vastness for our 'Big Friends'. And then we saw them com-

* Elmer Bendiner, *The Fall of Fortresses* (Putnam, New York, 1980).
† John Keegan, *General Motors Magazine*
‡ Bendiner, *Fall of Fortresses*.

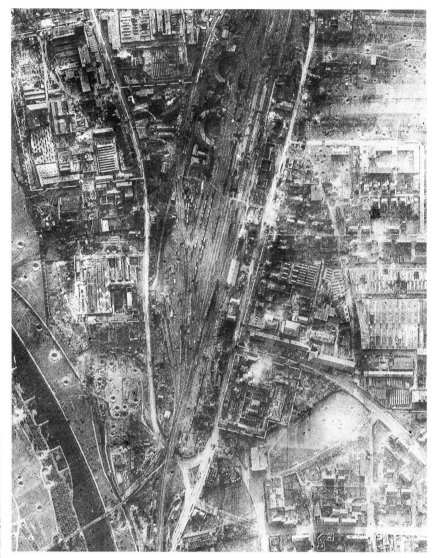

Schweinfurt after bombing by US Eighth

ing from afar – thirty miles or more. It was a sight I shall always vividly remember.

They were heading westwards into the declining sun which at our height of 23,000 feet was still well above the horizon. The sky was an intense blue and their windscreens and silver bodies glittered in the clear air.

About ten miles separated the two combat wings which had already been harried by flak batteries and fighters for more than four hours. Here, between Liège and Antwerp, the enemy fighter attacks intensified as the depleted bomber formations fought their way home. Messersch-

mitt 109s and 110s and Focke-Wulf 190s made white contrails well above the bombers which disappeared as they hurtled down into the warmer air. Heavy flak bursts fouled the sky. Stragglers, miles behind their parent formations, were being picked off. Hub Zemke's Thunderbolts fought valiantly over the rear combat wing but were about to withdraw. Here and there amidst this raging battle parachutes blossomed. Fortresses fell to the ground and two great columns of black smoke marked blazing bomber pyres.

Yet still they came on – these ragged yet somehow majestic forma-

tions, unflinching, somehow holding together and closing the gap between us until they were almost beneath us, and I was able at long last to lead my Canadians into the arena.

But, because of our limited range, we were too late. Of the 230 Fortresses that had left England, thirty-six aborted, for some reason or another. Of the remainder thirty-three were lost to fighters, one to flak and two fell into the sea. Many were damaged beyond repair and carried dead and wounded crews. The loss rate, nearly one-fifth of the force, was unacceptable, and Galland called it 'a disaster for the enemy'!

PEENEMUNDE: OPERATIONS HYDRA AND WHITEBAIT

Peenemunde! Even the name had a thrill about it in wartime. And then, as it gained currency with Bomber Command's famous attack on Germany's experimental rocket establishment on 17/18 August 1943, it began to assume an air of mystery. Secrecy surrounded the Allies' knowledge of the dramatic developments taking place on this thin peninsula lying on the east bank of the River Peene, and forming a part of the island of Usedom on Germany's Baltic coast.

For the staff working there in peacetime under *Oberst* Walter Dornberger, an officer of the Wehrmacht who had fought in the First World War, and with a brilliant young scientist named Wernher von Braun, it must have been an idyllic spot at which to be stationed. Nestling in the shelter of pine woods and dunes, hard by the secluded beaches of the Baltic, it was a dream location and yet an incongruous haven for the beginnings of what would become the enemy's A-4 rocket programme, the precursor of the V-2, potentially the most lethal of Hitler's so-called secret weapons.

Little but rumour was known of the developments of this establishment until one day, soon after the start of the Second World War. Britain's Naval Attaché in Oslo, much to his surprise, received an unsigned letter from a correspondent who purported to be a German scientist apparently well disposed to impart technical knowledge of the Nazis' plans for the long-range rocket and other scientific developments. Strangely, no financial consideration was attached to the offer. When the material was eventually passed over and examined, it revealed a variety of technical information including some details of the work said to be in train at Peenemunde's experimental and development centre.

British intelligence sources were at first highly sceptical, believing that the informant was probably a German 'plant' intended by the Nazis to encourage a time-wasting and protracted investigation that would, in the end, lead nowhere.

It was an understandable, if naive, misjudgement. Subsequent discoveries showed the information, although limited in its extent, to be soundly based. For a couple of years, however, what became known as the Oslo Report was largely and unwisely discounted. Meanwhile, under *Oberst* (later *Generalleutnant*) Dornberger and his colleagues the work was pressed ahead despite the inevitable set-backs. Test firings on the 300-mile range, running north-eastwards up the isolated Baltic, passed largely unnoticed.

Then one day in spring 1942 – it was 15 May, mark well the date – an exceptionally able young Royal Air Force officer named Flight Lieutenant D. W. Steventon ('Steve', inevitably) of 1 Photographic Reconnaissance Unit (PRU), was dispatched in his blue PR Mk V Spitfire, No. 7037, carrying cameras and excess fuel instead of guns, first to Kiel and then to Swinemunde, on the Baltic coast. His remit was to cover these two port installations and 'search and photograph any naval vessels'. It was the pilot's 213th operational sortie since war began – a sound base for the command of a squadron which would soon follow.

Donald Steventon already had an impressive record. He looked a certainty for advancement. Head boy at King Edward VIth's Grammar School at Stafford and captain of both the Cricket XI and the Rugby XV, he had passed well into Cranwell in 1937. By the time the Battle of Britain was fought, he was flying hazardous patrols in the Channel in ponderous Ansons with Coastal Command – nice pickings for the Messerschmitt 109s. Then came a call for volunteers for PRU. Steventon at once stepped forward. It was to prove an enlightened choice. The chance to shine was not long in coming . . .

Based now at Benson, in Oxfordshire, home of PRU, the reconnaissance volunteer set off on this fine May morning north-eastwards for Coltishall, in Norfolk, from there at once to set course on the first leg of his arduous five-and-three-quarter hours round-trip mission to the Baltic. Climbing steadily at 1,200 feet a minute to around 28,000 feet across the North Sea, Steventon had passed comfortably through the vapour trail height well before he approached the corridor linking Germany with Denmark.

With Kiel now lying straight ahead in clear visibility, he pushed the Spitfire up another 4,000 feet before making his run over the target area at an indicated airspeed of between 240 and 250 m.p.h. Having let the film run, he then turned slightly south of east to the second objective, Swinemunde, situated on the north German coast, between forty and fifty miles north and slightly east of Berlin and some fifteen to twenty miles from Stettin, near the mouth of the Oder.

Keeping his speed well up and maintaining his height steadily at around 32,000 feet on what became, after reconnoitring, an east-to-west run, the pilot set his cameras whirring again before switching off and heading west along the line of Germany's Baltic coast.

Three or four minutes after leaving Swinemunde, as he came up to the island of Usedom, Steventon's acute eyes picked up an airfield on the northern tip of a thin slither of land. On the east of this, in a well-wooded area, he noticed unmistakable signs of recent construction. Switching his cameras on again in the bright and clear sunlight, Steventon felt instinctively that his sighting was worth a few extra feet of film before heading out across the North Sea and, in due course, letting down over East Anglia and southern England for a landing back at Benson. Little did he realize at the time the importance of the information which would attach to the film he was bringing back.

When the reels were eventually developed, Constance Babington Smith, perceptive young WAAF officer at the Photographic Interpretation Unit at Medmenham, near Henley on the River Thames, immediately set about the task of interpreting the results of the pilot's last exposures. 'Something unusual caught my eye . . . I stopped to take a good look at some extraordinary circular embankments. I glanced quickly at the plot to see where it was and noticed the name, Peenemunde.'*

Ten months were, surprisingly, to elapse before a clever, if well-tried intelligence stroke settled the threat posed by Peenemunde beyond doubt.

Two of Rommel's subordinate generals from his Afrika Korps, Lieutenant-General Wilhelm von Thoma and Major-General Cruewell had been captured in the Western Desert in November 1942 and made prisoners of war. Four months later, towards the end of March 1943, after being kept apart during the interim, the two were put together in a thoroughly well-bugged room on the periphery of London. It was a jolly reunion for two spirited comrades-at-arms at which personal anecdotes, experiences and knowledge were freely traded.

Von Thoma, highly regarded by Rommel, was himself privy to much of the background to his country's rocket development programme, albeit in its earlier stages. He expressed his surprise to his colleague that by then – March 1943 – some of these projectiles had not already been launched at London.

* Constance Babington Smith, *Evidence in Camera* (David & Charles, London, 1957).

Top secret target: Germany's rocket development establishment at Peenemunde

light prevailing, would be sure to pose significant risks. None was left in any doubt of the effort which was being demanded of the squadrons to knock out this tiny and vital precision target. The code name of the operation was Hydra.

Timed to weaken and disrupt Germany's fighter defences – not least Major Hajo Hermann's single-engine *Wilde Sau** force, a potent factor in the moon period – B-17s and B-24s of the US Eighth Army Air Force were committed to make, in daylight, a deep-penetration raid to southern Germany on 17 August to take out the ball-bearing factories at Schweinfurt and the Messerschmitt works at Regensburg.

The night attack on Peenemunde within a few hours of the American raid on Schweinfurt and Regensburg was a minutely planned operation. The 596 bombers of the main force – Lancasters, Halifaxes and Stirlings – took off from their bases in eastern England in three separate waves, one for each of the three selected targets on the narrow peninsula. The Housing Estate, the southernmost aiming point, where the scientists and their staff lived, was to be attacked at 00.20. The strike against the middle target – the V-2 Production Works – was to go in sixteen minutes later, at 00.36, while the northern objective, the Experimental Works, was to be hit twelve minutes after that at 00.48. The aim was to concentrate the attacks by the three waves into forty-five minutes.

Masterminding things over the target throughout the duration of the raid was Wing Commander (later Air Commodore) John Searby, CO of 83 (PFF) Squadron, who made seven complete circuits of the target area during the attacks, exhorting the crews and giving bombing instructions in relation to the markers over the R/T. His two deputies, Wing Commander Johnny Fauquier, the outstanding Canadian commander of 405 (PFF) Squadron, and his Pathfinding counterpart in the van of 156,

This was quite enough for the two Generals' hosts. After further PRU sorties during the spring and early summer, culminating in a particularly effective Mosquito mission flown on 23 June 1943 by Flight Sergeant E. P. H. Peek and his navigator, plans for a major attack by four-engine, heavy bombers began to crystallize.

When eventually, all was prepared and the target disclosed, such was the secrecy surrounding it that its true content was withheld from the crews. Instead they were told that it housed the enemy's advanced experimental radar establishment with all that its work meant to the improved efficiency of the Luftwaffe's already formidable night-fighter force. Not a word was said about the rocket development. Its importance, however, was underscored when the crews were told that if the first attack did not succeed in its purpose a second mission would be ordered without delay.

Another clue was forthcoming about the need for the raid to succeed. The target was to be attacked from the abnormally low altitude of 7,000 feet which, in the bright moon-

* Wild Boar

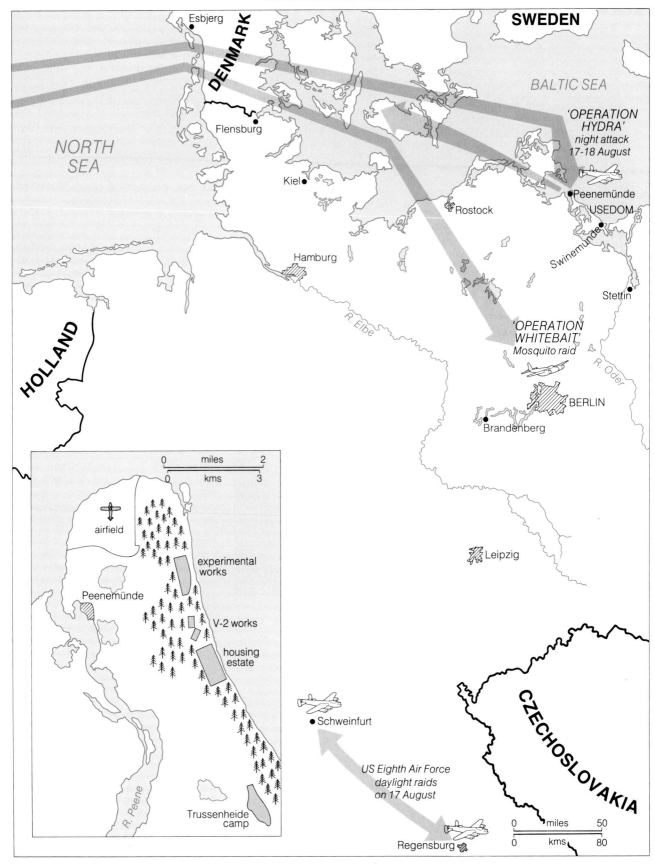

SWEDEN

BALTIC SEA

'OPERATION
HYDRA'
night attack
17-18 August

NORTH
SEA

DENMARK

Esbjerg

Flensburg

Kiel

Rostock

Peenemünde
USEDOM

Swinemünde

Stettin

HOLLAND

Hamburg

R. Elbe

'OPERATION
WHITEBAIT'
Mosquito raid

R. Oder

BERLIN

Brandenberg

Leipzig

0   miles   2
0   kms   3

airfield

experimental
works

Peenemünde

V-2 works

housing
estate

Schweinfurt

CZECHOSLOVAKIA

R. Peene

Trussenheide
camp

US Eighth Air Force
daylight raids
on 17 August

0   miles   50
0   kms   80

Regensburg

The leader – Wing Commander John Searby, Bomber Command

Left: A feint and the real thing. Bomber Command's Mosquitos attack Berlin while main force concentrates on Peenemunde: 17/18 August, 1943

– a loss rate of 6.7 per cent, well above the average tolerable percentage normally sustained in these major night attacks. It was at a level which could never have been endured over a protracted period.

To this loss had to be added the destruction of a single Mosquito on the Berlin raid with another written off on landing back at base. Nevertheless, nearly 1,900 tons of high explosive and incendiary bombs had been deposited by the main force on the night's prime target.

A few months before the Peenemunde operation, Fighter Command of the Royal Air Force had begun sending their night-fighters – Mosquitos and Beaufighters – now underused on home defence, out over Holland and north-west Germany to take on their opposite numbers as they prepared for their nocturnal interceptions of the main marauding force. Equipped with airborne radar called Serrate, the crews could readily pick up the radar emissions from the German fighters. While the results from this tactic may not have been in themselves dramatic, they had the effect of making the enemy night-fighter crews feel distinctly uneasy.

One Squadron, 141, equipped with its now almost obsolete Beaufighters, and commanded by Wing commander J. D. R. 'Bob' Braham, the most successful operator in the business, pioneered this specialist activity. Braham and his comparably able navigator, Flight Lieutenant (later Wing Commander) W. J. 'Sticks' Gregory, packed a killer punch having already shot down seven enemy aircraft since these Intruder operations were first started out of their much larger overall total.

There was, moreover, another crew in 141, the 'old firm' of Flying Officer (later Air Commodore) Harry White and his navigator, Flying Officer (later Flight Lieutenant) Michael Allen, who ran them close. White and Allen collected three Distinguished Flying Crosses apiece. They were a tenacious and good-humoured pair.

Wing Commander John White, remained in support until the last wave had come and gone. Here was a trinity of courage.

Sadly, some of the initial marking overshot and fell two or three miles south of the southernmost target, resulting in some heavy bombing of the Trussenheide labour camp which housed many foreign workers, notably Poles, some of whom had done their best to channel the experimental establishment's secrets to the Allies. Around 600 were killed.

A little over an hour before the main force had begun its attack, eight Mosquitos of 139 Squadron in the Pathfinder Force, dropping a profusion of Window, mounted a highly successful feint raid on Berlin after being routed just north of Peenemunde on the way in. This achieved the intended result. Code-named Operation Whitebait, it drew off the weight of the night-fighter defence sending it into absurd disarray and forcing much of it, through fuel shortage, to land at Brandenberg before topping up and taking off again for the Baltic coast. Chaos reigned on the airfield and some thirty aircraft – Junkers 88s, Messerschmitt 110s and single-engine Focke-Wulf 190s and Messerschmitt 109s – were written off.

Spoofed into thinking that Berlin was to be the target, the concentration of fighters around the capital meant that the initial two waves of Sir Arthur Harris's force had attacked the rocket establishment and were on their way out before the bulk of the defence could reach the target area. The third wave, however, suffered grievously from latent interceptions. Out of a strength of some 170 aircraft, twenty-nine were missing. In all, the Command lost 40 heavy bombers from its main force of 596 aeroplanes and pilotless weapon campaign (such as it was) was launched against London and the south-east. The first V-2, with a 200–210 mile radius, was fired from Holland and fell near Chiswick on 8 September; the first V-1 flying bomb had descended three months earlier, on 13 June.

By 7 April 1945, by which time the advancing Allies had overrun all the launching sites in Holland, 1,190 V-2s had been dispatched, of which no more than 501 reached the Greater London area. Of the 8,617 V-1s launched from northern France, only 2,340 had actually penetrated to Greater London, such was the effectiveness of the ack-ack and fighter defences. Nevertheless, 5,500 people had been killed and a further 1,600 badly wounded since the start of Hitler's V-weapon offensive some ten months before.

These facts are sufficient to make one pause and reflect what might indeed have happened to London, the southern part of Britain and Operation Overlord had Steventon not switched on his cameras high up over the Baltic that sunny day in 1942 as he passed over the island of Usedom.

Nine years after his historic flight, this accomplished officer was dead, felled in September 1951 when the Vampire jet he was piloting developed an engine fire and crashed in the circuit of the Royal Air Force's Flying College at Manby, where he was attending one of the first courses. It was a cruel way for a hero to go.

Brilliant reconnaissance pilot: Squadron Leader Donald Steventon *(centre)* with USAAF's Major General Barney Giles *(left)* and Brigadier General Arthur McDaniel *(right)*

Both these crews were at work during the Peenemunde assault, Braham and Gregory being off early during the attack, and White and Allen coming into their own towards the end. Remarkably, each popped a brace of enemy aircraft in the bag during their respective missions. Braham and Gregory had in fact landed back at Wittering before the 'old firm' was due to take off.

White, never one for missing a trick if he could help it, couldn't resist the mildest of digs at his ever-aggressive CO's somewhat premature return. 'Back early tonight, eh?'

Braham fell for it. 'Anyone who gets two,' he snapped, 'is entitled to be back early.'

How did the balance sheet look after the Peenemunde effort? While some had expected rather more telling results, it was undeniable that the experimental establishment had been critically damaged. Conservative estimates suggested, after subsequent pictures had been evaluated, that the enemy's V-2 weapon programme had been set back by two months and probably longer.

Among the 130 or so Germans who were killed were Dr Walter Thiel, the propulsion expert, and his entire family, and Dr Erich Walther, the chief engineer in the Production Works. Other than these two, there were no casualties among the principal scientists, Wernher von Braun being particularly fortunate to have escaped injury. General Dornberger was likewise unhurt.

For *Generaloberst* Hans Jeschonnek, Chief of Staff of the Luftwaffe, the attack on Peenemunde, coming only a few hours after the double-headed daylight raid by the Americans on Schweinfurt and Regensburg, was a shattering reverse. Bawled out first by Hitler and then by Göring, it was more than his highly strung temperament could take and he shot himself. A member of his staff found his body at the headquarters of the German Air Force early in the morning of 18 August 1943.

The retarding of the V-2 programme was vital for the Allies. As a result, they were able to mount Operation Overlord – the invasion of Normandy – and get the early June 1944 landings over before the Nazis' rocket

NUREMBERG

There are two quotes of Air Chief Marshal Sir Arthur Harris, Air Officer C-in-C, Bomber Command, from 22 February 1942 onwards until the war's end, which provide a useful backcloth for an account of his Command's attack on Nuremberg during the night of 30 and 31 March 1944.

The first is a general one and tells us something of the hazards of the great night offensive which Harris waged with his squadrons against Nazi Germany for more than three unrelenting years.

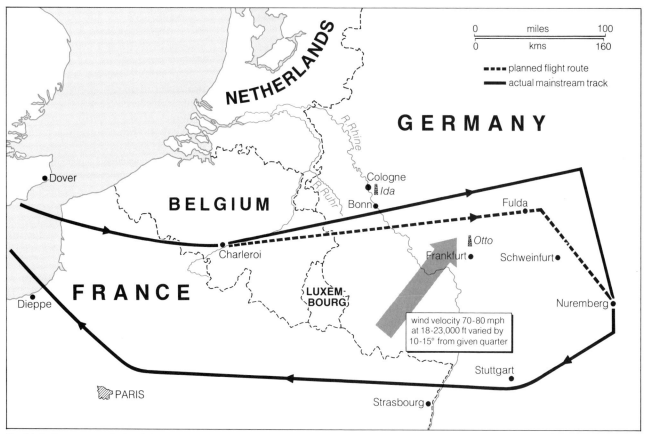

The night it all went wrong . . . fateful mission to Nuremberg: 30/31 March, 1944

There are no words with which I can do justice to the aircrews who fought under my command. There is no parallel . . . to such courage . . . in the face of danger over so prolonged a period . . . a danger which at times was so great that scarcely one man in three could expect to survive his tour of thirty operations.*

The second quote is specific. It refers to the Command's devastating reverse in the raid against the southern German city, seat of Hitler's Nazi party and scene of the famous war crimes trial which followed the ending of the Second World War.

Nuremberg – the one real disaster, and we were lucky not to have had a dozen.'†

What, then, were the circumstances of this ill-starred attack, set in the context of the most remorseless aerial campaign ever waged in war?

Against the Third Reich's stronghold 782 heavy bombers (Lancasters and Halifaxes) were dispatched, embracing some 5,500 aircrew. Fifty-two aircraft aborted for varying reasons. Of the remainder of the main force, only 512 are thought to have bombed the primary target. Many of the others, either by mistake or design, attacked the secondary objective, Schweinfurt, fifty-odd miles to the north-west. At the end of the operation, ninety-four aircraft (12 per cent of the main force) were missing, involving some 660 aircrew. Of these 545 were later known to have died. The figure of those who perished in this *one night* can be compared with the somewhat smaller total of 507 who were lost in the *four months* of the Battle of Britain nearly four years before.

Until the Nuremberg assault, the two heaviest reverses suffered by Bomber Command had been on 19 February 1944, when seventy-eight were lost on the attack on Leipzig, and on the night of 24/25 March 1944, when seventy-three bombers did not return from a raid on Berlin.

The route to the old Bavarian city, devised by Command HQ, and supported by a strong majority of Group Commanders, was vehemently opposed by the widely experienced and professionally accomplished Air Vice-Marshal Donald Bennett, the AOC, 8 Group, the Pathfinder Force. It became the butt of intense criticism and controversy – despite the diversionary 'spoofing' attacks which were also planned in conjunction with the same operation.

After reaching Charleroi in enemy-occupied Belgium, the sixty-mile-long stream of aircraft was required to fly a dead straight, easterly course for some 270 miles deep into Germany, in bright moonlight and clearing

* Sir Arthur Harris, *Bomber Offensive* (Collins, London, 1947; Greenhill Books, 1990).
† Extract from correspondence with Air Commodore H. A. Probert, then head of the Air Historical Branch (RAF), 7 November 1979.

cloud conditions, before reaching the next turning point just east of Fulda. From there the force would head south-east for seventy-five miles to Nuremberg and the selected targets. Flying at heights of around 18,000–23,000 feet, aircraft in the main stream were making tell-tale vapour trails – an open invitation to the twenty or so *gruppen* of German night-fighters (principally Messerschmitt 110s and Junkers 88s with some largely ineffective single-seat Focke-Wulf 190s and Messerschmitt 109s thrown in) which were active at night.

The objective was to be attacked in a tightly contained seventeen-minute spell between 01.05, when the Pathfinders were due to start marking, and 01.22, with 01.10 as the zero – a tidy assignment of the best of times for so concentrated a striking force but,

with the conditions prevailing, a virtually impossible task.

After bombing, the attackers were to withdraw to the south of Nuremberg before heading south-west and then on to a westerly course taking them south of Stuttgart, north of Strasbourg, north of Paris and eventually crossing out from the French coast just north of Dieppe. It was a 7½-hour flight for some crews, but for others who were struggling it would take as much as an hour longer.

The long, straight leg from Charleroi to Fulda, the contentious stretch of the operation, during which some sixty aircraft were lost, was routed south of Bonn and the heavily defended Ruhr, and then roughly midway between the enemy's two radio beacons at Ida, south-east of Cologne and Otto, north of Frankfurt,

collecting areas for the hordes of German night-fighters which would assemble there and await further instructions.

Bennett argued for an altogether more sophisticated and less direct route which gave the night-fighter beacons a wider berth, but he was over-ruled. The relationship between this forthright Australian, a product of Point Cook, and his blunt C-in-C, who had been openly opposed to the formation of a Pathfinder Force in the first place, was never particularly easy. Nor, indeed, was it with the intellectually able Ralph Cochrane, Bennett's opposite number at 5 Group, who had once served as a flight commander under Harris in peacetime in a squadron in the Middle East. 'The blood,' confided Bennett to a close colleague about

Briefing for disaster

those who opposed his argument, 'will be on their hands.'

Fickle meteorological conditions bedevilled the flight to the target. Few carried greater responsibility for these missions than the Command's forecasters upon whose predictions decisive judgements inevitably had to be made. Meteorology in wartime, aircrew were constantly being reminded, is not an exact science and on this occasion the dictum found its truth.

Exceptionally high winds, sometimes reaching 70 and 80 m.p.h., and clearing skies over the continental land mass, made a monkey of the earlier forecasts. Yet the final prediction, given later in the afternoon of 30 March, had aroused serious doubts about the advisability of proceeding with the operation. But Harris, the ultimate and lonely arbiter, had to discharge his hideous task. On the evidence before him, he said, the raid must go ahead.

In the event, the wind at 18,000 to 23,000 feet, which was veering by 10° and 15° from its given quarter, not only blew much of the main attacking force well to the north of its intended track, it also resulted in many captains making their final turn towards the target from a point noticeably further to the north and east of that designated near Fulda. And this, in turn, played havoc with the timing and accuracy of the critical run down to Nuremberg, which had now become largely obscured by a thick covering of strato-cumulus cloud up to a height of some 8,000 feet. All this put a weighty premium on competent and confident navigation. Here, the able and experienced navigators came into their own, but those aircraft navigated by the less able were to suffer badly.

Added to these problems, of course, was the furious and continuous onslaught by the Luftwaffe on the main striking force as it moved along the long, easterly leg, dangerously close to the enemy's two night-fighter collecting beacons. The twin-engined Junkers 88s and Messerschmitt 110s, many of them now

Control tower during Nuremberg bombing raid

equipped with the advanced SN-2 air-to-air interception radars and the comparatively new upward-firing 20-mm cannons – *schrage musik* – had a field-day. This lethal armament enabled the fighters to attack the Lancasters and the Halifaxes unseen, from below and slightly behind the bombers' blind spot.

The German crews fought the advancing bomber stream with all their customary courage, contesting every mile to the target. Exploding aircraft and plummeting fireballs became commonplace along the route. The results were deranging. For the Luftwaffe, the operation developed into an undoubted triumph and enemy claims of 107 bombers destroyed for the loss of some ten of their own aircraft (and eleven members of aircrew) came, in all the circumstances, remarkably close to the actual casualties.

An *oberleutnant* named Martin Becker, with seven heavy bombers destroyed during the night, following the six he had clawed down a week or so before during Bomber Command's

raid on Frankfurt, became a 'pin-up' with the German Press.

A combination of the enemy's repeated assaults in the moonlight, and the exceptional weather conditions, had of course had the effect of scattering over the long, easterly leg what had been intended to be a concentrated bomber stream, thus playing directly into the hands of the night-fighters. Whereas the aim had been for a sixty-mile long main force to be contained, for its own protection, within a width of some three miles, in the event it was spread across fifty miles and more of sky in the mayhem which prevailed.

With the bombers' GEE (an electronic navigational fixing device) being jammed by the enemy, the chances of recovering position for the run down to the target were then small. The damage, already done, proved to be irreversible.

As for the Pathfinders, when it came to marking the target they were presented with a formidable challenge. Even H2S, another electronic aid which provided a navigator with a radar picture of the terrain below, did not ease their task.*

Having to contend with a carpet of thick cloud on the one hand and excessive wind speeds on the other, and soon going out of range, their usual indicators were hidden beneath the strato-cumulus while the skymarkers dropped above it were soon carried away on the wings of the gale.

The upshot was that much of the marking which was done tended to settle down to the east (i.e. downwind) of the selected aiming point. Nuremberg got off lightly, but the Royal Air Force suffered hell.

It was hardly surprising that in the face of such an adverse balance sheet, rumours gathered strength about a serious lapse in Bomber Command's customarily tight security. Suggestions were rife that the Germans had obtained advance warning of the raid and the target. An 'authoritative' story was, years later, put about that a double agent was employed by the Allies to pass details of the impending attack to the Germans in order to convince the High Command of the man's dependability.

The alleged purpose of this unlikely ploy was to secure the confidence of the individual's former masters so that when the Allies wanted to have some 'disinformation' transmitted those in receipt of it would accept its accuracy without question. Thus when, a couple of months after the Nuremberg raid, the British wished to convey to the enemy that the Pas de Calais rather than Normandy was to be the place of the D-Day landings, a channel of communication would be ready to hand.

Martin Middlebrook, the distinguished military historian, in his minutely researched and cogently argued account of the Nuremberg mission, has torn the story to pieces.† So what then, when all was said and done, was the truth behind Bomber Command's greatest single disaster of World War Two?

The best answer is to be found in a revealing statement made thirty years afterwards by Air Marshal Sir Robert Saundby, Harris's deputy at the C-in-C's High Wycombe headquarters, in a conversation with the author and journalist, James Campbell. 'The weather conditions for Nuremberg were so bad that the timing went completely wrong. The marking was bad and the main force was late. It was a thorough shambles and one of the few occasions when everything went wrong.'‡

It is possible now, looking at the raid in retrospect, to reach a further conclusion. When, in the late afternoon of 30 March, the updated meteorological forecast suggested that there was more than a possibility of clearing skies in the moonlight over the chosen route, Harris was unwise to have taken a chance and put so massive an operation to the touch.

Easy to say this now, fifty years on. Yet it finds an echo in a comment made to Middlebrook by General Walter Grabmann, who at the time was commanding the Luftwaffe's 3rd Fighter Division. His *staffeln* were in the thick of the fighting in the early part of that historic night: 'It was a gross tactical error to make a major attack in such weather conditions.'†

Hard words . . . yet they bring home the measure of the responsibility which a great commander carried, almost continuously, for more than three years of war.

THE RUSSIAN SHUTTLE

The handful of American volunteers who had fought in the Battle of Britain had, by 1942, so increased that the Royal Air Force formed three Eagle Squadrons which were transferred to the US Eighth Army Air Force (USAAF) and became the Fourth Fighter Group. These pilots formed the hard core of fighter experience in the Eighth and the only difference in the tactics was that their squadrons

---

* This was a double-edged aid. Early on in its life, the enemy had acquired an H2S set from a Stirling bomber shot down over Germany. As a result, the Germans were themselves able to 'home' their radars on it. Among other advantages, this enabled them to pick up, at a considerable distance, the path of an attacking force. Its advanced successor in the electronic 'war', G-H, a blind-bombing device, became infinitely more accurate, effective and secure.
† Martin Middlebrook, *The Nuremberg Raid*, revised edition (Allen Lane, London, 1980).
‡ James Campbell, *The Bombing of Nuremberg* (Allison & Busby, London, 1973).

The US 56th Fighter Group's impregnable quadrilateral: Colonels Hubert Zemke, Francis Gabreski, David Schilling with Captain Frederick Christensen

Blakeslee of the Fourth

put four sections, each of four fighters, into the air while Royal Air Force squadrons – having fewer aeroplanes per unit – continued to fly in three sections.

One ex-Eagle pilot, tall, lean, vigorous Don Blakeslee, joined the Royal Canadian Air Force before his country was at war, and after a tour on Spitfires from Biggin Hill went to 133 (Eagle) Squadron and became its commander. Eventually he rose to be one of the best leaders ever to fight over Germany, but when he exchanged his blue uniform for khaki (and multiplied his pay four times) he wondered whether he had made a wise decision when he heard that he and his comrades were going to change their graceful Spitfire 9s for ungainly looking Thunderbolts, whose big cockpits seemed like old-fashioned bath tubs. Nor did Blakeslee and his contemporaries think highly of the Thunderbolt's six half-inch calibre machine guns. But the Thunderbolt had some good points, and her 2,000 horsepower Pratt and Whitney radial engine and rugged airframe could take a lot of punishment and still fly home. After his first flight, Don told me the Thunderbolt seemed very reluctant to leave the ground and very anxious to get back on it. When congratulated about its diving qualities, after destroying a Focke-Wulf just above the treetops, he retorted, 'It ought to dive. It sure can't climb!'

The Thunderbolt had much the same radius of action as the Spitfire, and wisely the few Luftwaffe squadrons in France and the Low Countries refused combat unless they had every advantage. But it was a different story when the Eighth began to enter Germany, for the enemy fighters waited until the escorting fighters turned back and then set about attacking the bombers, who were sometimes badly mauled.

The American reply was to slip drop tanks under the wings of their Thunderbolts and Lightnings, which theoretically doubled their radii of action. But the leaders went for the fighters when they crossed the Dutch coast, and the tanks were dropped immediately, since they reduced manoeuvrability and were highly inflammable. Having lost much of their petrol, the fighters had to return early, and the bombers were again sitting ducks for the German fighters.

Fortunately for Don Blakeslee and his contemporaries, some three years earlier the Royal Air Force had bought some Mustang fighters; but because of their disappointing high-altitude performance these aircraft had been used only for reconnaissance and close support. Later, when the Americans were seeking a long-range fighter, the Packard-built 1,520 horse-power Rolls-Royce engine gave the P-51D Mustang a much improved performance at height, with a top speed of 440 m.p.h. at 35,000 feet. Clever engineering gave her a tremendous amount of fuel, including some carried in two large drop tanks, one under each wing, and a belly tank which could be jettisoned. More than 2,000 P-51D Mustangs were ordered for the USAAF. They were capable of accompanying daylight bomber formations to their targets, and could still meet enemy fighters on equal terms after jettisoning their external fuel tanks. The Eighth's first Mustang escort mission was flown to Kiel in December 1943, and a few weeks later Mustangs accompanied bombers on the 1,100-mile round trip to Berlin. The Mustangs had seven league boots. They imposed a severe problem on the enemy's defence system, and added tremendous impetus to the daylight offensive.

There was great competition among American fighter pilots to get their hands on the Mustang, and Don

P-51D Mustang – the most significant fighter of the Second World War

Blakeslee pleaded with his general to exchange their old Thunderbolts for them. But a great daylight offensive was planned, the Normandy invasion would take place within three months, and so General Kepner answered that he did not see how Blakeslee's group could become non-operational for several weeks while they retrained on to the new fighter. 'That's OK, General, sir,' replied Don. 'We can learn to fly them on the way to the target!'

Blakeslee's remark was not made out of sheer bravado, but because he and many others like him had fought from Britain for a long time and knew something of the odds their countrymen faced in Fortresses and Liberators on their ten-hour flights. There was something very inspiring in the sight of a thousand bombers joining up over East Anglia; sorting themselves into great trains of aeroplanes,

and setting a steady course across the North Sea for Germany. To the escorting fighter pilots the bombers looked serene, unflinching, and eminently worthy of the great country whose star they bore.

The American planners were high-calibre officers who saw air fighting on a big canvas. They were determined not to repeat Göring's mistake in the Battle of Britain by failing to exploit the offensive qualities of their fighters. They did not therefore restrict their escorting fighters by keeping them near the bombers. They devised a shuttle escort service where the fighters escorted the bombers only for part of their route, so that, when relieved of these duties by other fighters, they had plenty of fuel left to roam and hunt as their leaders thought best. Realizing also that there is no such thing as absolute air superiority, and that it was impossible to

seal the air space round the bombers, they used more fighters on sweeps than on escort duties, and hoped by so doing that their pilots would get opportunities to attack climbing and assembling enemy fighters.

The Americans also remembered Göring's failure to take advantage of the radar gaps at low heights, and encouraged their fighter leaders to make their way home very low, not only because small formations were safer at this height but also because it afforded splendid opportunities for strafing the many airfields which lay in their path on the long return journey.

Blakeslee got his Mustangs and always led his group on the big shows, when some 800 Mustangs and Thunderbolts sometimes supported 1,300 bombers to Berlin and back. From his still expanding fighter force Göring could defend with about 900 interceptors, and the numbers of aeroplanes taking part in these air battles far exceeded those involved in the Battle of Britain.

There was little subterfuge about these great contests fought over Germany in 1944, for the Americans did not want their bombers to spend more time over hostile territory than was absolutely necessary, and usually routed them straight to the target, except when they detoured to avoid heavy flak concentrations. There was, of course, some jamming and 'spoofing', but it was difficult, to say the least, to disguise the straight approach of some 2,000 aeroplanes, and the Germans had ample time to reinforce the threatened area with plenty of fighters. The Americans were fully aware of the enemy's ability to switch squadrons from one area to another, and countered by routing their sweeps hundreds of miles ahead and on the flanks of the bombers. German fighters, especially the twins, tried to avoid Mustangs and Thunderbolts so that they could make concentrated attacks against the bombers, while American fighters were out to break up the German formations before they got to the bombers. With such numbers of attacking and defending aeroplanes, with such tactics and with such deep penetrations, the stage was set for the biggest air battles of all time.

Blakeslee led his group in much the same manner as wing leaders in Fighter Command, except that he controlled forty-eight Mustangs while Royal Air Force wings rarely exceeded thirty-six Spitfires. On one mission over Berlin he was authorized to direct the activities of all the supporting fighters, but it was impossible for one man cramped in a narrow cockpit to watch and assess the development of the air fighting round a bomber train twenty miles long, apart from all the skirmishes on the flanks many miles away. The idea of an airborne controller was sound enough, but at this time the right tools were not available for the job. (After the Second World War the US Navy developed the idea of fitting radars

and means of communication into large, four-engined aeroplanes, and so provided an airborne command post for the flying controller and his staff.)

Meanwhile, because the Spitfire was a short-range fighter, Fighter Command could not take part in these great air battles over Germany. Instead we were confined to unprofitable sweeps over the familiar and now barren hunting ground where a man could, and did, complete a tour of operations and never fire his guns in anger. We regretted this lack of vision about extending the range of our Spitfires which was entirely due to the Chief of the Air Staff, Charles Portal, whose 'obstinate resistance to the idea of a long-range fighter was a serious disservice'.*

Wrestling command of the daylight skies over Germany from the Luftwaffe, the long-range Mustangs flew beyond her eastern borders. On one famous occasion Blakeslee was detailed to escort bombers from England 1,600 miles across Europe to Poltava in Russia. James Goodson, one of the Fourth's most celebrated squadron commanders, has described the operation.

From Russia, the bombers would take off for Italy, bombing an oil refinery in Southern Poland on the way, escorted by the Fourth as far as the Yugoslav coast where Mustangs from the Fifteenth Air Force based in Italy would take over. From Italy, the bombers and their escorts would fly from Italy back to England, bombing railroad yards in France *en route*.

The 1,600 miles from England to Russia would be the longest leg, but it should take only seven and a half hours, and we had already been airborne for eight hours before. Nevertheless, every precaution was taken to assure success. Only 104 bombers were to be escorted to Russia and 1,000 bombers and their escort were to act as a diversion by bombing Berlin. The fighters were ordered not to engage in combat, nor to drop their wing-tanks until crossing the Polish–Russian border.

The group was to fly at only 15,000 feet across Europe to the Russian border and then drop to below 6,000 feet. As Blakeslee said at the end of the briefing: 'This whole thing is for show!'

Blakeslee was armed with sixteen

maps, but those covering Russia showed very little. In the event, none of them was necessary: there was cloud cover over the whole route. This meant that everything would depend on Blakeslee's ability to fly an accurate compass heading. He always maintained he was lousy at instrument flying, and flatly refused instrument practice in the Link trainer.

There were only two incidents on the flight to Russia, each resulting in the loss of a plane. Flying straight and level on one heading gave the German flak an excellent opportunity to line up their guns. South of Berlin a sudden intense barrage came up through the undercast. In spite of the accuracy only one Mustang was hit.

The other loss was a bomber, but a special bomber as far as I was concerned. Some of our crew chiefs and mechanics went along on the mission as gunners in the bombers so that they could service the Mustangs in Russia. East of Warsaw, they were hit head-on by ten to fifteen 109s. The B-17 which went down was the one in which my crew chief, Staff-Sergeant Bob Gilbert, was flying as waist-gunner. They were able to bale out and eventually joined up with a group of Russian partisans with whom they lived and fought for some weeks before finally getting back to England.

Estimated Arrival Time was 7.35 p.m. At 7.35 exactly the Russian flares floated up from the base. Blakeslee had hit it on the nose!'†

For the opposition the Fighter General takes up the story:

Apparently the first news of this event was brought by a German He 177, which hung on to the American formation and kept in touch with it. The German Command acted with lightning speed: 200 German bombers of the IV (Strategic) Flying Corps took off in the early evening of 22 June from their bases in East Poland to attack this worthwhile target in Russia 600 miles away. Our units had adopted the techniques of the night raids, with bomber stream, pathfinders and flares, which the British had brought to perfection. The weather was favourable, the defence slight. Without losses to themselves the German bombers dropped their load amongst the aircraft parked with peacetime carelessness, on the airfield of Pol-

* John Terraine, *Right of the Line* (Hodder & Stoughton, London, 1985).
† James A. Goodson, *Tumult in the Clouds* (William Kimber, London, 1983; Wingham Press, 1990).

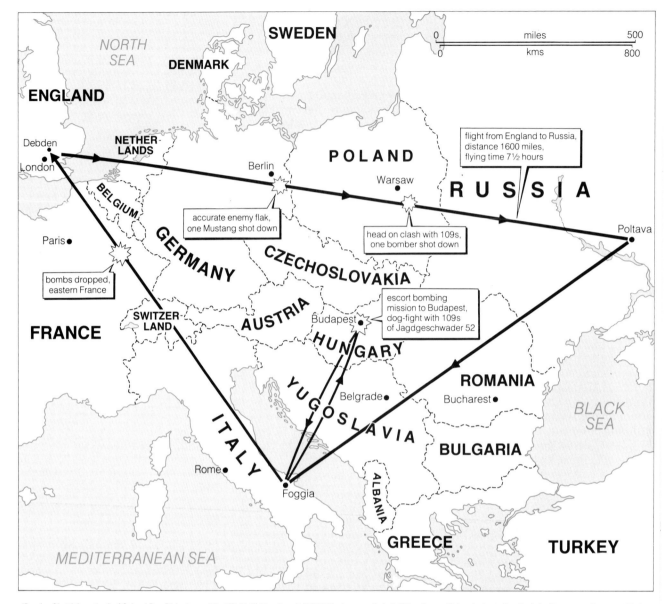

'Russian Shuttle' . . . track of Colonel Don Blakeslee and the US 4th Fighter Group's P-51D Mustangs on their 4,000-mile round-trip mission to Russia, Italy, Hungary and home to UK via Eastern France

tava: forty-three Flying Fortresses, fifteen Mustangs and several Soviet aircraft were destroyed and twenty-six damaged; 300,000 gallons of fuel which had been brought halfway round the world with so much trouble went up in flames.*

James Goodson continues the story:

In the meantime Blakeslee had been taken to Moscow to be wined and dined, and to make a radio broadcast to America. He hated anything to do with public relations, but acquitted himself nobly. Asked how he enjoyed it, he said, 'It was tougher than the trip over.'

The flight from Russian to Lucrera near Foggia in Italy was uneventful, but it was then arranged that the Fourth would join the Fifteenth Air Force on a bombing mission to Budapest. That was a different story. Lack of dust filters, and different sized nozzles on the drop tanks, led to many abortions, and the group arrived over Budapest with only twenty planes. 334 Squadron had only eight. The Fourth were flying top cover at 30,000 feet while the Fifteenth Air Force were flying some 10,000 feet lower.

Suddenly fifty to sixty 109s were screaming in to attack the bombers. Blakeslee called for the Fifteenth Air Force to come up and help, but in the event, the Fourth's twenty pilots were on their own. What they didn't know was that they were up against the unique squadron of aces, Jagdgeschwader 52, just transferred from Russia to Czechoslovakia. It included most of the top aces of all time: 'Bubi' Hartmann with 352 victories; Barkhorn, 301 victories; Rall, 275; Batz, 237; Graf, the *Kommandant*, 212; Lipfert, 203; Krupinski ('Graf Punski'), 197; and many others. Fifty or sixty of them now faced twenty of the Fourth, or perhaps eight of 334 Squadron, since they were mainly involved. The best

* Adolf Galland, *The First and the Last* (Methuen, London, 1955).

of the Luftwaffe against the best of the US Air Force.

In what was probably the last great dog-fight of the war the Fourth shot down seven, of which Blakeslee got one, and Deacon Hively got three, but they lost Hofer and George Standford, who ended up a POW. Hively and Siems were wounded, but managed to get back to Foggia.

It would be unfair to give the Fourth a score of 7 to 2. The Luftwaffe's priority was obviously to shoot down the bombers, and, in doing so, they took the risk of exposing themselves to fighter attack.

The fact that the Fifteenth Air Force didn't come up to help the outnumbered Fourth came in for some criticism, but not from Blakeslee. Most of us have often had the experience of being in the thick of the battle while other units, even in close vicinity neither heard nor saw anything, and didn't become involved. The first re-action is to jump to the wrong conclu-sions. In my experience, this overlooks three important factors. First, radio con-tact could not be relied on; volume and clarity dropped off dramatically with dis-tance, and short, shouted transmission from another group would probably be garbled, or so weak as to be drowned out, by other, closer signals.

With radio contact unreliable, reaction depended on visibility, but when one was flying in formation, escorting bombers, calculating speeds and times, it took a cool, and above all experienced fighter leader to spot, and identify as hostile, the minute specks far above or far below, against a dazzling sun or a background too bright or too dark.

But by far the most important factor in this sort of situation was one of time. When one was attacking or being attacked, it seemed like an eternity. In reality, the whole action was over in seconds, rather than minutes; and in those few seconds, enormous distances were covered, in all directions and alti-tudes, particularly in relation to planes fly-ing on a different course. Therefore, even if the leader of a distant group caught sight of the brief action and recognised the needs of assistance, the chances that he could bring his group up in time to be of any help, especially if he didn't have the advantage of superior altitude, were nil.

But the shuttle shouldn't be judged by the number of bombs dropped, or 109s shot down. Blakeslee was right when he said: 'This whole thing is for show!' And it showed a lot. It showed that no corner of

Germany's world was safe from the air. In 1944, Churchill said: 'Hitler did make Europe into a fortress, but he forgot the roof.' Quite independently, Lieutenant-General Adolf Galland took 'Fortress Without a Roof' as the title of a chapter of his book, and Lieutenant-General 'Macky' Steinhoff's book is entitled *They Had For-gotten the Roof*. All three saw this air supremacy as the basis of the Allied vic-tory. The shuttle raid underlined the fact that Allied air supremacy was complete, and the end of the war only a question of months.*

TIRPITZ: SHADOW ACROSS THE ARCTIC

Winston Churchill could make mis-takes over small things, but seldom was he wrong about the big ones. For him, *Tirpitz*, the German Navy's 45,000-ton battleship, launched at Wilhemshaven in Hitler's presence on 1 April 1939, was a Big Thing. The great capital ship remained in the forefront of his maritime thinking as the Battle of the Atlantic and opera-tions in Arctic waters moved on re-lentlessly towards the crisis of 1942 and '43. And she stayed there until the end came in November 1944.

A minute which the Prime Minister dictated on 22 January 1942 to General Sir H. L. 'Pug' Ismay, his Chief of Staff, makes his appreciation of the warship's importance quite plain. He had then particularly in mind the Führer's mistaken (as he saw it) determination to retain the battle-ship, and additional surface vessels, defensively in Norwegian waters rather than release them – as his admirals were urging him to do – for operations against Allied convoys in the Atlantic. From Prime Minister to General Ismay, for COS Committee:

The presence of *Tirpitz* at Rondheim has now been known for three days. The des-truction or even crippling of this ship is the greatest event at sea at the present time. No other target is comparable to it . . . A plan should be made to attack both with carrier-borne torpedo aircraft and with heavy bombers by daylight or at dawn. The whole strategy of the war turns at this period on this ship, which is hold-ing four times the number of British capital ships paralysed, to say nothing of

the two new American battleships re-tained in the Atlantic. I regard this matter as of the highest urgency . . . I shall men-tion it in Cabinet tomorrow and it must be considered in detail at the Defence com-mittee on Tuesday night.

From this executive instruction various attacks on *Tirpitz*, some of them heroic in character, were to flow over the next two, almost three years. The difficulty in finding ways into the vessel as she nestled in fjords set among Norwegian hills and mountains, was obvious. Moreover, the presence of early-warning radars, and an ever-ready protective smoke-screen, compounded the problem. But this did not stop the Royal Navy and its Fleet Air Arm, and the Royal Air Force, from pressing their indivi-dual assaults to the limit.

Bomber Command raided the battleship in Aas Fjord, hard by Tron-heim, at low level with thirty-one Hali-faxes and twelve Lancasters during successive nights on 27/28 and 28/29 April 1942 with inconclusive results and at the expense of six Halifaxes, one Lancaster and some fifty aircrew. In the first attack, a Halifax flown by Wing Commander D. C. T. Bennett, Australian CO of 10 Squadron, later to become an Air Vice-Marshal and AOC, 8 Group, the Pathfinder Force, was hit by heavy gunfire on the run-up to the target and set on fire. Bennett and his crew baled out. Four weeks later, after making his way with his Wireless Operator/Air Gunner through mountain passes and across rivers out of Norway and into Sweden, the future Pathfinder leader was back at his base at Leeming, fifteen miles north of Ripon in Yorkshire. He at once resumed command of 10 Squad-ron, and so rounded off another stir-ring episode in a rare and varied career.

Another attack on *Tirpitz* followed. In March 1943, just after Grand Admiral Erich Raeder, for fourteen years C-in-C of the German Navy, had re-signed after some rough exchanges with Hitler and had handed over re-

* Goodson, *Tumult in the Clouds*.

sponsibility to Grand Admiral Karl Donetz, the U-boat chief, the battleship was moved far northwards, right up to Alten Fjord in the Arctic Circle, not far from the North Cape.

Here, the Royal Navy planned and executed one of the truly heroic operations of the war. Between 11 and 28 September 1943 six of its specially designed and constructed midget submarines, submerging by day and surfacing by night, were towed a thousand miles or so from Scotland by their underwater parents to a release point west of Kaa Fjord, a spur of Alten Fjord, where *Tirpitz* now lay alongside.

With immense courage, the commanders of two of the six midgets, Lieutenants Donald Cameron and Godfrey Place, with their gallant crews, penetrated the anti-submarine nets and other defences to reach the target area. Timed explosive devices were then secured against the hull of the battleship. Explosions at the appointed hour caused widespread damage and ensured that the German prize would be out of commission for months.

There could hardly have been two more deserving awards of the Victoria Cross in wartime than those bestowed a year later upon Cameron and Place who had, thankfully, survived to become prisoners of war.

Some seven months later, on 3 April 1944, after a Norwegian agent and Ultra's busting of the enemy's Enigma-coded cyphers had, between them, kept the Admiralty appraised of progress with repairs to the ship, the Fleet Air Arm struck at *Tirpitz* just as she was about to embark upon fresh sea trials.

In an imaginatively conceived sortie, embracing the Fleet carriers *Victorious* and *Furious*, and the auxiliaries *Emperor*, *Pursuer* and *Searcher*, Barracuda bombers, with Corsair, Hellcat and Wildcat fighters in support, took off at 04.30 on a beautiful Arctic morning to press a two-wave attack on the capital ship.

After keeping tight down on the water and well under radar cover for much of the flight, the first formation pulled up fast to some 8,000 feet as it approached the coast. Clearing the mountains, the leaders got an instant view of *Tirpitz* lying, apparently unawares, at the head of Kaa Fjord. With no fighter opposition to contend with, pilots of the forty Corsairs, Hellcats and Wildcats tore down on the battleship with typical Fleet Air Arm verve, strafing it from bow to stern in an aggressive attempt metaphorically to clear the decks for the twenty-one Barracudas which, with their 1,600-pound armour-piercing bombs, were following immediately behind.

Diving well below their accredited height of 3,000 feet, the Barracuda crews drove home their attack, scoring hits all over the ship, with a thoroughly accurate display of bombing in the teeth of strong resistance from waterborne and land-based defences. Only one Barracuda was lost in the concentrated assault which was all over in little more than a minute.

An hour later, the second wave of aircraft delivered a similar attack investing it with all the same determination. Now fully alert, the defending gunners mounted a sharp response as the protective smokescreen settled over the ship. Once again, only one Barracuda was lost.

Damage was extensive – and so too were enemy casualties. Word both from the well-placed agent and Ultra's decrypts confirmed the Fleet Air Arm's hopes. Once more the battleship could be expected to be immobilized for weeks if not months. The belief was now beginning to gather strength at German Naval Headquarters that the likelihood of the capital ship ever again being returned to ocean-going worthiness was slim.

For the Naval flyers, this latest attack, which had resulted in 122 Germans being killed and 316 wounded, had added another glittering chapter to their already well-filled record book.

However, despite the damage meted out in these last two attacks, it quickly became clear that nothing short of total destruction of the battle-ship was going to satisfy Churchill, the War Cabinet and the Chiefs of Staff. At this propitious moment, a fresh development now entered the reckoning and brought the attainment of the War Cabinet's goal much closer.

The genius of Dr Barnes Wallis, which had earlier produced a bomb capable of breaching the walls of the Mohne and the Eder Dams, now provided Sir Arthur Harris and his two 5 Group Lancaster Squadrons, 9 and 617, with a weapon similarly able to terminate finally the warship's chequered life. A 12,000-pound bomb of 21 feet in length – dimensions which soon secured for it the pseudonym Tallboy – now opened a new window of opportunity. No ship, no matter how strong, was going to withstand the penetrative and explosive power of such an instrument of war.

But before precise plans could properly be laid for the scientist's invention to be used against the battleship, it was necessary first for photographs to be obtained to establish exactly her position in the vicinity of Alten Fjord and its offshoot, Kaa Fjord, in Norway's far north region.

The responsibility for flying this important and testing mission fell to the Photographic Reconnaissance Unit's 544 Squadron and to one of the outstanding crews in the photographic business, the exceptionally competent Squadron Leader (later Air Vice-Marshal) Frank Dodd and his accomplished observer, Flight Sergeant (later Pilot Officer) Eric Hill, who, post-war, was to play several seasons of first-class cricket for Somerset.

The sortie, which was flown on 12 July 1944 in a blue Mark XVI unarmed Mosquito, equipped with the largely untried 100-gallon wing drop tanks, lasted in all for a gruelling nine hours and twenty-five minutes. It was to come to be regarded, in this highly professional unit, as one of the classic photographic missions of the war.

Masterly Arctic reconnaissance, 12 July, 1944. Squadron Leader Frank Dodd and Flight Sergeant Eric Hill's outstanding photography of *Tirpitz* in Alten Fjord

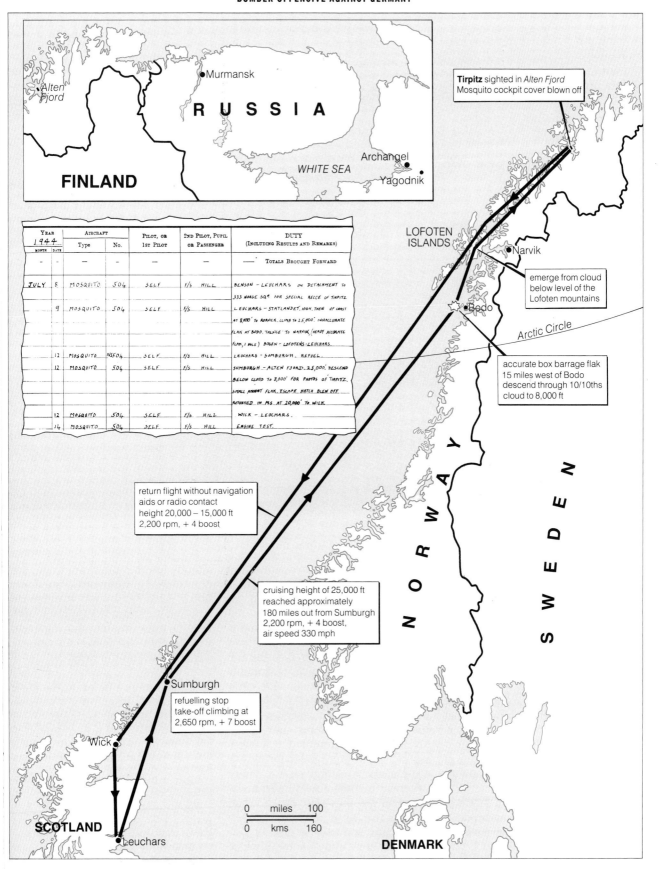

Tirpitz sighted in *Alten Fjord*
Mosquito cockpit cover blown off

emerge from cloud
below level of the
Lofoten mountains

accurate box barrage flak
15 miles west of Bodo
descend through 10/10ths
cloud to 8,000 ft

return flight without navigation
aids or radio contact
height 20,000 – 15,000 ft
2,200 rpm, + 4 boost

cruising height of 25,000 ft
reached approximately
180 miles out from Sumburgh
2,200 rpm, + 4 boost,
air speed 330 mph

refuelling stop
take-off climbing at
2,650 rpm, + 7 boost

Year 1944		Aircraft		Pilot, or 1st Pilot	2nd Pilot, Pupil or Passenger	Duty (Including Results and Remarks)
Month	Date	Type	No.			
—	—	—	—	—	—	— Totals Brought Forward
—	—	—	—	—	—	—
July	8	Mosquito	504	Self	F/S Hill	Benson – Leuchars on detachment to 333 Norge Sqn for special recce of Tirpitz.
	9	Mosquito	504	Self	F/S Hill	Leuchars – Statlandet. High, then up coast at 8,000' to Norvik. Climb to 25,000'. Innacurate flak at Bodo. Thence to Narvik (heavy accurate flak, 1 hole). Bogen – Lofotens – Leuchars.
	12	Mosquito	NS504	Self	F/S Hill	Leuchars – Sumburgh. Refuel.
	12	Mosquito	504	Self	F/S Hill	Sumburgh – Alten Fjord. 25,000'. Descend below cloud to 8,000' for photos of Tirpitz. Small amount flak. Escape hatch blew off. Returned in MS at 20,000' to Wick.
	12	Mosquito	504	Self	F/S Hill	Wick – Leuchars.
	14	Mosquito	504	Self	F/S Hill	Engine Test.

The *Tirpitz* at bay

Denied airfield facilities by the Russians at Murmansk, Dodd and Hill moved first to Leuchars, in Fife, and thence up to Sumburgh in the Shetlands, the most northerly airfield in the UK capable of taking a heavily laden Mosquito.

After climbing steadily and economically on a north-easterly track towards the Arctic Circle, the crew began their reconnaissance of the Norwegian coastline at 25,000 feet just west of Bodo and south of Narvik. They were met, somewhat unexpectedly, by a vicious box barrage of anti-aircraft fire predicted exactly to their height.

Then came the first of a series of supreme tests. With the weather deteriorating quickly and no navigational aids to guide them, the pair began

their long, blind descent through thousands of feet of unbroken tentenths cloud to a point close to where they estimated the Lofoten Islands, with their treacherous mountain terrain, would be.

With absolutely no predetermined information about the likely height of the cloud base and, therefore, the altitude at which they might reasonably expect to see land again, the crew were obliged to rely on Dead Reckoning, the ultimate navigational examination both for observer and pilot.

'Happily,' commented Hill afterwards, 'our D/R navigation turned out to be correct and there were no "hard centres" to the clouds!' (What he failed to say was they broke cloud *below* the level of the Lofoten mountains and only a mile or two west of them – a really intrepid piece

of navigational flying.)

Pressing on north-eastwards at low altitude towards the North Cape, the crew turned to starboard in the direction of Alten Fjord where Intelligence believed the ship would still be found. Let Hill, the journalist who, in peace, was to join the *Somerset County Gazette*, pick up the story:

As we cleared the hills before the Fjord, we saw *Tirpitz*, naked without a smokescreen and with only desultory flak to greet us. However, as Frank was hauling the Mossie round in a tight turn and I was busying myself setting the camera controls there was an explosion.

'God,' I thought, 'these Germans are bloody good.'

Maps, navigation bags, wireless telegraph (W/T) gen, dust and goodness knows what flew all round the cockpit and we thought we had been hit. In fact, the

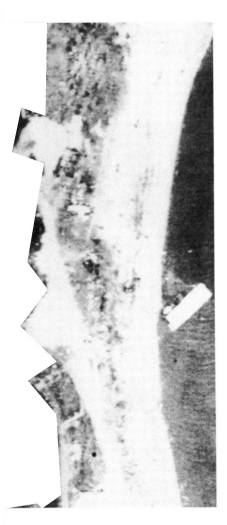

perspex top of the cockpit – the bubble – had parted company with the rest of the aircraft.

Much to our relief we realized that neither had been injured and, once accustomed to the wind noise of open-cockpit, high-speed flying, and satisfied that both engines were still in position, we continued with the photographic run.

Deranging though the experience must have been, the job was in fact brilliantly executed with a combination of precision and skill and determined low-level flying under the whip. It represented the acme of PRU work.

The four-hour return flight south-westwards to Scotland, over a thousand miles and more of sea, turned out to be almost as agonizing as the traumas through which the crew had just passed. Dodd and Hill knew that

the fuel situation was to become critical as they neared home; but what they hadn't bargained for was the earlier blow-out from the cockpit and the loss of papers giving essential code information to enable them to answer the repeated challenges over the W/T, which now came from the ground stations as they approached the Scottish mainland.

Once again without electronic aids, and with cloud-base and visibility lowering by the minute, and with the fuel gauges hovering on zero, there was nothing else for it but to trust in the Almighty and the accuracy of their advanced Dead Reckoning navigation to see them through. Eric Hill again:

With sundry parts of the crew's anatomies twitching naggingly, a break in the cloud was spotted ahead. Great was the joy when land was seen through the gap and even greater when Wick airfield was spotted. Frank made a perfect landing and with all gauges now reading zero we just about managed to taxi to flying control.

After filling up the empty tanks, the crew headed south for Leuchars immediately. To the delight of Intelligence and to Dodd's and Hill's undisguised relief the pictures of *Tirpitz* turned out to be excellent.

Armed now with indisputable photographic evidence of the battleship's location, it was the turn of Harris's heavy bombers to move to centre stage. There was, however, a problem to overcome. Alten Fjord was outside the acceptable radius of the Avro Lancaster operating at the extremity of its range from Lossiemouth in Morayshire. There was, therefore, only one thing for it. Seek the Soviet Union's permission to use an airfield south of Archangel and make the strike from the east. This would offer an added bonus. Apart from the surprise element, the German radars guarding the fjord and the warship would provide shorter warning of an assault if the bombers attacked from the Russian mainland. And this, in turn, would allow the enemy less time in which to activate the protective smokescreen.

Arrangements were thus made with the Soviet Union – not, however, without considerable difficulty – to use the *grass airfield* (editors' italics) at Yagodnik, twenty miles south-east of Archangel. It was a field more suited to light training aircraft than to heavy bombers each loaded with a 12,000-pound Barnes Wallis Tallboy.

Willie (Tirpitz) Tait

The flight to northern Russia from the Squadron's bases in Lincolnshire, in eastern England, took more than ten hours to complete. Once there, many were the frustrations which had to be faced before the redoubtable Wing Commander J. B. 'Willie' Tait, the overall leader of the operation, was ready to make the attack on *Tirpitz* with thirty-one Lancasters of 9 and 617 Squadrons as the massive ship was lying alongside in Kaa Fjord. The day selected for the strike was 15 September 1944.

With no special navigational assistance to call on, and with the Russians flatly refusing to give Squadron Leader Tom Bennett, the navigation leader of 617, and the other navigators, accurate, up-to-date maps for the mission, pin-pointing at speed and at relatively low-level posed an exacting challenge.

Nevertheless, the attack, delivered after a late, fast climb from around

'The Sinking of the Tirpitz' portrayed by Gerald Coulson

12,000 feet, was a palpable success. Willie Tait's Tallboy hit the ship fair and square in the bows. This, coupled with other near misses, caused serious damage and at once aroused fresh doubts about the capital ship's future usefulness.

Returning to Yagodnik after being airborne for more than seven hours, the Squadrons set out for home the next day. One aircraft was lost *en route* in southern Norway, due, it was thought, to a navigational error. The Germans forced the local inhabitants to bury the crew in a shallow mass grave.

A month later, after undergoing superficial repairs, *Tirpitz* was moved south at a steady 7 knots to Tromso, there to shelter in the lee of nearby Haakoy Island.

New and much more convenient plans could now be laid for further attacks. Tromso was within the tolerable operational radius of Lancasters, modified to take extra fuel, and flying from Lossiemouth, an adequate northern base for four-engine aircraft.

On 29 October, therefore, with Tait still in the van, 9 and 617 struck a second time, this day in thoroughly unfavourable weather. A single near-miss further disabled the stricken warship, but she was still afloat and neither the Prime Minister, the War Cabinet nor the Chiefs of Staff would rest content until she had been conclusively dispatched.

One more heave was thus ordered on 12 November when, in clear weather, thirty Lancasters from the same two squadrons, with Tait leading a third time, sallied forth to administer the *coup de grâce*. A photographic Lancaster from the Royal Australian Air Force's 463 Squadron accompanied the heavily-laden force to obtain a pictorial record of the historic deed.

There was no doubt about the effectiveness of this final assault. Four Tallboys straddled the prize, and with others achieving near-misses irreparable damage was done. This was the end. Slowly *Tirpitz* heeled over to port until, with water flooding in, this once proud vessel capsized completely, her vast superstructure sticking fast in the sea bed and exposing an inelegant view of the ship's shining keel.

Valiant efforts were made by the Germans to save those of the ship's company who were still alive. Out of a total complement of 1,900, some 900 crew members perished during the attack which lasted for no more than three terrifying minutes. Of those who did survive, 600 or so were taken from the surrounding water, while nearly ninety were rescued miraculously from the hull when it had seemed that hope had all but gone.

Professor R. V. Jones, the celebrated scientist, in his book *Most Secret War*,* wrote a fitting epitaph to those who died serving *Tirpitz* to the end: 'With their ship capsized, the doomed men inside were heard singing "Deutschland uber Alles" as the waters rose. What a tragedy it was that men like that had to serve the Nazi cause.'

* R. V. Jones, *Most Secret War: British Scientific Intelligence, 1939-1945* (Hamish Hamilton, London, 1978).

13 · AIR–SEA POWER: BATTLE OF THE ATLANTIC

BISMARCK AND HER BATTLE-CRUISERS

Until the spring of 1940 the war at sea had gone steadily in the Allies' favour, but the German occupation of Norway, the defeat of France and the Low Countries, and the entry of Italy into the arena meant that the enemy now had widespread bases from which his battleships and cruisers, U-boats, E-boats and maritime aeroplanes could sally forth and attack the British lifeline – the ocean convoys that carried food and supplies. During the Battle of Britain we held our Island base, we endured the Blitz, but our survival depended upon our mastery of the ocean routes.

From airfields on the French Atlantic coast the long-range Focke-Wulf 200, known as the Condor, could take off, fly right round the Islands and refuel in Norway, from whence it could harass our North Sea shipping and make the return journey when necessary. These Condors could search for our inward or outward bound convoys and, having found them, could either attack with bombs, or direct the lurking U-boats to the scene. Further south, Mussolini's ships and aeroplanes, with bases on Sardinia, Sicily, Southern Italy and the Dodecanese, threatened our short route to the Middle East and made us take the long voyage round the Cape.

In the second half of 1940 more than three million tons of Allied shipping were sunk by the Germans. Most of this tonnage fell to U-boats, about one-tenth to the Condors and the remainder to mines and surface raiders.

The spring of 1941 saw the climax of the struggle. New ocean-going U-boats, more Condors, and the surface raiders *Hipper, Scharnhorst, Gneisenau* and *Scheer* all combined in sending, in March alone, more than half a million tons of our shipping to the bottom. To add to our gloom a newly completed enemy battleship, *Bismarck*, of immense power, and described by the Prime Minister as a 'masterpiece of naval construction', now entered the lists.

Before the sinking: German battleship *Bismarck* pictured lying off Norway from battlecruiser *Prinz Eugen*, May 1941

123

German strategy was that their great battleship, which they claimed was more than a match for anything afloat, would, together with the battle-cruisers *Scharnhorst* and *Gneisenau* form a powerful strike force to wreak havoc on our trade routes.

On 28 March 1941 photographic reconnaissance confirmed that the two battle-cruisers were at Brest, and although Bomber Command flew more than a thousand sorties against them only four direct hits were made. As the Commander-in-Chief understated at the time: 'We are not de-signed for this purpose and we are not particularly effective in execution.'*

On 6 April 1941 four Beauforts of 22 Squadron, Coastal Command took off for Brest and *Gneisenau* but only one, captained by Flying Officer Kenneth Campbell, a young Canadian, located the target on that misty morning.

Gneisenau was lying in the inner harbour alongside one of the shore quays. To her seaward was a long stone mole; behind her was sharply rising ground; in dom-inating positions all round were anti-air-craft guns – some 270 of them. Three *flak* ships moored in the outer harbour and the battle cruiser's own formidable arma-ment added to the strength of the defences.†

A small, fast-weaving fighter, flying very close to the sea might have stood a faint chance of getting through the curtains of steel. The lumbering twin-engined Beaufort had none. But un-daunted and with matchless courage the young Canadian and his three-

* Sir Charles Webster and Noble Frankland, *The Strategic Air Offensive Against Germany, 1939-1945* (HMSO, London, 1961).
† Denis Richard, *Royal Air Force, 1939-1945* (HMSO, London, 1953), vol. 1.

Destruction of Germany's most powerful battleship: the sinking of *Bismarck*, 26 May, 1941

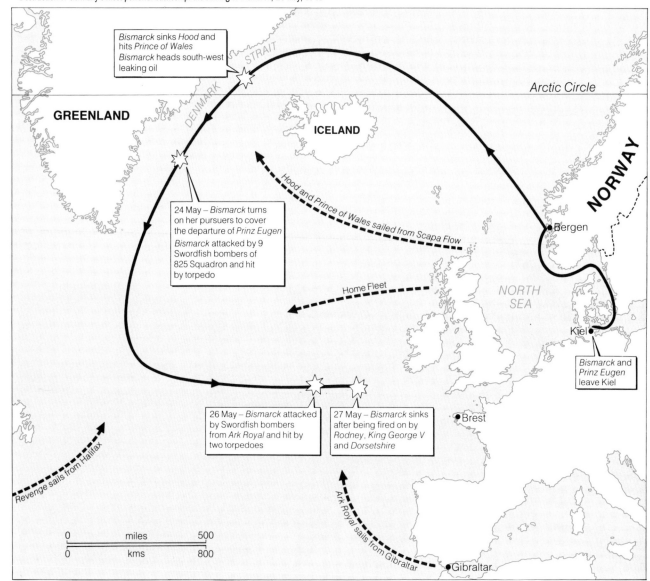

0   miles   500
0   kms   800

man crew bored in below mast height to get at the battle-cruiser. The Beaufort was shot out of the sky by the storm of flak, but not before it had released its torpedo which ran true to hit *Gneisenau*'s stern beneath the water line. Eight months later she was still under repair. Flying Officer Campbell received a posthumous Victoria Cross.

Bomber Command continued to attack both *Gneisenau* and the *Scharnhorst* at Brest; the former was hit and some of her crew killed and the latter's refitting was delayed by damage to the docks.

Deprived of her battle-cruisers, *Bismarck*, accompanied by the cruiser *Prinz Eugen*, left Kiel and were first sighted sailing through the Kattegat. They were seen near Bergen by a PRU Spitfire and then subsequently shadowed by air and sea units until in the early morning of 24 May 1941 HMS *Hood* opened fire and minutes later was sunk by *Bismarck*. *Prince of Wales* also was struck by the enemy battleship's guns, but not before she had damaged *Bismarck* which made off to the south-west, leaking oil.

Scenting a kill, My Lords Commissioners summoned all available ships

Above: Eugene Esmonde VC – beyond the call of duty

Swordfish of the Fleet Air Arm off on a strike

to the chase. *Rodney*, 500 miles to the south-west, was diverted. *Ramilies* was ordered to leave her homeward-bound convoy and position herself westward of *Bismarck*, and *Revenge*, from Halifax, was ordered to intercept. Cruisers covered a possible enemy break-back to the north and east, and another naval force steamed northwards from Gibraltar.

On the evening of 24 May the great battleship turned on her pursuers and there was a brief encounter; but this was a clever ruse to cover the departure of *Prinz Eugen* which made off to the south-east. Ten days later, after re-fuelling at sea, she reached Brest.

At 22.00 the same night, the aircraft carrier *Victorious* launched the nine Swordfish torpedo-bombers of 825 Squadron, Fleet Air Arm, against the enemy battleship. These old-fashioned biplanes, obsolescent both in design and performance, were led by Lieutenant Commander Eugene Esmonde, a highly efficient and courageous officer. It was a foul night with rain, scudding low clouds and a strong head-wind, but helped by wireless instructions from HMS *Norfolk*, the squadron commander led his old 'Stringbags' at a steady 90 knots

Aftermath of the Atlantic battle – HMS *Dorsetshire* taking aboard survivors from sunken *Bismarck*

towards his quarry. Somehow two hours later, in darkness, he found *Bismarck* and attacked in the face of heavy fire. They scored one torpedo hit under the bridge and set course for home.

Home, of course, was the carrier *Victorious*. The weather, on this pitch-black night, had worsened with a stronger wind and heavy rain showers. The pilots had little practice in deck-landing even in daylight and, to make matters worse, the ship's homing beacon had failed. Their squadron commander, however, brought them back to *Victorious* where, with the help of searchlights and signal lamps, they all landed safely.

Despite the torpedo hit which slowed her down, *Bismarck* shook off her pursuers but on 26 May she was found by a Catalina of Coastal Command, then lost again but soon spotted by Swordfish from *Ark Royal*. The enemy battleship was now sur-

rounded by many of the Royal Navy's capital ships and cut off from Brest. But there was still confusion.

HMS *Sheffield* was sent forward to close and shadow the German vessel, but *Ark Royal* was not informed and her Swordfish attacked *Sheffield* instead of the enemy battleship. *Sheffield* happily recognized the String-bags and did not fire, and at least one FAA pilot realized his appalling mistake because he signalled to *Sheffield*: 'Sorry for the kipper!'*

The penitent Stringbags returned to their carrier where, after refuelling and rearming, they took off shortly after 19.00 the same day, and were diverted to their prey by the forgiving *Sheffield*. This time there was no mistake and two torpedoes, and possibly a third, struck *Bismarck*. She was seen by a shadowing aeroplane to make two complete circles and seemed out of control. At 08.47 on 27 May, *Rodney* opened fire and was joined by *King George V* and *Dorset-*

shire, but it was not until 10.40 that the great ship went down.

So ended the saga of *Bismarck*. A triumph for air–sea operations, especially 825 Squadron's epic mission on that daunting Atlantic night.

ATLANTIC MIRACLE

After the 'Stringbag' attack on 24 May the shadowing force of cruisers, *Norfolk* and *Suffolk*, had lost radar contact with *Bismarck*. It had been a major misfortune at that stage in the chase. The next day, a rough, uninviting day of poor visibility and low, scudding clouds, 825 Squadron had been ordered to fly individual searches to find her. The outcome makes a compelling narrative.†

One of the aircraft, piloted by Lieutenant Pat Jackson RN (Commander P. B. Jackson RN), with Lieutenant D. A. 'Dapper' Berrill RN, observer, and Leading Airman Sparkes, gunner, making up the three-man crew, swept its designated area to the limit. Then catastrophe! *Victorious* couldn't be found on return. Stark reality faced the Captain of the Swordfish. 'We were lost,' he said, 'in mid-Atlantic.'

Jackson, down to the last few pints of fuel, had no alternative but to 'ditch'. Just as this was about to happen, Dapper Berrill, in a billion to one shot, spotted an object in the sea. Jackson himself now takes up the story. Nearly five decades have done nothing to dim its fearful detail.

There, directly below the aircraft, with waves washing over it, was the outline of a ship's lifeboat. We instantly decided to ditch; the perilously low state of our fuel tanks left no other choice. Having dropped a smoke-float to ascertain the wind direction, we made a deck-landing approach twenty yards beyond it. By the time we had struggled, drenched and chilly, into our life raft, the aircraft was almost submerged with just the tail showing above the surface. The only other thing visible was the lifeboat, its shape

* Winston S. Churchill, *The Second World War: The Grand Alliance* (Cassell, London, 1950). 'Kipper' was Naval slang for a torpedo.
† Extract from Laddie Lucas, *Out of the Blue* (Hutchinson, London, 1985).

outlined by white, breaking water. We drifted downwind towards it.

The only available tools which resembled balers were our flying boots. With these we baled steadily until at first one, and finally, all three of us could board the lifeboat and shelter from the bitter wind. By now, anxiety and the rough seas had made us all desperately sick; it was some time before we were able to take stock of our bleak surroundings.

The boat came from a Dutch ship, the SS *Ellusa*. There was a grim, soaking bundle amidships which, when opened up, produced not bodies but a sail-bag containing a lug-sail and foresail; sweeps and mast were lashed to the thwarts. There were also a rusty axe and knife, a suit of clothes and trilby hat, a waterlogged tin of fifty cigarettes and a bottle of 1890 Napoleon brandy. The lockers contained ship's hard biscuits and a securely stoppered water beaker. We also had the Very light pistol and cartridges and navigation equipment and compass rescued from the aircraft.

For two days we sailed, at first eastwards towards Scotland, then, because of a severe easterly gale, westwards towards North America. Once, the boat was completely swamped in the heavy seas, but with frantic baling and the help of a makeshift sea anchor, we stayed afloat. It was about now that we sighted another boat. Everything about it was black, the sail and the figures lining its hull. Only their faces were white, although the eyes showed white in black rings. They were Norwegian, the only survivors from a coal burner in a convoy torpedoed a fortnight before. There were several dead men on the bottom boards. They were heading for Greenland, but had been driven back by gales. They advised that our westward heading would lead to death from cold in the ice off the Labrador coast. Their officer suggested that some of his crew should join us and we should sail northwards in company. My decision to reject this offer was hard, but our boat was lighter and faster and our chances of survival were better alone. We passed over cigarettes and biscuits and went our different ways, ours westward and theirs into oblivion . . .

The weather continued to alternate between strong and gale-force winds; the violent seas made sleep difficult and the long nights nightmarish. We tried to sleep by watches during the daylight, since it was during the night that we had been swamped by breaking waves. Exhaustion

led to fantasies which might have proved fatal had one been alone. The biting cold, and cold, water-soaked biscuit diet, caused severe jaw and toothache, and we all had a great longing for hot food. The brandy we kept for medical purposes only, being too strong for our empty tums.

Boils appeared, and a slowing of the blood circulation in feet and legs. In the case of Sparkes this soon became chronic, perhaps because he wore soaking wet flying boots at all times. (Dapper and I had removed ours in order to move freely, and because we needed to bale with them.) A deterioration in Sparkes's condition caused us to alter course due north for the nearest landfall, Greenland. Though the possibility of landing near habitation was remote, the chance had to be taken . . .

Sea birds began to reappear, an encouraging sign that land was near, but the foul weather persisted and the sails showed signs of wear. It was a miserable boatload, being driven before a sleet-ridden gale, which eventually sighted a vessel,* passing about a mile distant. Despite our Very lights it seemed at first that the ship would pass without the lookouts seeing us, but our last smoke-puff went off with a rather louder 'ponk' than usual and

an answering blast came from the ship's siren. It was a lovely sound, and the sight of her crew as they leapt into our boat to help us aboard was one to remember . . .

CHANNEL DEBACLE

Operation Fuller, issued in 1941, warned that the German battle-cruisers *Gneisenau* and *Scharnhorst*, and their cruiser *Prinz Eugen*, would, sooner or later, leave their well-defended base at Brest and attempt the narrow and dangerous passage of the Straits of Dover to break out into the northern seas. They would have to sail the whole length of the English Channel, which, since 1690 (when Tourville defeated the Anglo-Dutch fleet off the Isle of Wight), had never seen strong enemy naval forces.

During that summer the three enemy vessels were photographed at Brest and were attacked many times

* It was the Icelandic ship *Lagerfoss*, bound for Reykjavik from Halifax, Nova Scotia. Captain Gistlassen was the skipper. He was helpful and hospitable once he knew the survivors weren't German.

Channel epic, February 1942: German battlecruisers *Scharnhorst* and *Gneisenau* in company with *Prinz Eugen* breach the Dover Straits in daylight

Bomber Command Halifaxes over Brest – but still Germany's battlecruisers escaped

by Bomber and Coastal Commands. On 23 July, a PRU Spitfire photographed *Scharnhorst* at La Pallice and on the next day fifteen new Halifaxes of Bomber Command, with fighter escort, made a daylight attack, and at a cost of one-third of the bombers scored five direct hits. The damaged *Scharnhorst* returned to Brest where, with her two sister ships, she was bombed throughout the late summer and autumn, once by a force of more than one hundred bombers.

On Christmas Eve Group Captain 'Gus' Walker, pre-war England Rugby scrum-half, drew three crews of 144 Squadron out of a hat to fly their obsolescent Hampdens, in daylight, against the enemy ships protected by the heaviest concentration of anti-aircraft guns in the world. One Hampden failed to return, another lost half its tail to a balloon cable but struggled back and the third returned with a wounded navigator.

On 25 January 1942 all three ships were photographed in the harbour, and soon they were joined by German escorting vessels, destroyers, torpedo boats and minesweepers. Thus, in early February, the Admiralty was convinced that the break-out would soon be attempted and the enemy ships would pass through the Straits of Dover by night. The stand-by arrangements detailed in Fuller were brought into force. No large British ships were available but the Channel light naval forces were strengthened. Coastal Command flew additional patrols, torpedo-bombers were alerted and heavy bombers were brought to a readiness state of two hours.

On 11 February a PRU Spitfire photographed the ships still at Brest. Sixteen Wellingtons were dispatched

against them and did no damage. That evening the German commander, Vice-Admiral Ciliax, put to sea and began his daring voyage.

The Germans had done their homework well. Hitler himself had chaired a meeting at his 'Wolf's Redoubt' when the importance of the fighter umbrella was stressed and 'Dolfo' Galland, the Fighter General, was made responsible for the fighter protection of the ships which would dash through the Straits in daylight. After this meeting Galland flew to the Pas de Calais to establish his various sector headquarters at Caen, Le Touquet, Schiphol and Jever, to test his communications and research his relays of fighters.

February 1942: Naval 'steal' of World War Two – German battlecruisers breach the Dover Straits in daylight

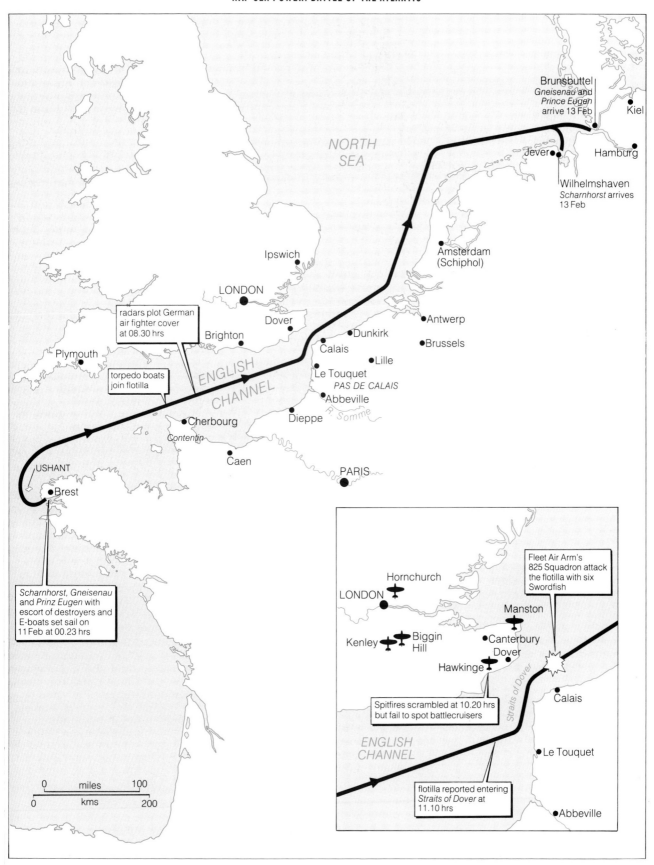

NORTH
SEA

Brunsbuttel
Gneisenau and
Prince Eugen
arrive 13 Feb

Kiel

Jever

Hamburg

Wilhelmshaven
Scharnhorst arrives
13 Feb

Amsterdam
(Schiphol)

Ipswich

LONDON

Dover

Antwerp

Dunkirk

Brussels

Brighton

Calais

Lille

Le Touquet

radars plot German
air fighter cover
at 08.30 hrs

PAS DE CALAIS

Plymouth

ENGLISH

Abbeville

CHANNEL

Dieppe

R. Somme

torpedo boats
join flotilla

Cherbourg

Contentin

Caen

PARIS

USHANT

Brest

Hornchurch

LONDON

Fleet Air Arm's
825 Squadron attack
the flotilla with six
Swordfish

Manston

Kenley

Biggin
Hill

Canterbury

Dover

Scharnhorst, *Gneisenau*
and *Prinz Eugen* with
escort of destroyers and
E-boats set sail on
11 Feb at 00.23 hrs

Hawkinge

Straits of Dover

Calais

Spitfires scrambled at 10.20 hrs
but fail to spot battlecruisers

ENGLISH
CHANNEL

Le Touquet

flotilla reported entering
Straits of Dover at
11.10 hrs

Abbeville

0   miles   100

0   kms   200

Admiral Ciliax, too, had done his homework. He sailed four nights before the full moon which would give him a flood tide up the Channel. His minesweepers had swept our minefields and marked his deep water course which, as far as possible, avoided our low-scanning radars. He had arranged diversionary raids against British harbours and airfields, and had direct links with Galland's several headquarters.

Undetected the German squadron, consisting of the two battle-cruisers, the cruiser, an outer screen of seven destroyers and an inner screen of between eight and fifteen E-boats, rounded Ushant in the early hours of 12 February, and making about 30 knots, set course for the Channel. Off Cherbourg a flotilla of torpedo boats reinforced the outer screen. Dawn found the squadron off the Cotentin peninsula; the weather was cloudy with a 1,500-feet ceiling but the visibility was relatively good.

At 08.30 our radars began to plot Galland's fighter umbrella but our controllers thought they were air–sea operations, and it was not until 10.20 that two Spitfires were scrambled from Hawkinge. In poor visibility the pilots saw destroyers and E-boats but not the capital ships. At 10.00, still unhampered by all the air and sea forces at our disposal, the intrepid Ciliax and his sailors were off the mouth of the Somme – but forty miles from the neck of the English Channel.

When the weather did not permit wing formations – as on this day – the more fearless spirits of Fighter Command, flying in pairs, flew over the Channel and the Pas de Calais hoping to come across a stray Messerschmitt or two. One such courageous pilot was Group Captain Victor Beamish, the eldest of four distinguished brothers and Station Commander at Kenley, who on this fateful day elected to take his Wing Commander Flying, Finlay Boyd, on their own private sortie over the Channel.

They were airborne at 10.10 and when within sight of the French coast came across two Messerschmitt 109s of Galland's umbrella. Diving to

attack they found themselves over the German squadron and saw the battle-cruisers with their screens of destroyers and E-boats. The two Spitfire pilots were set upon by more 109s, so they dived into the flak barrage – through which the 109s did not follow, fired at an E-boat and escaped 'on the deck'. They landed at 11.10 and a few minutes later the almost unbelievable news was out that the enemy flotilla was entering the Straits of Dover.

Even at this late stage in this sorry catalogue of events, there should have been a big bomber attack, but the hundred or so bombers earmarked by Fuller had, for some reason, been released to a readiness state of four hours and could not attack before 15.00, when the light would be fading on this cloudy February afternoon. The unsavoury fact, after months of warning, was that from the hundreds of strike aeroplanes based in the UK only seven Beaufighters from Thorney Island and six old Swordfish from Manston were available to strike within the next two hours.

The Swordfish of 825 Squadron, still commanded by Eugene Esmonde, had been based at RAF Manston since 4 February to participate in Fuller. They were stationed there on the understanding that they would only operate at night when they would have a better chance of survival. However, on 12 February, Esmonde was told the bad news that his six old 'Stringbags' were to fly in daylight after all, and that they would be protected by five squadrons from Fighter Command.

Soon after noon the controllers at Biggin Hill and Hornchurch informed Manston that their squadrons would be a few minutes late for the rendezvous at 12.25 with the Swordfish. Indeed, the Hornchurch controller spoke personally to Esmonde who said that he must set course on time. At 12.20 he led his small force into the air and circled Manston. At 12.28, three minutes late for the rendezvous, 72 Squadron joined up with the Swordfish. Meanwhile, 401 Squadron,

Royal Canadian Air Force, part of the fighter escort, for some extraordinary reason was told to orbit Canterbury for several minutes, from whence they could actually see the enemy ships.

With only one fighter squadron of ten Spitfires the supremely brave Lieutenant Commander, upholding the very finest traditions of the Senior Service, set course in his lumbering Stringbag for the enemy and certain death. Poor visibility soon caused the ten Spitfires to lose contact with the plodding Stringbags, and then Esmonde and his six aircraft were flying alone towards the immensely powerful enemy, now ten miles north of Calais.

They approached in two flights of three. Before reaching the powerful destroyer screen they were engaged by the enemy's most modern fighters in strength. Esmonde's own aircraft was the first to be badly damaged. His port mainplanes were 'shot to shreds' (according to a survivor) but the Stringbag kept flying as Esmonde headed at low level over the destroyers towards the capital ships they encircled. Both the pilots with him, Kingsmill and Rose, were also hit but flew on, though Rose was badly wounded, his air gunner killed, his petrol tank shattered by cannon fire. Esmonde's aircraft crashed into the sea when hit again some 3000 yards from the battle cruisers. Kingsmill and his observer, Samples, were wounded, the aircraft further damaged. But they closed within range of their target, *Scharnhorst*, and Kingsmill could aim and drop his torpedo before being forced to ditch. Rose did much the same: he pressed home his torpedo attack, also on *Scharnhorst*, and was able to turn back over the destroyers before his engine succumbed.

The second flight, led by Lieutenant Thompson, and flying astern of Esmonde, was never seen again.

So ended the most incomprehensible, most badly planned, most gallantly led operation in the history of naval aviation. No hits were scored on the enemy fleet. Of the eighteen officers and men taking part, thirteen were killed and four seriously wounded. Lee, who was Rose's observer, alone emerged unscathed.*

* Laddie Lucas, *Wings of War* (Hutchinson, London, 1983).

Esmonde was awarded a posthumous Victoria Cross. The four surviving officerrs, all RNVR sub-lieutenants, were awarded DSOs and the surviving gunner, a Conspicuous Gallantry Medal. Months later Esmonde's body was washed ashore at the mouth of the Medway.

During the rest of this grim day some 242 bombers were dispatched in three waves against the enemy squadron, but only thirty-nine succeeded in bombing. No damage was done. A few torpedo boats and some ancient destroyers also failed to harm the ships.

A subsequent Board of Inquiry whitewashed the whole disgraceful affair, finding that no one was to blame. Galland, the Fighters' General, was far nearer the mark when he recorded that the break-out was 'a great and impressive victory', and that the Royal Air Force had been sent into action 'with insufficient planning, without a clear concept of the attack and without systematic tactics'.*

AIR BATTLE OVER DIEPPE

The 12 Group Wing consisting of 485 (New Zealand) Squadron, 411 (Canadian) Squadron and 610 (County of Chester) Squadron flew to West Malling, Kent, 'where,' writes 'Johnnie' Johnson, 'on the evening of 18 August 1942 our Wing Commander Flying 'Jamie' Jameson, briefed the pilots about Operation Jubilee, a big raid on the French town of Dieppe.'

Jubilee was devised by Vice Admiral Lord Louis Mountbatten, Chief of Combined Operations and a member of the Chiefs of Staff Committee. His imaginative and audacious personality was soon apparent in the successful but costly attack on the German-controlled port of St Nazaire. On this occasion an old destroyer rammed and blew up the gates of the dry dock, one of the largest in the world; this 'brilliant and heroic exploit', to use Churchill's tribute, made Mountbatten's planners cast round for another target and what better than the small coastal town of

Dieppe. It was within easy reach of an assault from southern England, had good beaches and was well within the limited range of our fighters.

According to the official history of the Dieppe raid, which was first called Operation Rutter, the troops were embarked on 2 and 3 July, briefed and sealed on board. However, because of the weather, the operation was cancelled and the troops were disembarked, but not before the German bombers had attacked the ships lying in the Solent. The Canadian historian says, 'As the troops had been fully informed of the objective of the proposed raid, once they left the ships it would no longer be possible to maintain complete

'As a mouse going into a trap'

secrecy. General Montgomery recommended that the operation should now "be off for all time".'†

Six weeks later, Montgomery left for the Desert and the assault, renamed Jubilee, was on again. Some 6,100 troops, of whom 4,963 were Canadian and about 1,075 British, would make the attempt. There were also fifty US Rangers and a few French Commandos and anti-Nazi nationals. The Naval Force Commander had the difficult job of controlling a fleet of 237 ships and landing craft. Leigh-Mallory would control the air effort by

* Adolf Galland, *The First and the Last* (Methuen, London, 1955).
† *The Canadian Army, 1939–45*, Ottawa.

seventy-four squadrons from his headquarters at Uxbridge, and he had a representative in the headquarters ship, HMS *Calpe*.

Johnnie Johnson continues his eye-witness account:

Our first thoughts at the briefing were that we preferred our own task in the air to that of the troops on the ground. We were pleased that we were airmen and not soldiers, for some of us had flown over this part of France for almost two years and had a healthy respect for the German defence and gunners. Quite a few of our own pilots had been shot down in this area to return with tales of bristling defences and a heavily fortified coastal belt. Our own opinion of Dieppe was hardly in accord with the official intelligence estimate, which indicated that the town was only lightly defended.

As we walked away from the briefing room a French pilot, from 610 Squadron, remarked that his family always spent their summer holidays at Dieppe. He described the narrow, shelving beaches overlooked by high cliffs, where the Germans had sited their defences, and said he could not imagine anywhere less suitable on the coast of Europe for a big raid.

At dawn on the next day, 19 August, we took off and crossed the Channel at low level to avoid radar detection. About ten miles off Dieppe we began to climb to our allotted height of 10,000 feet, and as we climbed we heard the excited chatter of fighter pilots:

'Break right, now.'

'Watch those bastards at six o'clock above.'

'109s coming down.'

'I shall have to bale out.'

'Break right.'

'All Elfin aircraft get out. I say again. All Elfin aircraft get out.'

Jameson called the fighter controller in HMS *Calpe* to report our position. There was no reply.

My Squadron was top cover to the Wing and as we levelled out at 10,000 feet, we saw Spitfires, Messerschmitts and Focke-Wulfs milling about the sky. I saw several of the formidable Focke-Wulf 190s above and told my pilots to turn and keep turning. Then the experienced Denis Crowley-Milling called the break, and three finger-fours of 610 Squadron swung round together, the wingmen slipping into line astern as they turned steeply for their lives. 190s could not stay with Spitfires in a steep turn and suddenly, and surprisingly, I saw several 190s ahead and at the same level. I gave one long burst with the maximum deflection from the maximum range. To everyone's astonishment it began to smoke, the wheels dropped and it fell away to the sea. Crow said: 'Good shooting, Johnnie.'

But it was only a temporary lull in this violent air battle, for the Messerschmitts and Focke-Wulfs came down on the Squadron from astern and the flanks. The 190s, superior in speed, climb and armament to our Spitfire Vs, were full of fight and we could do little but turn and break and turn and break. During a steep turn I caught a glimpse of a strong formation of enemy fighters heading towards Dieppe from inland. Swearing violently I informed the Wing Leader about the enemy reinforcements. Jameson acknowledged and warned me to watch my language.

I reckoned that we were surrounded by more than a hundred enemy fighters. When they came at us we turned so steeply that we blacked-out momentarily, and our Spitfires protested and shuddered as we approached their stalling speeds. The Squadron had lost its cohesion. Section was separated from section and wingmen lost their leaders. I saw three of my own lads shot down, two in flames, and the third was my own wingman, 'South' Creagh from Australia, who glided down streaming white glycol from his engine.

I parted company with another Spitfire when we broke in opposite directions to avoid an astern attack, but a 109 hung on to my tail and I lost a lot of height before I shook him off.

I was alone over Dieppe and it was time to go home, when I spotted a solitary Focke-Wulf 190. At the same time he saw me and snaked towards me – almost head-on. We both turned hard to the left and whirled round on opposite sides of what seemed to be an ever-decreasing circle.

I learned, the hard way, that this pilot could stay with me in the tightest of turns, but turning does not get you home, and I could not dodge round the spires and cliffs of Dieppe much longer.

Eventually I managed to get rid of him by breaking all the rules and flying fast and low at a British destroyer which, of course, fired everything it had at both friend and foe. Flak and tracer came at me from the destroyer and slower tracers, like yellow golf balls, passed over my cockpit from the 190. At the last moment I pulled over the destroyer, then slammed the nose down and eased out a few feet above the sea. I broke hard to the left and searched for the Kraut, but he was no longer with me. Either the flak had put him off or had nailed him. I made off at high speed to West Malling.

Group Captain Harry Broadhurst, flying over Dieppe on that fateful morning, noticed that the Germans were working their fighters in pairs and fours. The enemy aeroplanes were flying about five miles north-east of Le Treport, getting well up into the sun and then diving straight down through our patrols towards our ships lying off Dieppe. Some attacked the ships and some went for the patrolling Spitfires. Broadhurst noticed that immediately our wings – each of three squadrons – reached the French coast they were bounced by the higher, faster Focke-Wulfs when the Spitfires were badly split up. He thought we would be better off flying, like the enemy pilots – in the more flexible pairs and finger-fours and after landing at Northolt he telephoned Leigh-Mallory and put his case. The AOC, as we have already seen, was very much a 'Big Wing' man and could not be persuaded to alter his tactics; his Group Captain

'The greatest air battle of the Second World War' . . . Dieppe, August 1944

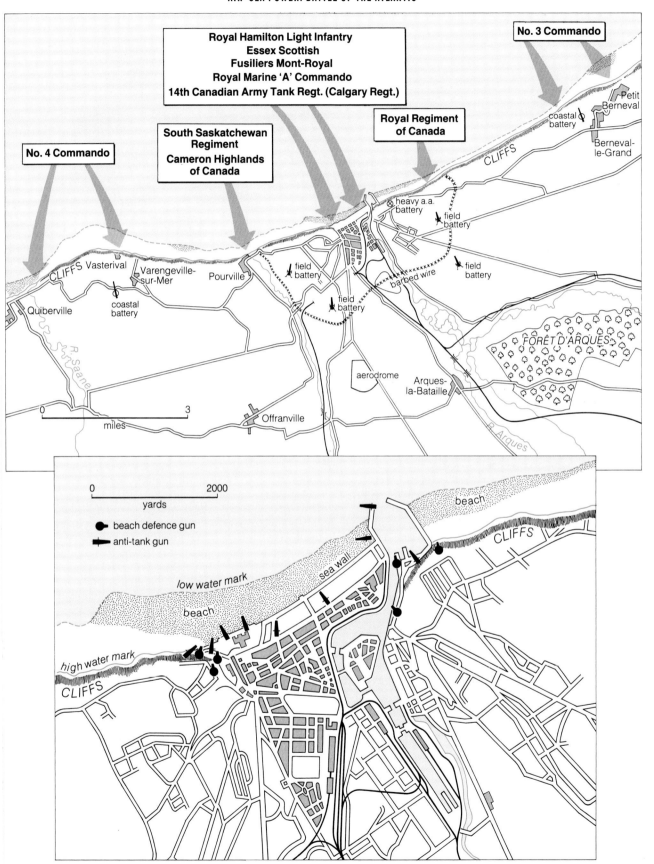

Failure at Dieppe

persisted and knew he had lost the debate when Leigh-Mallory suddenly became quite pompous and the familiar 'Broady' was replaced with 'Broadhurst'!

The 12 Group Wing flew four times that day and Jameson never established radio contact with HMS *Calpe*. We fighter pilots were not aware of the bloody and terrible situation below where, at 09.00, the various commanders realized that orders for withdrawal must be issued. This was timed for 11.00.

But some fighter pilots coming out at low level over the shelving shingle of the Dieppe beaches caught fleeting glimpses of the debris of a lost battle – overturned tanks, shattered and blackened landing craft and the grotesque huddled shapes of the Canadian dead and dying.

Later, after the survivors returned, we heard that those soldiers who made it through the surf were mowed down by machine gun fire and shelling from the cliffs. A Royal Navy officer called the debacle 'a sea version of the Charge of the Light Brigade'. The commander of a German battery said: 'We felt very sorry for the enemy because he had no chance. He was as a mouse going into a trap!'*

By the end of this day the Royal Air Force and the Luftwaffe had fought the greatest air battle of the Second World War. We lost 106 aeroplanes, of which eighty-eight were fighters and seventy-one pilots were killed or missing. The Germans lost forty-eight aeroplanes.

The Dieppe raid was, and still is, a highly controversial affair. Tactically it must be regarded as a complete failure, for none of its stated objec-

tives was achieved in full measure. It is a record of poor security, of faulty intelligence, of inadequate communications between air and ground, of a confused and bloody ground situation over which central co-ordination could not be exercised. It is a story of great gallantry and heavy loss of life. The record of the (Canadian) Essex Scottish, who brought back fifty-two personnel, of whom twenty-eight were wounded, out of a force of 553, gives some indication of the desperate situation on the ground. Perhaps Chester Wilmot made the best assessment of the operation when he stated that the Dieppe raid 'yielded bloody warning of the strength of the Atlantic wall'!*

* T. Murray Hunter, *Canada at Dieppe* (Canadian War Museum, Ottawa, 1982).

14 · ALLIED INVASION OF EUROPE

D-DAY

Here is Johnnie Johnson's account of this momentous day.

After three years with the fighter squadrons, I was posted, early in 1944, to the planning staff of 11 Group Headquarters, Fighter Command. Our main task was to provide fighter escort and fighter support wings for the various bomber forces which belonged to four different organizations. These were the Lancasters of Bomber Command; Fortresses, Liberators and fighters of the US Eighth Air Force; Marauders and Havocs of the US Ninth Air Force; and Bostons, Mitchells and Mosquitos of our own 2 Group. Day in, day out, thousands of bombers, escorted in daylight by fighters, ranged far and wide across occupied Europe and Germany wrecking the enemy war machine and paving the way for D-Day.

Fighter Command,* with its underground concrete operations rooms, its permanent communications and airfields, was a static, defensive organization. Its squadrons could move, but not its essential being. Thus it was decided that although the defence of Britain, the base for the invasion, should remain Fighter Command's responsibility, the fighters that would maintain air supremacy over and beyond the Normandy beaches must belong to a more flexible organization geared to the needs of the invading armies. The new force must be mobile, it must be able to build airfields, lay communications, establish its own radar warning, and move ever forwards.

It was decided that this Allied air force would consist of two parts – the British Second Tactical Air Force (TAF) to support the British and Canadian group of armies, and the US Ninth Air Force to support the American group of armies. These two forces, together with what remained of the Air Defence of Great Britain, were combined together in what soon proved to be an unnecessary organization called the Allied Expeditionary Air Force which was respon-

* From November 1943 until October 1944 Fighter Command was called the Air Defence of Great Britain.

D-Day in Normandy. US troops penetrate the defences

'He that outlives this day and comes safe home will stand a tip-toe when this day is nam'd'

sible for the planning and co-ordination of all aircraft operating in the support of the invasion on D-Day. Two experienced airmen, 'Mary' Coningham, of desert fame, and Harry Broadhurst (Mr 'Cab Rank') were appointed to command Second TAF and its fighter-bomber subsidiary 83 Group.

Beside the colossal power of the strategic air forces, placed at the call of Air Chief Marshal Tedder, the Deputy Supreme Commander, the Allies would have a great armada of 2,000 British and 1,300 American fighters and fighter-bombers, eighty-eight British and 550 American medium bombers, 972 British and 1,619 American gliders, 500 British and 1,666 American transport aircraft, 102 artillery observation aircraft, ninety-eight rescue aircraft, and more than 100 tactical reconnaissance aircraft. It was directed from a Combined Control Centre at Uxbridge where, less than four years before, when the Battle of Britain had reached its zenith, Keith Park told Winston Churchill that he had no fighter squadrons in reserve.

Although I was not on the staff of the Allied Expeditionary Air Force

those officers with recent combat experience often attended the D-Day planning conferences, and on one occasion we discussed how many sorties fighter pilots could fly each day over the Normandy beaches. I stressed that the average fighter pilot was capable of flying four sorties per day, but he would soon be exhausted if he flew at this intensity for several days. This was accepted, and preparations were made for fighter squadrons to fly four sorties on D-Day (6 June 1944), three on D + 1, and two thereafter. The tasks given to the fighters were to maintain air supremacy, to reconnoitre enemy dispositions and movements, to disrupt enemy communications and his flow of reinforcements and supplies, to provide close support for the invading troops, to attack enemy naval forces and to escort the airborne forces.

Drawing on the lessons of previous years the planning staffs set down the routes to the beaches, the schedules of our patrols, the areas for armed reconnaissance and offensive action, the routes and targets for bombing operations, patrol areas for coastal traffic, reinforcement plans and

emergency plans. When these plans were complete, checked and re-checked, they were put together into an operation order known as a 'Form D', which was fed into the teleprinters on the evening before D-Day and sent to the waiting squadrons.

By this time I had returned to the contest and on the forward airfields of southern England we had completed our preparations except for one last thing. With such a mass of aircraft in the sky there must be no mistaken identities, and so it was that large tins of black and white paint were produced, and every aeroplane was painted with thick black and white stripes running fore and aft across the wings and on the fuselage near the tail.

On the evening of 5 June (D−1) I briefed my Canadian fighter pilots on our particular task – to protect the eastern flank of the assault from enemy air attack. The briefing was soon finished, and there were few questions. Everyone knew his job, and there was a feeling of relief that after four years of flying over the Channel we should soon be on the other side. As I walked to my quarters I heard the roar of a multitude of aircraft overhead, and through a break in the low clouds I saw Lancasters pounding their way through the night to herald the invasion of France.

On the early morning of Tuesday, 6 June, I led my Canadian Wing of thirty-six Spitfires across the choppy, grey Channel to patrol the eastern flank of the assault beaches. The cloud base was about 2,000 feet and the visibility between five and six miles, which meant that a great many aeroplanes were compressed into a small air space. I called George Keefer, the Wing Leader of the Spitfires we were about to relieve, and told him we were on our patrol line. Had he seen an enemy fighter? 'Not a bloody thing,' he replied, 'but there's plenty of ours milling about and the flak is pretty hot.' I called the fighter direction ship below and asked if

Return to France: Allied landings in Normandy, June 1944

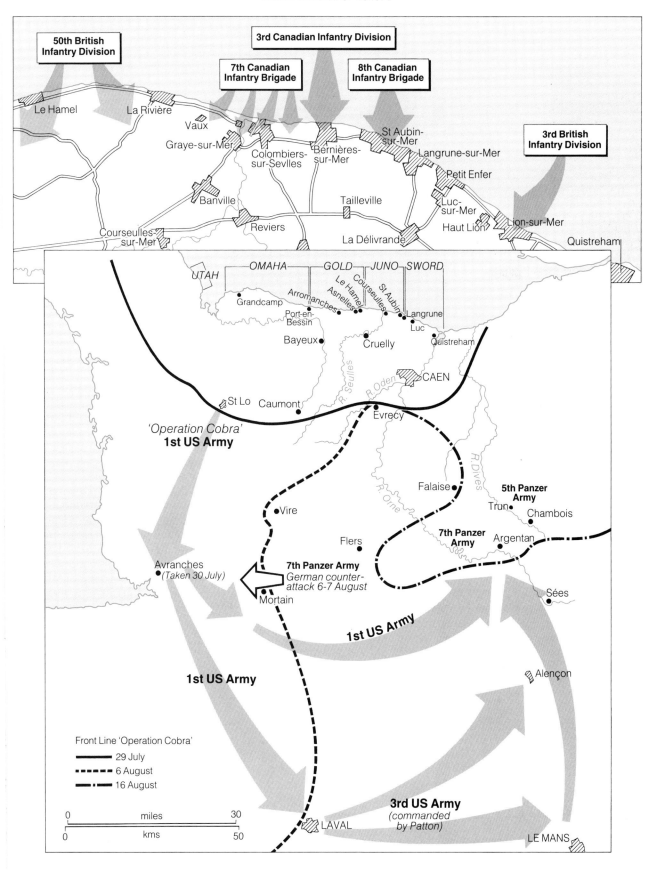

50th British Infantry Division

3rd Canadian Infantry Division

7th Canadian Infantry Brigade

8th Canadian Infantry Brigade

3rd British Infantry Division

Le Hamel

La Rivière

Vaux

Graye-sur-Mer

Colombiers-sur-Sevlles

Bernières-sur-Mer

St Aubin-sur-Mer

Langrune-sur-Mer

Petit Enfer

Banville

Tailleville

Luc-sur-Mer

Haut Lion

Lion-sur-Mer

Courseulles-sur-Mer

Reviers

La Délivrande

Quistreham

UTAH

OMAHA

GOLD

JUNO

SWORD

Grandcamp

Arromanches

Port-en-Bessin

Le Hamel

Asnelles

Courseulles

St Aubin

Langrune

Luc

Quistreham

Bayeux

Cruelly

R. Seulles

R. Oden

CAEN

St Lo

Caumont

Evrecy

'Operation Cobra'
1st US Army

R. Dives

Falaise

R. Orne

5th Panzer Army

Trun

Chambois

Vire

Flers

7th Panzer Army

Argentan

7th Panzer Army
German counter-attack 6-7 August

Avranches
(Taken 30 July)

Mortain

1st US Army

Sées

1st US Army

Alençon

1st US Army

Front Line 'Operation Cobra'

—————— 29 July

- - - - - - 6 August

—·—·—·— 16 August

0 ——— miles ——— 30

0 ——— kms ——— 50

LAVAL

3rd US Army
(commanded by Patton)

LE MANS

Canadians in Normandy: Prime Minister meets their leader Wing Leader Johnnie Johnson

MORTAIN: THE TYPHOONS COME INTO THEIR OWN

Operation Overlord called for the capture of Caen on D-Day, 6 June 1944, but weeks later, the Allies were still stuck in the beachhead and to try and break through the German defences two operations, Goodwood and Cobra, were attempted. Goodwood began on 18 July when Bomber Command, the Eighth and Ninth US Air Forces attacked the positions of Panzer Group West, south-east of Caen. By the end of that day some 4,500 Allied aeroplanes had taken part in the awesome air attack against ground troops. After the bombing Dempsey's Second Army, with some 750 tanks, forced a way through the demoralized Germans to the Caen–Falaise open plain but two days later the attack foundered and was called off. Montgomery had previously told Eisenhower that if he could have the heavy bombers 'My whole eastern front will burst into flames . . . '* and the Supreme Commander commented 'that it had taken 7000 tons of bombs to gain seven miles and the Allies could hardly hope to go through France paying a price of 1000 tons of bombs per mile'.†

Cobra, devised by General Omer Bradley to free the Americans from the dreadful Normandy bocage, got off to a bad start when errors in carpet bombing by the Eighth Air Force on 24 and 25 July killed and wounded hundreds of US soldiers. But the German troops, thin on the ground compared to Caen, were so devastated by the bombing that they began to give way. Bradley, the outstanding general in Normandy, sensed that this was his opportunity, and on 29 July launched four armoured divisions towards Avranches, the 'corner town' between Normandy and Brittany. At long last they were out of the hedgerow country and, as the armour rolled at high speed into the enemy's rear areas, the admirable and aggressive

there were any plots of Hun formations. The controller came back with the guarded reply that for the moment he had nothing for me.

We swept parallel to the coast beneath a leaden sky, and I positioned the Wing a few hundred yards off-shore so that the enemy gunners could not range our Spitfires. We were forced down to a low altitude by the intermittent cloud. The air space became dangerously crowded as fighters, fighter-bombers, light bombers, medium bombers, reconnaissance aeroplanes and gun spotters twisted and turned above the grey, choppy sea. The danger was not from the Luftwaffe, but from a mid-air collision.

Once the controller asked me to investigate 'bogey' aircraft flying south, but these turned out to be Typhoons.

Our patrol line ended over the fishing village of Port-en-Bessin and further to the west lay the two American beaches, Omaha and Utah.

As I made a wide turn a wing of American Thunderbolts harried our progress, and for a few uneasy seconds we circled warily round each other. We had seen their black and white stripes, but had they seen ours? Formations of different types of Allied aircraft had attacked each other throughout the war, and we all knew the Americans were very fast on the draw. They tended to shoot first and ask questions later. Fortunately, they sheered off, and we continued our flight to the Orne.

Four times that day we made our way across the Channel and never a sign of an enemy aeroplane. My pilots were bitterly disappointed with the Luftwaffe's failure to make an appearance on this day – one of the most momentous in our long history of war. But the truth was that the once-vaunted Luftwaffe was crumbling into defeat on all fronts – beaten into the ground by the might of Allied air power.

* John Terraine, *The Right of the Line* (Hodder & Stoughton, London, 1985).
† Stephen E. Ambrose, *The Supreme Commander* (London, 1970).

Major General Ellwood 'Pete' Quesada, heeding all the lessons of tactical air power learned in North Africa, unleashed his fighter-bombers of the Ninth Air Force. Each command tank carried an Air Force Officer in constant touch with the prowling Thunderbolts and Mustangs which, in open country and good weather, fell upon anything German that moved. The long straight roads were soon lined with wrecked and burned guns, tanks, armoured cars, command cars and, here and there, horse-drawn vehicles. This was the first time since D-Day that German defences had yielded to an Allied attack. Brad-

ley's break-out was becoming a break-through, and waiting to exploit it was the flamboyant, pistol-packing, mercurial, aggressive, controversial Texan, George Patton, anxious to make amends after the humiliation of being sacked in Sicily.

Thus it was Bradley's, not Montgomery's, front that had 'burst into flames', and once Avranches was taken (30 July) it was decided that the German Seventh Army should be trapped before it could escape across the Seine. On 3 August Bradley ordered Patton, now commanding his newly formed Third Army, eastwards to Paris. However, before Pat-

ton could get moving Hitler ordered what proved to be his last counter-attack in Normandy.

But Ultra had already intercepted the vital messages, including those detailing Field Marshal von Kluge's fierce opposition to the movement of German armour for their attack on Mortain. Thus Air Vice-Marshal Harry Broadhurst had time to make plans for his fighter-bombers, especially the hard-hitting Typhoons with their eight sixty-pound rockets. He arranged with Pete Quesada that his Thunderbolts and Mustangs would roam farther afield, for Ultra had also revealed that 300 enemy fighters would protect their armoured columns. Broadhurst's plan worked well.

The German counter-attack came on the night 6/7 August and penetrated several miles south-west of Mortain before being contained by US reinforcements. The day dawned with

Planners all: General James Doolittle (*right*), Commander of the US Eighth Air Force, 1944-45 with staff members Brigadier Banfill and General Orvil Anderson

Eisenhower – the Supreme Commander

summer mists and in the late morning the forward tank crews of the 30th (US) Division saw enemy tanks clattering through the haze. This division had only recently moved into the Mortain sector, it was not well established and at noon the situation became critical. Fortunately the day cleared and within half an hour Broady's Typhoons, armed with rockets, were on the job.

The Typhoon pilots of 127 Wing, led by a splendid aggressive

'Typhoons over Falaise' (Frank Wootton)

Rhodesian, Charles Green, fell to with a will, relishing their first opportunity in Normandy of attacking concentrated German armour, including the formidable Tiger tanks. Their first target was some 200 enemy vehicles and sixty tanks to the north of Mortain.

There was little flak. What remained of the Luftwaffe in France was elsewhere so that Green and his pilots, and other Typhoon squadrons, blasted their targets with deadly effect, first attacking the front and rear of the German columns. Thus the columns were halted in their tracks and those in the middle were trapped.

Usually the Typhoons flew in squadron strength of twelve fighter-bombers, but the AOC did not want his squadrons to waste time on the ground whilst all twelve aeroplanes were being refuelled and re-armed. He therefore ordered that the Typhoons were to operate in pairs and fours, keeping a 'shuttle service' over the doomed columns.

After two hours of repeated strafing with rockets and cannon, Green reported that the battle area was so covered in dust and smoke that their targets were almost invisible. However, at about the same time, Broady heard that a contact car near Vire was asking for immediate air support against a German attack. He at once switched some Typhoons to Vire which destroyed the tanks and the attack petered out.

Before dusk fell the Typhoons of 83 and 84 Groups flew nearly 300 sorties and the AOC had demonstrated, as he had in the Desert, that action by the Allied tactical air forces in a land battle could be decisive. Broadhurst called it 'Blitzkrieg in reverse', and was happy that, at last, the Typhoons had come into their own. Later, an American infantry officer told him that he was at Mortain and saw German crews abandon their tanks immediately they spotted the Typhoons and sometimes even before the fighter-bombers attacked.

'Just before Mortain,' Broady commented, 'we had received a report from Solly Zuckerman* stating that our sixty-pound rockets were pretty useless against tanks!'

FALAISE: THE KILLING GROUND

On 7 August 1944, Montgomery launched the First Canadian Army against Falaise and on the next day Bradley, delighted with his progress so far, thought if he could contain the German Army at Mortain for another two days it would give Patton's Third Army time to get to Argentan – some twelve miles south of Falaise. Thus Falaise and Argentan were the objectives – the jaws of a trap from which, it was hoped, the enemy could not escape. At this stage Bradley did not intend to seal the Falaise–Argentan Gap.

On 12 August, Major General Haislip reported to Patton that his XV Corps were close to Argentan and asked for further instructions. Patton, who knew the Canadians were stalled north of Falaise, instructed his Corps Commander to 'push on slowly in the direction of Falaise . . . upon arrival . . . push on slowly until you contact our Allies'.†

Bradley, however, had obtained his objective, Argentan, and was fearful of a head-on collision with the Canadians, whose advance elements contained a Polish Armoured Division. There were grave dangers involving recognition, especially at night, and he ordered the Texan not to proceed north of Argentan. During this conversation Patton, with his customary lack of tact said: ' . . . shall we continue and drive the British into the sea for another Dunkirk?'‡ Bradley was not amused and neither were the British.

On 16 August the Canadians reached Falaise, and on the next day Broadhurst, who was closely monitoring events from his headquarters, began to get reports from his tactical reconnaissance Mustangs that German armour was retreating eastwards in the Chambois area. However, the ground situation was uncertain because leading elements of the Polish Armoured Division also reported their position near Chambois when they were, in fact, some distance away at a place with a very similar name, and when Broadhurst telephoned Crerar, commanding the First Canadian Army, the latter would not agree that the Typhoons should be let loose.

* Professor S. Zuckerman, Scientific Adviser to the Allied Expeditionary Air Force Bombing Committee.
† Message, Third Army to XV Corps, 12 August 1944.
‡ From Col. Hansen's unpublished diary, 12 August 1944.

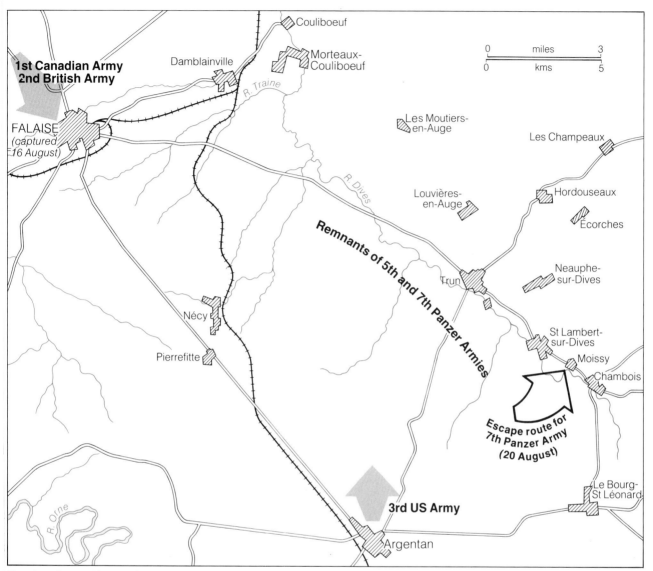

Victory for the Typhoons, 19 August, 1944. German armour decimated at Falaise

Crerar's decision was perhaps understandable because his Canadians had been bombed, suffering heavy casualties, by both Bomber Command and the Eighth Air Force, bringing into doubt, and not for the first time, the wisdom of employing heavy bombers, with their imperfect bombing techniques, in close support of land forces.

The identity of the east-bound columns had to be re-established beyond all doubt, so Broadhurst immediately dispatched his most experienced ground-attack leader, Charles Green, who soon reported that the retreating columns were Ger-

man and on being pressed by his AOC said, 'I saw their black crosses – and the square heads of their drivers.'

Broadhurst immediately telephoned Montgomery explaining the golden opportunity, but also pointing out that since the Canadians were so close to the Germans there could be casualties on our side. Montgomery said he would call back in fifteen minutes, which he did and said: 'Go, there will be no recriminations.'

When they arrived over that small triangle of Normandy bounded by Falaise, Trun and Chambois, the Typhoons trapped the desperate enemy on the narrow dusty lanes by

using the Mortain tactic of sealing off the front and rear of a column by the accurate dropping of a few bombs. The transports were sometimes jammed together four abreast, which made the subsequent rocket and cannon attacks comparatively easy. Some of the armoured cars and tanks attempted to escape their fate by making detours across the fields and wooded country, but these were soon spotted by the Typhoon pilots and were accorded the same treatment as their comrades on the highways and lanes.

Immediately the Typhoons withdrew from the killing ground the Spit-

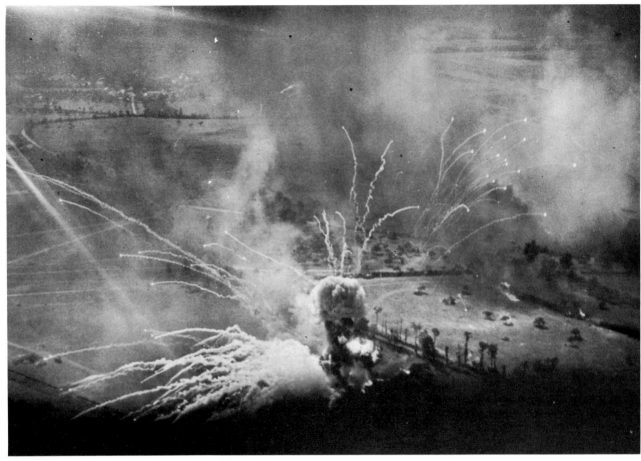

The 'heavies' support the land battle

fires raced into the attack. The tactics of the day were low-level strafing attacks with cannon shells and machine guns against soft-skinned transports, including all types of trucks, staff cars and lightly armoured vehicles. Here and there amongst the shambles on the ground were a few of the deadly Tiger tanks, and although the cannon shells had little effect against their tough armour plate, a few rounds were blasted against them for good measure. As soon as the Spitfires had fired all their ammunition, they flew back at high speed to their airfields, where the ground crews worked flat-out in the hot sunshine to rearm and refuel the aircraft in the shortest possible time. The Typhoons, with their rockets, did far more damage than the Spitfires.

Throughout this day, and on all subsequent operations in the Falaise gap, the Luftwaffe failed to provide any degree of assistance to their sorely pressed ground forces. Faced with the threat of losing their forward airfields to our advance, they were busily occupied with withdrawing to suitable bases in the Paris area, so our fighter-bombers enjoyed complete air supremacy over the battle area. Quick to exploit such a great tactical advantage, Broadhurst once again issued instructions that, until such time as the Luftwaffe reappeared to contest our domination of the Normandy sky, all his aircraft would operate in pairs. Detailed briefings were unnecessary since all the pilots knew the area and the position of our own ground troops. Valuable time was saved, and it was possible to put the maximum number of missions into the air. Before Falaise an individual fighter pilot had rarely flown on more than three or four missions on any one day, but now it was not uncommon for a pilot to fly six times between dawn and dusk.

The hedgerows and small woods, in full foliage, afforded some cover to the Germans, who tied large green branches and shrubs on their trucks in an effort to conceal them from the eyes of our pilots. A gleam of reflected sunshine on metal here, a swirl or eddy of dust there, or fresh tracks leading across the fields were sufficient evidence to bring down the fighter-bombers with their assorted armoury of weapons. When darkness fell to bring some relief to the battered Germans there was time to take stock of the situation and to add up the score. The pilots turned in immediately after dinner, for they would require all their energy for the new day. As they settled down to sleep they heard the continuous drone of our light bombers making their flight across the beach-head to harry the enemy columns through the short night.

The pattern was much the same on the following day. They breakfasted well before the dawn, and the first pair of Spitfires retracted their wheels as the first hint of a lighter sky flushed the eastern horizon. The Germans were making strenuous efforts to salvage what equipment they could from the debacle and get it across the Seine. Broadhurst had anticipated this move and some Typhoons were diverted to attack barges and small craft as they ferried to and fro across the river. Once more other fighter-bomber pilots turned their attention to the killing-ground and attacked all manner of enemy transports wherever they were to be found. They were located on the highways and lanes, in the woods and copses, in small villages and hamlets, beneath the long shadows of tall hedges, in farmyards and even camouflaged with newly mown grass to resemble haystacks. During the previous night many of the enemy had decided to abandon a great proportion of their transports: they could be seen continuing the retreat on foot and in hastily commandeered farm carts. Sometimes the despairing enemy waved white sheets at the fighter-bombers as they hurled down to attack, but these signs were ignored; our own ground troops were still some distance away and there was no organization available to round up large numbers of prisoners.

On this day, 19 August, thousands of transports were destroyed or damaged, and many were left burning. Afterwards, our efforts in the Falaise gap gradually petered out, for the transports and personnel of the German Seventh Army had either been eliminated or had withdrawn across the Seine. The Falaise gap ranks as one of the greatest killing-grounds of the war, and is a classic example of the devastating effects of tactical air power when applied in concentrated form against targets of this nature. During these few days, pilots of the Second Tactical Air Force flew more than 12,000 missions and

Fighter-bomber targets

turned an enemy retreat into a rout. But many thousands of Germans escaped across the Seine and lived to fight another day.

Johnnie Johnson, in a personal reflection, recalls a later visit to the battlefield:

Long after the Battle of Normandy I walked over the ground with Major General George Kitching who commanded the Fourth Canadian Armoured Division during the fighting, and Oberst Hubert Meyer who was Chief of Staff of 12 SS Panzer Division throughout the Normandy campaign. We were accompanied by a gaggle of middle-aged Canadian officers.

Kitching's Canadian soldiers, recently arrived from England, were no match for their tough, veteran German opponents, and his armour could not be compared with the enemy's Tiger and Panther tanks with their formidable 88-mm and 75-mm guns – far better than any Allied gun.

Compassion in Caen. The British Army lends a helping hand

Kitching told us of changing orders from his Corps Commander – to seize the small town of Damblainville, which, after the attack had gone in, was changed; to capture Coulboeuf and advance to Trun, which was changed again to halt north of that town.

He, George Kitching, told us of lack of communications (except for dispatch riders), navigation errors, brave yet decimated units and of his difficulties with 'boundary lines' which were lines drawn on maps, running roughly from north to south, over which his armour must not cross – otherwise it would be treated as hostile by both friend and foe. Also, the General told us of his difficulties with the Polish Armoured Division on his left flank because he 'never knew exactly where they were'.

The General told us too, of how on 21 August his Corps Commander, Guy Simons, invited his Divisional Commander to breakfast and said: 'George, I'm afraid you will have to go!' Naturally, Kitching was shocked and emotionally upset but remembers that there were no harsh words.

The three of us stood on some high ground (360 feet) overlooking the Falaise Gap between Lambert-sur-Dives and Chambois where Canadian, British, Polish and German soldiers were so interlocked that it was impossible to provide close air support. Meyer showed us how he and fourteen of his comrades escaped in daylight through the Gap.

Should the Falaise Gap have been sealed thus preventing the escape of some 20,000 Germans who would fight again? The dignified, still-erect George Kitching did his best, but we wondered whether he was of the right stuff for the rough cut-and-thrust of the Falaise fighting. Hubert Meyer said we should have sealed the Gap and we, nearly half a century on, agreed with his verdict. We concluded that the main reason for our failure was, in plain Canadian language, our 'screwed-up command and control organization'!

15 · THE EASTERN FRONT: STALINGRAD

In the summer of 1941 Hitler's *Blitzkrieg* technique against Russia scored again – its fifth resounding success since the conquest of Poland in 1939. But in the winter the German offensive ground to a halt in snow and ice surrounding Moscow.

After this failure Hitler split his 1942 offensive between the Caucasus oilfields and Stalingrad on the Volga – the gateway to the north and the Urals. However, General Friedrich Paulus's Sixth Army attack on Stalingrad was held at bay by the defenders, whereupon Hitler, obsessed by its capture, diverted forces from the Caucasus front to strengthen the onslaught on the defiant city.

For the onslaught against Stalingrad some 1,000 combat aeroplanes, including fighters, reconnaissance aircraft, dive-bombers and medium-range bombers were grouped together in *Luftflotte* 4 under the short-fused Colonel General Frieherr Wolfram von Richthofen, of Condor Legion fame, the architect of *Blitzkrieg* and no admirer of Army generals.

At this time the Russian Air Force was still recovering from the crippling blows it had suffered at German hands during the summer and autumn of 1941. Now it was being modernized and strengthened from its own factories (east of the Urals and thus out of range of German bombers), and their latest fighters, the new Lavochkin 5 and Yakovlev 9, were of much improved design and performance, and the IL-2 Stormovik, with heavy armament and rockets, was superior to the Stuka as a close support weapon. However, these new aeroplanes were only reaching the hitherto poorly equipped squadrons as they fell back before the Ger-

man onslaught, offering little resistance to the Luftwaffe. Indeed, General S. I. Rudenko, commanding the Sixteenth Air Army, thought that his fighter pilots lacked discipline, failed to protect the bombers and fighter-bombers, broke off combat too soon and had little technical knowledge about their new fighters.

Between 17 July and 4 August 1942 the bulk of the ground fighting took place inside the Don Bend as Soviet forces tried to slow down the German advance and gain time to improve the defences of Stalingrad.

Richthofen's dive-bombers were able to respond within minutes to information passed from tactical reconnaissance aeroplanes. On 25 July, when Russian troops, stragglers and civilians, panic-stricken because of rumours of panzers nearby, herded

Stalingrad blazing

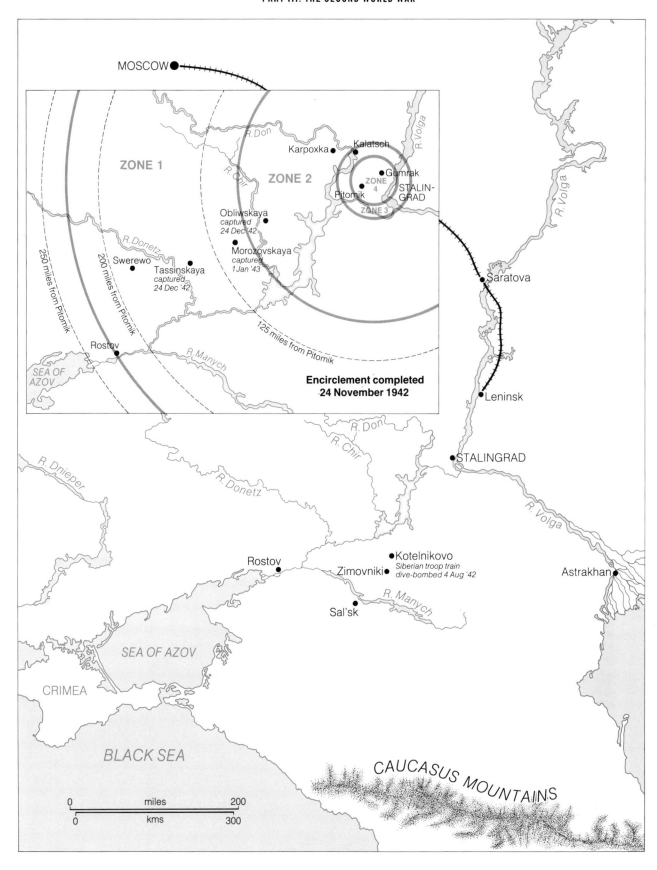

MOSCOW

ZONE 1

ZONE 2

ZONE 4

ZONE 3

R. Don

R. Chir

R. Volga

R. Volga

Karpoxka

Kalatsch

Gumrak

Pitomik

STALIN-GRAD

Obliwskaya
*captured
24 Dec '42*

Morozovskaya
*captured
1 Jan '43*

R. Donetz

Swerewo

Tassinskaya
*captured
24 Dec '42*

Saratova

Leninsk

250 miles from Pitomik

200 miles from Pitomik

125 miles from Pitomik

Rostov

R. Manych

SEA OF
AZOV

**Encirclement completed
24 November 1942**

R. Dnieper

R. Donetz

R. Chir

R. Don

R. Volga

Rostov

Kotelnikovo
*Siberian troop train
dive-bombed 4 Aug '42*

Zimovniki

STALINGRAD

Astrakhan

Sal'sk

R. Manych

SEA OF AZOV

CRIMEA

BLACK SEA

CAUCASUS MOUNTAINS

| 0 | miles | 200 |
| 0 | kms | 300 |

together at a crossing of the Don, they were decimated.

On 4 August a troop train unloading Siberian troops at Kotelnikovo Station was savaged by both dive-bombers and tanks; the losses were so appalling that the commander of the troops, now fleeing towards Stalingrad, was found in a state of complete shock.

During August, Richthofen flew on some reconnaissance missions, visited various Army headquarters and found the Russians much weaker than he expected. The Luftwaffe general never thought much of his Army colleagues, and noted in his diary that 'the Army always seems to have far too high an opinion of the enemy'.*

Two days later he received a sudden alert and put the whole of *Luftflotte* 4 into the air. Some 600 bombers attacked the city, killing some 40,000 people and reducing much of it to rubble. All thirty miles of Stalingrad's waterfront was enveloped in flames. As a result of his bombing a panzer corps advanced sixty kilometres against very light opposition and reached the Volga.

During September, the air fighting intensified but the Germans usually had the upper hand because they had more aeroplanes and the Russians did not have radio telephones to speak to each other and their ground stations; soon, however, radio telephones became available and they established a radio guidance network and ground stations passed what information they had to pilots in the air. There was no sophisticated radar control such as we had in the West.

At this desperate time Russian fighter-pilots, fighting for their homeland, used a desperate tactic – ramming. On 14 September, young Chumbarev, 237 Fighter Air Regiment, flew his Yakovlev 1 into a Focke-Wulf 189 reconnaissance aeroplane and sent it down, but the Russian had to crash-land. A few days

General Chuikov – defender of Stalingrad

later there were two rammings when Chenskiye, 283rd Fighter Air Division, downed a German aeroplane and himself parachuted to safety, and Binov, 291st Fighter Air Division, destroyed a Messerschmitt 110 and then crash-landed. These rammings called for incredibly brave pilots but, as the score suggested, they did not win air battles.

In mid-September Richthofen flew with General Fiebig, Commander Eighth Air Corps, to Pitomik airfield, accompanied several missions and was not impressed with the dive-bombing. A few days later, again at Pitomik, he thought his airmen

... were slack and lacking in enterprise and were not pressing home their attacks ... Sorties lacked dash and determination ... As the Army is a lame duck, the Air Force cannot do very much. But with a little more combined and spirited action we could finish off Stalingrad in a couple of days.*

The period 13 September to 18 November saw the historic battle within the city and General Vasily Ivanovich Chuikov declared, 'We shall either hold the city or die here.' Although his attacks, before daylight, met with some local successes, once

the sun was up German bombers, in gaggles of fifty or sixty, stopped his troops and then counter-attacked with dive-bombers, motorized infantry and tanks.

The wily Chuikov soon realized that the bombers could not hit pinpoint targets and neither could the Stukas which were doing well if they could plant their bombs within thirty-five yards of their aiming point. Therefore, Chuikov reasoned, if he could bring the German infantry to really close quarters so that no-man's-land never exceeded 'the distance of a hand-grenade throw', it would keep his front line immune from air attack. He found, too, that his men were better fed and clothed than the Germans, and that they were superior at hand-to-hand night fighting. Also, the mountains of rubble accumulating in the streets of Stalingrad from the bombing, hindered the German tanks and favoured the ambush tactics of the defenders. Highly favourable to Chuikov, too, was the powerful fire of the artillery and Katyuska mortars from their reasonably secure positions on the far side of the Volga

Defence of Stalingrad – 'the longest and most crucial battle of World War Two': August 1942 to February 1943

* Walter Goerlitz, *Paulus and Stalingrad* (Methuen, London, 1963).

which harassed the Germans throughout the siege.*

In late September the Germans began their first big offensive against Stalingrad's industrial area. Hordes of dive-bombers attacked Russian positions and the Germans, despite heavy losses, made some headway. Chuikov commented, 'One more such day, and we would have been thrown into the Volga' and sent an SOS to the War Council asking for reinforcements and more help in the air.

On 14 October three German infantry and two panzer divisions stormed Chuikov's 62nd Army positions on a five-kilometre front; Richthofen's airmen flew some 3,000 missions in support and although it was a sunny day the smoke and debris from the bombing reduced visibility to a few yards.

That day saw the beginning of a ground battle unequalled in its ferocity and cruelty through the Stalingrad campaign. Fierce hand-to-hand struggles, sometimes with knives and daggers, with quarter neither asked for nor given, were fought for shattered factories and workshops. At night there was more blood-letting. Rooms and cellars might change hands three times in a night and resistance ended only when the whole building was smashed by artillery fire. Whole platoons, companies and battalions were slaughtered and finished as fighting units. The dead froze where they fell. The dying were left in the searing cold of the ruined city.

One Russian battalion fought for several days for the railway station and finally only six survivors, all wounded and out of ammunition, left behind their dead and badly wounded comrades, made their way to the Volga, improvised a makeshift raft and drifted downstream where they were rescued and sent to hospital. They had not eaten for three days.

Chuikov's position would have been hopeless but for the Russian artillery and mortars on the other side of the river, the guns of the Volga flotilla, ground reinforcements from across the Volga and the ground-attack Stormoviks which, despite

heavy losses, began, at last, to break through the German fighter screen and attack the advancing enemy troops. Towards the middle of October it seemed to the defenders that German attacks lacked their former punch, and by 30 October Chuikov began to feel he had a chance of winning.

At the beginning of November the Germans, who occupied seven-eighths of the city, made their last major attack but achieved only little progress, and after one day the offensive petered out. They were then but a hundred yards from the Volga, now covered with ice floes, and the hard winter was upon the poorly clothed German troops.

The preparations for the Russian counter-offensive had been conducted with great secrecy. Despite their air superiority the Germans had little idea of how much equipment and how many troops were being moved, mainly at night, to the area north of the Don and to the two main Russian bridgeheads inside the Don Bend. Vast numbers of troops were transported along the railway line east of the Volga, and pontoons and ferries took them across the near-frozen river under the very noses of the Germans.

The Russian offensive began on the early morning of 19 November and because of bad weather, poor visibility and clouds 'on the deck', few aeroplanes were used by either side. The Romanian and Italian troops were the first to crack and in three days Russian troops advanced some seventy-five miles. Soon after, Russian forces from the north and south joined together at Kalatsch, but not before Lieutenant-Colonel Hitschbold and his pilots had flown off from the airfield leaving much of their equipment behind. At Karpoxka airfield a few Stukas managed to take off led by Hans-Ulrich Rudel, who later became the celebrated 'tank buster', flying no less than 2,530 missions in the east.

The German Sixth Army was trapped and Paulus, knowing Hitler's

maniacal views about withdrawing, announced that he would continue to defend Stalingrad and that he expected that his army of some 250,000 men would be supplied by the air. Richthofen thought it 'stark raving madness!' and so informed his superiors back in Berlin. Should the airlift fail, Paulus wished to retain the right to save his army by a break-out, but Hitler refused this request.

At the beginning of the airlift there were about ninety serviceable transports, and all available Junkers 52s, Heinkel 111s and Junkers 90s were sent to the east. Further small numbers of Heinkel 117s, Focke-Wulf Condors, Junkers 290s, and even aged Junkers 86s, were pressed into service; but during the next two months the majority of the Junkers 86s either fell to Russian fighter pilots or succumbed to the harsh winter. The flight to the Cauldron, as the German pocket was called, normally took about fifty minutes, with the aircrews following a radio beacon to Pitomik; but the Russians were quick to harass the flight corridor with both fighters and anti-aircraft guns.

During the first half of December the daily tonnage flown into the Cauldron gradually increased, and the returning transports brought out wounded soldiers. The vital Pitomik airfield had to be continually cleared of drifting and freezing snow and Junkers 52s had to be dug out of the snow by hand. Poorly clothed groundcrews wore gas masks to prevent frost-bite and sometimes their fingers froze to engines. Russian fighter-bombers strafed the airfield by

* Incredibly, Richthofen failed to take out the great Russian arsenal on the far side of the Volga where, throughout the siege, artillery and mortars continued to harass and kill the invaders. Further, the vital railway link, Moscow–Saratova–Leninsk, carried all the supplies and reinforcements for the besieged garrison; and it was at Leninsk, where the railway terminated, that all the supplies were sorted and dispatched across the Volga. Yet Leninsk remained intact, and although the railway lifeline was repeatedly attacked it functioned throughout the siege. Thus Richthofen failed to observe one of the basic tenets of tactical air power – isolation of the battlefield.

Ring of steel round Stalingrad: Russian anti-aircraft defences

day and at night Stormoviks and old Po-2 biplanes maintained the pressure; but all the while artillery shells rained down as the Russian grip tightened on the Cauldron.

The weather remained bad and planned reinforcements from the Caucasus front were unable to reach the Stalingrad front. The Russian troops pressed on, vital German airfields were threatened and on 26 November a motley collection of groundcrews, administrators, stragglers and men returning from leave drove back an attack on their airfield at Obliwskaya, supported from the air by a few anti-tank Hs 129s and a squadron of obsolete Hs 123 biplanes, whose groundcrews defended and held the runway. During this contest Richthofen landed and asked for General Fiebig, but someone said, 'He's out there manning a machine gun, *Herr Generaloberst*.'*

Richthofen was not amused and told Fiebig that he was supposed to be leading his Air Corps and organizing a vital airlift – not indulging in hand-to-hand fighting with the Soviets.

Air superiority was passing from the Luftwaffe to the Russian Air Force

as Colonel V. A. Kitayev ably demonstrated on 30 November when his 238th Fighter Air Division came across a gaggle of Junkers 52s, escorted by a handful of Messerschmitt 109s, and knocked down five over Gumrak airfield. As they progressed from defensive to offensive air fighting, the fighter leaders were given more freedom of action 'to roam in the allotted areas' and these *Oknotniks* (free hunters) seized their opportunities to exploit all the inherent qualities of their fighters – speed and surprise – to destroy the lumbering German transports. Such were the pickings that even the ground-attack Stormoviks, being faster than the three-engined Junkers 52s, took a successful hand in the air-fighting.

Having surrounded the city, the Russians imposed a carefully planned air blockade consisting of four zones, each with detailed tasks. The first, or outer zone, included the German airlift airfields, Morozovskaya, Tassinskaya, Sal'sk, Novocherkassk and Rostov. The second zone consisted of the area between the inner and outer Russian fronts which was itself divided into five sectors

with fighters stationed in each sector. Surrounding the Cauldron, the third zone was about nineteen miles wide and here the Soviets based their anti-aircraft batteries along the flight paths of the German transports. The fourth zone was the Cauldron itself which contained at this time four German airstrips – Gumrak, Basargino, Voroponovo and Bol'shaya Rossoshka – from which some forty Messerschmitt 109s tried to keep open the lifeline of the Sixth Army. Soviet fighters, ground-attack, reconnaissance and bomber units were based in the five sectors and moved from airfield to airfield according to the tactical situation.

On the ground the Soviet forces moved steadily to reduce the circumference of the Cauldron and to capture its airstrips. Hitler would still not permit the Sixth Army to attempt to break out, even after the airlift had proved inadequate and an attempt to relieve Stalingrad from the west, made at the end of November had failed. Hitler made one last big

* Cajor Bekker *The Luftwaffe War Diaries* (Macdonald, London, 1967).

attempt to relieve Stalingrad when the prestigious Field Marshal von Manstein, 'the victor of the Crimea', formed the 'Don' Army Group, which included all German troops and their allies between the Middle Don and the Astrakhan steppes.

On 12 December Manstein's Group, including some 250 tanks and supported by hundreds of bombers and fighters, began operation Wintergewitten (Winter Tempest) when they struck out on a narrow front along the railway from the Caucasus. Two days later they reached the Myshkova river, the last natural barrier between them and Stalingrad – only forty kilometres distance. There they were halted by the Second Guards Army who had force-marched over 125 miles from beyond the Volga, at twenty-five miles a day, through the snow-covered steppe in a howling blizzard. The élite Guards had to fight with only infantry and artillery, but on Christmas Eve both tanks and Stormoviks joined the party and drove the Huns back to the Axai river, to Kotelnikovo, then to Zimovniki and finally beyond the

River Manych, sixty miles south-west of Kotelnikovo, from whence they had started.

Also on Christmas Eve, freezing fog hid a Soviet attack on the Tassinskaya airfield and as the shells fell some transport began to burn. The rest of the aeroplanes, more than a hundred of them, waited with engines running, for General Fiebig to give the order to go. But despite the shelling and the burning Junkers, Fiebig insisted on getting clearance from his chief, Richthofen.

Eventually, at 05.30, Fiebig gave the word, and with engines roaring, and snow cascading from their wheels, the Junkers 52s lumbered through the fog from every direction. Visibility was down to fifty yards and there was a violent explosion as two transports collided. Others taxied into each other, some hit other aeroplanes whilst taking off and smashed wing-tips and tail units. Burning wreckage littered the airfield and Russian tanks were reported just a kilometre or two away. At 06.15 the last Junkers 52 left the burning airfield. It was flown by

Sergeant Ruppert and on board was Fiebig and members of his Air Corps staff. The pilot climbed into cloud and after seventy minutes landed at Rostov-West.

From the Tassinskaya debacle 108 Junkers 52s and sixteen Junkers 86s came out unscathed and landed at other airfields. One was flown out by Captain Lorenz, of Signals Regiment 38, who had never before flown an aeroplane; that evening Richthofen gave him an honorary pilot's badge.

Typical of Soviet aggression was the mission of Captain I. P. Batkin who, on 2 January 1943, led seven Stormoviks escorted by Yakovlev fighters to the Sal'sk airfield. Once over the German lines the ground-attack leader let down to the tree tops. Then he found Sal'sk, strafed the German transports, repeated the attack six times and eventually claimed seventy-two enemy aeroplanes destroyed.

The Soviet advance to the south-west deprived Richthofen of his forward airfields and compelled him to withdraw both his fighters and dive-

Street fighting in the beleaguered city

Ice road across the Volga

bombers to more secure airfields, thus placing Stalingrad outside the range of his Messerschmitt 109s. Moreover, with the opening of the Allied offensive in Libya and Tunisia further withdrawals were necessary to strengthen the Luftwaffe in the Mediterranean.

Russian fighters strengthened their patrols along the air corridors and struck repeatedly at the five remaining German airfields. Pitomik, the main supply airfield, was bitterly contested and once the issue was beyond doubt the remaining Heinkels were flown to Gumrak and the Junkers 52s to Swerewo. At Pitomik, the Germans had a big concentration of pillboxes which finally had to be smashed by a powerful barrage of guns and mortars. Within twenty-four hours Swerewo was bombed and fifty-two Junkers 52s destroyed. Russian superiority allowed their fighters to be based within fifteen to thirty miles of the Cauldron, whilst bomber and ground-attack bases were within forty to sixty miles.

In mid-January only Gumrak remained to handle the German transports. Lowering morale among both soldiers and officers was rapidly becoming more marked, and there were ugly scrambles with officers paying large bribes to airmen for a seat on the last departing planes.* Gumrak saw, according to another witness, the biggest slaughter of Germans ever. 'The place is just littered with thousands of them; we got them well encircled and our *katyushas* let fly. God what a massacre!'*

With Pitomik and Gumrak now lost, Richthofen's airlift was confined to dropping canisters by parachute; but in mid-January, Paulus reported that many of the canisters were never found because his poorly clad men were too weak to look for them. The last horses had been eaten and some of his troops had not been fed for four days. Later, he told von Manstein of the

... frightful conditions in the city where about 20,000 unattended wounded are seeking shelter in the ruins. With them are about the same number of starved and frost-bitten men, stragglers, mostly without weapons ... Last resistance will be offered on 25 January ... Tractor factory may perhaps hold out a little longer.†

Manstein made a last attempt plea to Hitler to allow a surrender, but was refused. One of the last officers to leave Gumrak saw Hitler on 23 January and spoke of the suffering and the unattended wounded and ended: 'The troops at Stalingrad can no longer be ordered to fight to the last round because they are no longer physically able to fight and no longer have a last round.'†

Hitler replied, 'Man recovers very quickly,' and left the room to send yet another signal to Paulus forbidding surrender.

On 30 January, the Führer promoted Paulus to field marshal hoping that he would remember that no German field marshal had ever surrendered. But on the following day his headquarters in the basement of a large department store was surrounded and shelled, and Paulus surrendered what was left of his Sixth Army to the Russians.

So ended the longest and most crucial battle of the Second World War. Total German, Romanian and Italian casualties killed, missing, wounded or captured could never actually be assessed, but between August 1942 and February 1943 the most reliable estimate put the figure at approximately 1,500,000 men.

Go, tell the Spartans, thou who passest by,
That here obedient to their laws we lie.

* Alexander Worth, *Russia at War, 1941–1945* (Barrie Books, London, 1964).
† Geoffrey Jukes, *Stalingrad* (Macdonald, London, 1968).

16 · PACIFIC THEATRE

If a week is a long time in politics, four particular days in the Far Eastern and Pacific theatre of World War Two seemed like an eternity. For the Allies, the inclusive span between 7 and 10 December 1941 was shocking and deeply humiliating. There seemed to be no end to the set-backs. For the Japanese, on the other hand, it was a spell when the Rising Sun moved up to its zenith to shine upon success.

Consider the scoresheet.

Soon after first light on 7 December* the Japanese, without so much as declaring war, but with infinite guile and stealth, launched an unprovoked air assault against the US Pacific Fleet lying peacefully at anchor in Pearl Harbor, on the Hawaiian Island of Oahu. Concurrently with this strike, brainchild of Admiral Yamamoto, attacks were also made upon the neighbouring air bases at Hickam and Wheeler Fields.

At the end of the short offensive, the US Navy was decimated. Of the ninety-four vessels lying alongside, the great capital ships had plainly been singled out for the attention of the attacking aircrews. At a stroke, the battleships *Arizona, California* and *West Virginia* were sunk, *Oklahoma* was capsized and *Nevada* heavily damaged. Indeed every capital ship bar *Pennsylvania* (fortunately isolated in dry dock) was either destroyed or put out of commission for weeks. Mercifully, the Navy's aircraft carriers were in service elsewhere, and not involved, but three cruisers, three destroyers and a minelayer, as well as important air and naval installations, all received severe, if not terminal damage.

Of the existing US air strength in the area, eighty-seven out of a force of 169 naval aircraft on Oahu, were writ-

Architect of the Pearl Harbor attack – Admiral Isoroku Yamamoto

ten off while casualties among Navy and Marine Corps personnel were horrendous, 2,086 officers and other ranks being killed outright or fatally wounded, with a further 749 wounded, some severely.

There were, however, a few items to place on the credit side of the US balance sheet. The lack of warning meant, inevitably, that the defending fighters on the small airfield at Haleiwa, which had largely escaped attack, were still on the ground. Here a few spirited officers of the 47th Pursuit Squadron grabbed whatever transport they could find and dashed for their aircraft as the assault developed.

Acting with the Navy's customary bravado, but without any orders or authority, these pilots took-off in their P-40s and 36s and, at full bore,

climbed to attack. Lieutenants Harry Brown, Robert Rogers, Kenneth Taylor, John Webster and George Welch, all in the van, were soon pitching into the attack. In his 'crowded hour', George Welch stood out from among his comrades with four enemy aircraft claimed as destroyed.

This 'free enterprise' lead was immediately taken up by a handful of P-40 pilots from the 44th Pursuit Squadron based at Bellows Field, but sadly with less happy results. Lieutenants Hans Christiansen, George Whiteman and Samuel Bishop were on the point of taking off when elements of the Japanese escorting fighters spotted them from high above. Peeling off in pairs, their speed gathering quickly in the dive, the Nippon pilots pounced on their prey, killing Christiansen as he climbed into the cockpit of his aircraft, felling Whiteman as soon as he was airborne and shooting down Bishop into the ocean moments later. Such was the bitter fruit of endeavour.

Churchill described the effect of the Imperial Navy pilots' successful but 'treacherous blow' against the US Fleet at Pearl Harbor in global terms. 'The mastery of the Pacific had passed into Japanese hands, and the strategic balance of the world was for the time being fundamentally changed.'†

Meanwhile the Royal Navy was joining hands in catastrophe with its US counterpart. With the Japanese currently striking out strongly with their seaborne invasion convoys from

* The reader will appreciate that dates in this narrative appear out of sequence owing to events occurring on either side of the international date line. Local times are adhered to.
† Winston S. Churchill, *The Second World War: The Grand Alliance* (Cassell, London, 1950).

French Indo-China, across the Gulf of Siam, to establish landing points along the east coast of Malaya, the recently commissioned battleship *Prince of Wales*, and the 25-year-old battle-cruiser *Repulse*, under the overall command of Admiral Tom Phillips, had sailed northwards during the evening of 8 December from Singapore to meet the enemy threat. Accompanying the capital ships were the destroyers *Electro, Express, Vampire* and *Tenedos*.

Although Japanese bomber and torpedo-strike aircraft were known to be based in strength around Saigon in southern Indo-China, the Admiral saw it as his duty to proceed up the Malayan coast to a point east and a little north of Kota Bharu, to give whatever support he could to the defenders during the initial stages of the landings. The weather, with low cloud, poor visibility and frequent rain squalls, seemed likely to hamper air reconnaissance and, therefore,

detection. Even without the promise of fighter protection the risks seemed to be justified.

But then the Admiral's luck changed. With a sudden and marked improvement in the weather, to continue to steam north would be to court discovery and the certainty of subsequent aerial attack. A decision was therefore taken to turn about and head south for Kuantan where a fresh Japanese landing had, wrongly as it turned out, been reported.

Japan attacks! Pearl Harbor, 7 December 1941

USSR

Vladivostok

KOREA JAPAN

Nagoya Tokyo
Kobe Yokohama
Osaka

KURILE ISLANDS

PAC
OC

LUZON
Lingayen Gulf

Iba

MANILA

Bataan
Peninsula

Cavite
CORREGIDOR

Canton

Hong
Kong

FORMOSA

RYUKU ISLANDS

BONIN
ISLANDS

MARCUS
ISLAND

Calcutta

BURMA

Rangoon

SIAM

FRENCH
INDO-
CHINA

Saigon

Gulf
of
Siam

ANDAMAN
ISLANDS

Kota Bharu

MALAYA

Kuantan

Singapore

BORNEO

South
China
Sea

LUZON

Manila

PHILIPPINE
ISLANDS

MINDANAO

PALAU

GUAM

MARIANA
ISLANDS

TRUK

CAROLINE
ISLANDS

WA
ISLA

MARSHALL
ISLANDS

GI
IS

SUMATRA

CELEBES

Surbaya

JAVA

TIMOR

Darwin

NEW
GUINEA

Lae

Port
Moresby

ADMIRALTY
IS

NEW IRELAND

NEW
BRITAIN

BOUGAINVILLE

CHOISEUL

FLORIDA

GUADALCANAL

NAURU

CORAL
SEA

NEW
HEBRIDES

AUSTRALIA

NEW
CALEDONIA

The sweep of the Pacific War: Emperor versus President – dominance of the aircraft carrier

KODIAK
ISLAND

ALEUTIAN ISLANDS

VANCOUVER
ISLAND

CANADA

● San Francisco

USA

I C
N

MIDWAY
ISLAND

●Haleiwa

OAHU

Pearl Harbor

GUADALUPE ◊
ISLAND

HAWAIIAN
ISLANDS

JOHNSTON
ISLAND

PALMYRA ISLAND

CHRISTMAS ISLAND

Equator

CANTON
ISLAND

PHOENIX
ISLANDS

ELLICE
ISLANDS

SAMOA

SOCIETY
ISLANDS

FIJI
ISLANDS

FRIENDLY
ISLANDS

AUSTRAL
ISLANDS

| 0 | miles | 1000 |
| 0 | kms | 1600 |

This change of plan proved, in the end, calamitous. On 9 December a Japanese submarine had sighted the British force heading north, and now, before first light on the following day, a further sighting revealed the British squadron sailing southwards on a reciprocal track. The 22nd Flotilla of the enemy's 11th Air Fleet, comprising a force of some eighty-five bombers and torpedo strike aircraft from its Saigon bases, was at once briefed to search the waters of the South China Sea as far south as Singapore.

However, an extensive sweep found no trace of the British force and the Japanese, resigned to an abortive mission, were heading north for home. Then chance intervened. A lone aircraft from the Flotilla sighted the British squadron moving south at speed. With its position reported in mid-morning, the Royal Navy braced itself for the attack it knew must follow.

It came within the hour, delivered in waves, first by bombers of the Minoro Air Group, flying in at heights between 12,000 and 14,000 feet, and then by torpedo-strike aircraft of the Kanoya and Genzan Groups, pressing their onslaught right home at low level. Finally, the attacks were rounded off by bombers of the Takeda Group making a last, high-level run over the Prince of Wales.

Vigorous anti-aircraft fire from the British ships gave the attackers a hard time of it, although it is fair to say that the defensive fire against the low-level torpedo carriers was less effective than that aimed at high level. What was never in question, however, was the British squadron's determination to resist to the end.

Repulse, under the command of Captain Tennant, was the first to go, an hour and a half after the first attack had been launched. It took fourteen direct hits from torpedoes and one from bombs to dispatch the battle-cruiser to the bottom of the sea. Prince of Wales lasted some fifty minutes longer. Hers was a remarkable defence for the great battleship was struck by five of the first seven torpedoes fired against her,

thus reducing her speed to no more than 8 knots. The killer punch came when two 500-kilo bombs, dropped from altitude, scored direct hits, exploding one of the ship's powder magazines.

The aftermath of this tragedy saw British seamanship at its most skilled with crews of the accompanying destroyers rescuing 2,000 officers and men from the two ships' total complement of some 3,000.

Admiral Phillips, totally disregarding the pleadings of his staff to leave the bridge of Prince of Wales and take his chances with the rescue operation, went down with the stricken ship; so, too, did his Flag Captain, John Leach.

For the Japanese 22nd Air Flotilla, and the Groups within it, this was an outstanding triumph for land-based aircraft, operating at extreme range, against capital ships at sea devoid of fighter escort. Important lessons flowed from the victory. The first was the realization on the part of the Americans and the British that the daring and efficiency of the Nipponese aircrews, and the effectiveness of their aircraft, far exceeded anything for which they had hitherto been credited.

The second was the discovery that no matter how heavily armed, capital ships without fighter cover were sitting ducks for land-based aeroplanes capable of carrying bombs and torpedoes and operating even at maximum range. An altogether new chapter had to be written in the manual of naval/air warfare.

There is a poignant and prophetic passage in Sir Arthur Harris's Bomber Offensive* in which the wartime C-in-C of the Royal Air Force's Bomber Command recounts his parting with Tom Phillips, following their Deputy Chiefs of Staff meeting in King Charles Street in 1941, before Harris left for the USA and Phillips for the Far East. As they said goodbye, the then Air Marshal made his good-natured point:

Tom, you've never believed in air. Never get out from under the air umbrella; if you do, you'll be for it. And as you flutter up to

heaven all you'll say is, 'My gosh, some sailor laid the hell of a mine for me!'

Poor Tom Phillips, he was the bravest of the brave. He and John Leach, captain of Prince of Wales, another old and valued friend of mine from Staff College days, walked down the side of the ship together and into the sea as she rolled over and sank.*

The Emperor's air forces now had their tails right up. Fighter and bomber leaders felt they were on top, no matter what the circumstances. For Churchill, the loss of the two British ships was a wounding blow, the news of which hit him as hard as any reverse during the whole war:

I was thankful to be alone . . . As I turned over and tossed in bed, the full horror of the news sank in upon me. There were no British or American capital ships in the Indian Ocean or the Pacific except the survivors of Pearl Harbor, who were hastening back to California. Over this vast expanse of waters Japan was supreme, and everywhere we were weak and naked.†

Nor was this the end of the rise of Japanese air power. At the same time as these events were unfolding in the Hawaiian islands and off the coast of Malaya, the enemy was unleashing a meticulously planned operation against US and Filipino forces in the Philippines. For the overall commander, General Douglas MacArthur, and the Air Force's chief, Major General L. H. B. Brereton, this was the start of one of the bloodiest and most vicious campaigns of the Pacific War.

News of the Pearl Harbor attack had reached the US commanders in the Philippines before dawn on 8 December and air and military bases were alerted well before Washington confirmed that a state of war now existed with Japan. Fortunately for the defence, unfavourable weather over Luzon, in the north of the islands, delayed the enemy's first air strikes which had originally been

* Marshal of the Royal Air Force Sir Arthur Harris, Bomber Offensive (Collins, London, 1947; Greenhill Books, 1990).
† Churchill, Second World War.

Bomber escort: Zero fighters taking off from carrier *Akagi*

planned to coincide as closely as possible with the timing of the attack on Pearl Harbor. In fact, the opening of the assault was delayed by as much as nine crucial hours thus giving the defending forces a valuable breathing space before the opening of hostilities.

During this lull, General Brereton, believing that attack would prove to be the best force of defence, made representations to the Commanding General's Chief of Staff, Brigadier General Richard Sutherland, to be allowed to strike at once with his small force of B-17s at Formosan bases, from where the Japanese invasion forces were being launched.

What happened after this request was entered has been the subject of prolonged controversy, with General MacArthur himself claiming, some years afterwards, that he had never been informed of Brereton's recommendation. Sutherland, for his part, held that Brereton had accepted the premise that attacks on Formosa would achieve little without prior re-

connaissance sorties. But Brereton's understanding appeared to refute this, his belief being that the Chief of Staff had himself given the go-ahead for preparations for an offensive to start at once; in the meantime, he would obtain MacArthur's confirmation for an air attack to begin.

The records are scanty and inconclusive, so the truth about the controversy is unlikely ever to be known. What is plain, however, is that the confusion resulted in the Japanese finding two squadrons of B-17s grounded at Clark Field, the principal air base on Luzon, when they launched their aerial bombardment.

Raids were mounted the next day against Nichols Field, the fighter airfield close to Manila, and against its two counterparts at Iba and Del Carmen where, with Clark Field, P-40s of the 3rd, 17th, 20th, 21st and 34th Pursuit Squadrons were deployed.

After a single day's hostilities, and in the face of the enemy's relentless pounding, the US Far East Air Force

was cut to pieces with at least half its bomber and fighter strength being destroyed either on the ground or in the air. Air Force casualties were heavy with fifty-five officers and men killed and more than a hundred being wounded at Clark alone.

Not only was the Japanese bombing remarkably accurate, the strafing of the airfields by Zero fighters was also lethal in its effect against ground aircraft. Many of Japan's fighter aces shone in these airfield attacks (as they did in such combats as took place) – the great Saburo Sakai, Toshio Ota, Shizuo Ishi-i, Kaneyoshi Muto, Juniichi Sasai, Sada-aki Akamatsu and Masayuki Nakase being among those who made their mark in the early fighting.

As for the defence, Lieutenant Joseph Moore, commanding the 20th Pursuit Squadron, got enough of his P-40s off the ground at Clark to allow a few successful interceptions to take place. This gave Lieutenant Randall Keator his chance to gain the distinction of destroying the first Zero over the Philippines, while Moore himself seized the opportunity to score twice.

The 3rd Squadron was not so fortunate. Returning with their fuel tanks almost empty after a long and fruitless search over the South China Sea, the Squadron's twelve P-40 pilots were preparing to land at Iba, west of Clark Field, when some thirty or forty Japanese Bettys (bombers), with strong Zero escort, set upon the airfield. While Lieutenant Jack Donalson turned into the attackers, claiming two aircraft destroyed, Zeros accounted for five of the remaining eleven P-40s. Three others, out of fuel, force-landed on nearby beaches, all three pilots being saved. Such was the Nippon superiority that two-thirds of the Squadron had been wiped out in a few minutes.

Two days later, on 10 December, the enemy let loose the heaviest attack yet against the naval base at Cavite, south of Manila and north-east of the island of Corregidor. The results were devastating with naval installations, supply depots and power plants being set on fire while the US Navy's submarine *Sea Lion*, lying alongside, was also destroyed. It was the culmination of four days of appalling reverses for the Allies.

With General Brereton's Far East Air Force now unable to offer more than token resistance, the Japanese quickly landed at several points on Luzon. On 21 December the main invasion force, with strong air support, had little difficulty in establishing a bridgehead in the Lingayen Gulf before breaking out and striking southwards for Clark Field, other adjacent airfields, and for Manila itself, the capital.

Weeks and months of cruel fighting followed with US troops, Marines and Filipinos performing heroics in the jungles and hills of the Bataan peninsula and, eventually, in the final stronghold of the Malinta Tunnel on the island of Corregidor. Greater valour was not seen in the Pacific war; but with the weight of the Japanese ground and air offensive there could be but one end.

When Washington insisted on the withdrawal of the remnants of the Far East Air Force to Darwin, in northern Australia, and the movement of General MacArthur and his staff, first, to Mindanao, in the extreme south of the Philippines, and thence to Australia, the Commanding General mounted a characteristically defiant response. Threatening to resign his commission, MacArthur declared that he was ready to volunteer to fight alongside the defending forces in the jungles of Bataan.

Persuaded eventually to retire to Australia with his staff, and his wife and son, MacArthur handed over control to Lieutenant-General Jonathan Wainwright who was to hold Corregidor until all hope was gone, when he would then sign the final surrender. This he did at midnight on 6 March 1942 some six months after the Japanese had first landed on Luzon, and after one of the historic stands of World War Two.

Soon after landing at Batchelor Field, outside Darwin, Douglas MacArthur met the world's Press. Shortly to be appointed Supreme Commander of Allied forces in the South-West Pacific, the General claimed, with typical aplomb, that he was in Australia to gather forces for an offensive against the Japanese, one of the principal aims of which would be the eventual liberation of the Philippines. 'I came through,' he declared, in an oft-quoted phrase, 'and I shall return.'

The three episodes of Pearl Harbor, the sinking of the two British warships and the capture of the Philippines had ensured an altogether new respect for Japanese air power in the Allied mind. Erased forever was Britain's and the USA's underestimation of the Nippon ability to produce military aircraft and aircrews to a standard to match the West.

For the moment Japan, having confounded her doubters, was marching relentlessly from triumph to triumph. The outlook was indeed bleak for it was not until later that her fatal failure to appreciate the extent of the US manufacturing and recuperative

capability became glaringly apparent.

It would take the size and sweep of the forthcoming battles of the Coral Sea and Midway finally to establish in the Nippon mind the overwhelming strength of American naval, air and industrial might.

OCEAN VICTORY: NIMITZ TURNS THE PACIFIC WAR

Events of governing importance were now about to transform the Pacific War. They were to occur after a run of seemingly unstoppable Japanese victories and, paradoxically, at a time when the enemy's High Command had been critically divided over a question of strategy.

The attack on Pearl Harbor, the landings in Malaya and the capture of Singapore, the sinking of *Prince of Wales* and *Repulse* and the invasion of the Philippines had all combined to give the opposition a daunting ascendancy over the Allies across great areas of land and ocean.

At the end of it, the Nipponese admirals and generals had been confronted at the summit of their ascendancy by what appeared to be a relatively straightforward military decision: whether to drive on aggressively at once and push the Pacific frontiers still further east and southwards – as the Imperial Navy wanted to do – or rest for a while and consolidate the massive gains which had already been made, the generals' option.

It was a power struggle in which the admirals, buoyed up by the success of their air and naval might, and led by the forceful and determined Admiral Isoroku Yamamoto, Commander-in-Chief of the Japanese Combined Fleet, prevailed. Eyes were now trained on goals in the south-eastern, eastern and north-eastern Pacific areas with heady thoughts about enveloping Australasia and probing forward even to the west coast of the United States. It was a daring and sweeping scenario.

An American thrust of quite extraordinary imagination and courage may well, at this moment, have influenced the outcome of the argument and handed Yamamoto a sword to flash at his military colleagues. On 18 April 1942 a short, stocky and ramrod-straight US Army Air Force colonel named James Doolittle had led sixteen B-25 medium bombers from the US Navy's carrier *Hornet* across almost 800 miles of ocean to bomb Tokyo, Yokohama, Nagoya, Osaka and Kobe, and had then headed south-west for China and for hair-raising bale-outs and forced landings in Cheiang Province and also in Japan ... Some dreadful Japanese executions followed.

It was a stirring operation, small in relation to tonnage of bombs dropped, but imposing in its psychological impact upon the Nipponese mind. It electrified the United States at a juncture of low morale; at the same time it acted as a stab to the stomach of the Imperial High Command. On his return, and amid all the euphoria whipped up by the raid, Doolittle received a telegram from his old friend, Roscoe Turner, a fellow air racer of pre-war days. 'Dear Jimmy,' it ran, 'you son of a bitch. Roscoe.'

Whatever the attack's consequences for Japan's strategic thinking, the enemy's forward plans had by now been crystallized. They rested upon three clear premises:

1   The capture of Tulagi on the island of Florida, opposite Guadalcanal, in the southern Solomons. Here would be created a naval and air base from which reconnaissances could be flown all over the eastern approaches to the Coral Sea. Thereafter the possession of Port Moresby, in the south-eastern corner of New Guinea, north of Darwin, would follow. From there, aerial mastery could readily be obtained over the Coral Sea and over the routes linking Australia with the United States.

2   The capture of Midway Island in mid-Pacific and, at the same time, of islands in the western Aleutians away in the north-eastern segment of the ocean. This was designed to secure the defence of Japan's extended east-

ern perimeter and encourage the US Pacific Fleet into a show-down with the Imperial Navy, a clash much desired by Admiral Yamamoto.

3   Lastly, the invasion and capture of New Caledonia, Fiji and the Samoa Archipelagos to the south and south-east of the Coral Sea. This last capture would ensure the severance of the lifeline joining Australia and the United States.

It was the enemy's attempted discharge of the first of the foregoing plans which provoked the initial clash of major carrier-borne forces in the Pacific war. This historic encounter became known as the Battle of the Coral Sea. Taking account of the preliminaries, it covered a period of nine days, from 1 to 9 May 1942, and its principal features, including the great advantage which accrued to the Allies from the busting of the Japanese naval code, can at once be seen.

Intelligence informed the US Navy's C-in-C, Pacific, Admiral Ches-

ter Nimitz, in late April and early May, that the enemy was marshalling his forces for a drive southwards from the main naval base of Truk, in the Carolines, and from Rabaul, his forward base in New Britain, first against Tulagi, in the southern Solomons, and then against Port Moresby, the south-eastern port of New Guinea. The taking of Port Moresby would complement the earlier landings on New Guinea's northern coast and greatly strengthen the security of Nipponese operations from Rabaul. It would also, with the possession of Tulagi to the east, increase the enemy's mastery of the Coral Sea with all that this would mean to Australia's eastern seaboard.

In the face of this southerly thrust to the Coral Sea, Nimitz, 'a man of monumental patience and optimism, indispensible to the US cause in the Pacific',[*] at once dispatched all available elements of his Fleet to the

[*] Samuel Eliot Morison, *Coral Sea, Midway and Submarine Actions, May 1942–August 1942* (Little, Brown, Boston, 1949).

Pacific leaders: General Douglas MacArthur *(left)* with Admiral Chester Nimitz, C-in-C US Pacific Fleet

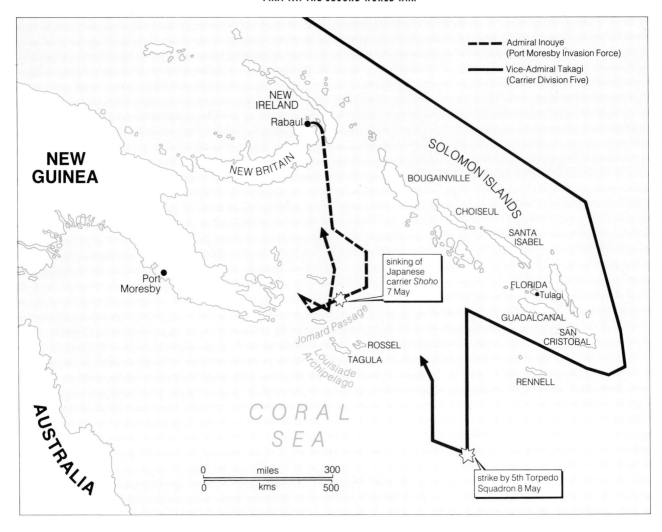

Battle of the Coral Sea: first carrier battle of Pacific War, 1-9 May, 1942

threatened area. These were formed into three separate and effective entities: the first under Rear Admiral Frank J. 'Frank Jack' Fletcher in the US Navy carrier *Yorktown*, with a full complement of aircraft and supported by three heavy cruisers and a screen of destroyers; the second with Rear Admiral Aubrey Fitch flying his flag in the US Navy carrier *Lexington*, attended by three cruisers and destroyers; and a third, with a combined US Navy and Royal Australian Navy presence, under the command of the Royal Navy's Rear Admiral J. G. Crace. Fletcher in *Yorktown*, as the C-in-C of the Carrier Striking Force, would be in tactical command of the three groups.

Ranged against this formidable array of naval air power, the Nipponese Admiral Inouye would pit his Port Moresby Invasion Force of five transports, four cruisers and the escort carrier *Shoho*, complete with her squadron of fighter aircraft. As the force headed steadily south for the Jomard Passage and the Louisiade Archipelago, Inouye's Carrier Division Five, which included two of the Imperial Navy's latest carriers, *Zuikaku* and *Shokaku*, with 125 bomber, torpedo and defensive fighter aircraft aboard, was also sailing south at speed well to the east of the Solomons and far beyond the practical compass of Allied reconnaissance aircraft. The remit of this impressive

group was to swing westwards round the southern Solomons and the island of Cristobal, enter the Coral Sea from the east and then steam north-west to converge with and give full cover to the Port Moresby Invasion Force.

Throwing the full weight of his torpedo bombers against the carrier, Fletcher quickly had *Shoho* in terminal trouble. An hour or so later, the escort carrier sank, taking some 500 of the 1,200-strong crew with her. Deprived of their air cover, Inouye's invasion transports, and their surface escorts, at once turned tail to head northwards for Rabaul having failed to penetrate the Jomard Passage.

Now Fletcher's main concern was for the whereabouts of Vice-Admiral

Takagi's Striking Force with its two powerful aircraft carriers and their torpedo-launching and dive-bombing capability. Intercepted signals and the US ships' radars confirmed that, during the night of 7/8 May, the two groups were quite close, but neither was apparently prepared to risk the hazards of a night-time engagement. By daybreak, the opposing forces had become well separated with one contending with noticeably different weather conditions from the other.

As the morning wore on, Fletcher's group was bathed in bright sunshine and sailing under clear skies with unlimited visibility. The Japanese contingent, on the other hand, had the comforting shield of low cloud, rain squalls and poor visibility. There was no doubt where the advantage lay.

At this point Fletcher, husbanding his own strike squadrons in *Yorktown* and anxious once more to keep himself in the picture on the movement of the two Japanese carriers, dispatched a strong reconnaissance mission of some twenty aircraft from *Lexington*. Within two hours, and in exceptionally unfavourable weather, at first Lieutenant J. G. Smith and then Lieutenant Commander R. E. Dixon of the US Navy reported sighting the Japanese carriers lying between Cristobal and the Louisiades to the northwest of Fletcher's force. At much the same time, Nipponese aircraft had established from afar the position of the US carriers steering north-east towards Takagi's group in bright sunlight.

Knowing from a decoded enemy message that an attack was now imminent, Fletcher at once ordered a major strike with some eighty aeroplanes from *Lexington* and *Yorktown* – SDB Dauntless dive-bombers and TBD Devastator torpedo-launchers, with Wildcat fighter escort, against the Japanese Task Force. Despite the lack of surprise, the assault against the enemy, led by Lieutenant Commander Joe Taylor of the 5th Torpedo Squadron and involving a force of about sixty dive-bombers followed by torpedo-carriers, went in soon after 11.30 on 8 May.

The first carrier battle of the Pacific war had now been joined. At its peak it would last little more than forty-five minutes.

Shokaku, bearing the brunt of the US attack, took three direct hits with bombs which at once set the carrier alight. *Zuikaku*, on the other hand, with deft seamanship befitting Admiral Hara's flagship, was able to make good use of the heavy rain squalls and worsening visibility to keep out of the US pilots' sight.

As soon as the engagement was over, the enemy's Carrier Division Five, following the course of its invasion charges, withdrew northwards for Rabaul, with *Shokaku*, although substantially damaged, still able to make way under her own steam.

Meanwhile, Fletcher's force, in disconcertingly good weather, had been subjected to vigorous retaliatory attacks, pressed home with boundless courage. Despite suffering extensive damage and casualties, *Yorktown* and her escorting cruisers had fended off the aerial onslaught with notable skill, but *Lexington* – Lady Lex to the US Navy – with Rear Admiral Fitch and his Flag Captain, Captain 'Ted' Sherman, very much in control, had not been so fortunate, taking the full force of the Nippon bombing and torpedo assault.

On fire, with three boiler rooms flooded, and now listing 7°, Lady Lex stayed afloat for a while thanks to the superhuman exertions of her indomitable crew. In the course of overseeing emergency repairs to the carrier, Commander 'Pop' Healy, the Damage Control Officer, telephoned the Captain. 'Sir,' he said, 'I can report that the torpedo damage is shored up, the fires are out and soon we shall have the ship back on an even keel. But I would suggest, sir, that if you have to take any more torpedoes you take 'em on the starboard side.'

Sadly, a series of heavy explosions incapacitated the 'flat-top' still further and eventually, with all hope gone, she had to be sunk on the orders of Admiral Fletcher by a torpedo fired from the US destroyer *Phelps*, but not before her crew had been

rescued successfully by the busy destroyers.

From this encounter, in which sixty-six US aircraft had been lost, many lessons were learnt which would prove to be invaluable for the navy pilots and crews in the critical contest for Midway Island which would now shortly follow. The carrier battle of the Coral Sea – a strategic success for the United States – was an indispensable preliminary for the larger carrier battle for Midway.

Moreover, coming so soon after the impact of Doolittle's Tokyo raid, it acted as a further fillip for American morale at home which, after the earlier succession of Japanese triumphs, was still close to its lowest ebb. Never again would the Imperial Navy attempt to force a way through the Jomard Passage and past the Louisiades, for a frontal assault on Port Moresby; nor would its warships return to operate in this area of ocean, lying to the north-east of Australia beyond the Great Barrier Reef. The Nipponese advance southwards had been halted once and for all; and all this for the loss of *Lexington*, the destroyer *Sims*, and the oiler *Neosbo* – not a heavy price to have paid for so much gain . . .

But now the massive carrier-borne resources both of Japan and the United States were hastily being marshalled in mid-ocean for the great Island battle which would decide irrevocably the future course of the Pacific war.

The capture of Midway Island, an isolated atoll lying to the west of Pearl Harbor in the central Pacific, was a necessary prerequisite for the establishment of Japan's forward eastern base. Midway – 'the sentry to Hawaii' – represented in Admiralissimo Yamamoto's fertile mind a stepping stone to other glittering prizes, not least the sought-after confrontation with Admiral Nimitz and the US Pacific Fleet.

Using a diversionary attack on the western Aleutians, away to the north-west, as a feint, Yamamoto now readied himself, with his subordinates,

Admirals Nagumo and Kondo, for the tests with the enemy which must surely follow. He was flushed with confidence and an undisguised conceit in his maritime strength following the US Navy's Pearl Harbor calamity only six months before, and the recent sinking of *Lexington* and damage to *Yorktown* in the Coral Sea.

Moreover, Yamamoto appreciated one fact accurately – a realization not shared by his colleagues in the Imperial High Command. The US Pacific Fleet must be annihilated this year – in 1942 – otherwise, with America's recuperative strength and her manufacturing and productive might, the war would eventually and inevitably be lost. The Japanese Naval leader knew it was now or never. Well might he repeat with the poet:

He either fears his fate too much,
  Or his deserts are small,
That puts it not unto the touch,
  To win or lose it all.

The future of the Japanese Navy, over which he presided with such authority, would now be on the line. Fight a major battle with the US Navy soon, win it and the Pacific Ocean would belong to Japan. He made his immediate intention clear in a brisk and simple declaration to his subordinate commander: 'The C-in-C, Combined Fleet, will, in co-operation with the Army, invade and occupy strategic points in West Aleutians and Midway Island.'

What the Admiralissimo did not know, however, was that his greater naval air strength would be compromised not only by the United States' possession of radar, but also by her Ultra-secret ability to bust the Japanese Naval code and decypher the coded messages passing between his Headquarters and elements of his Fleet and their staffs. With the last days of May and the first critical week of June 1942, many of Yamamoto's

tactical plans thus became known to the United States in advance. This was to prove his undoing. In the end, it would also account for his own premature demise.

Reduced to its rudimentary form, Yamamoto's battle plan was as uncomplicated as it was direct.

The Western Aleutians Occupation Task Forces under Admirals Omori and Kakuta would weigh anchor in northern Japanese waters between 24 and 28 May with the aim of reaching these island outposts on 3 June. All measures would be taken to convince Admiral Nimitz and his immediate subordinates, Admirals Raymond Spruance and Frank Jack Fletcher, heading up Task Forces 16 and 17 respectively, that this feint was, in fact, the main Japanese eastwards thrust.

Meanwhile, Yamamoto's principal assault forces – his own Main Body, with the Admiral flying his flag in the

Evasive action in mid-Pacific: carrier *Hiryu* being attacked, 4 June 1942

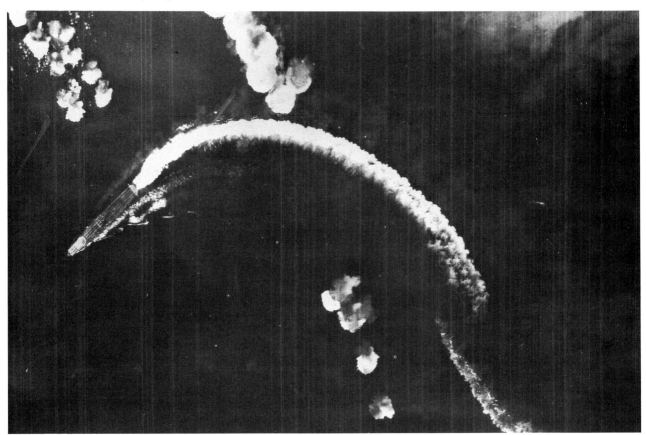

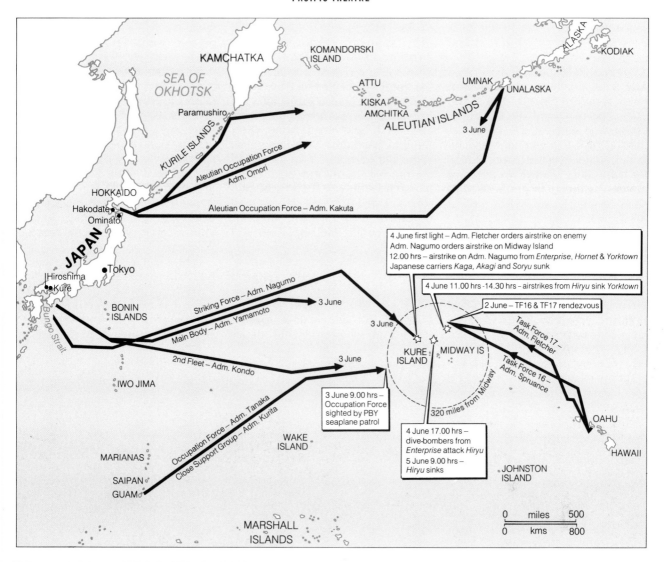

The map contains the following labels:

KAMCHATKA
KOMANDORSKI ISLAND
ALASKA
KODIAK
SEA OF OKHOTSK
ATTU
KISKA
AMCHITKA
UMNAK
UNALASKA
ALEUTIAN ISLANDS
3 June
Paramushiro
KURILE ISLANDS
Aleutian Occupation Force Adm. Omori
HOKKAIDO
Hakodate
Ominato
Aleutian Occupation Force – Adm. Kakuta
JAPAN
Tokyo
Hiroshima
Kure
Bungo Strait
BONIN ISLANDS
Striking Force – Adm. Nagumo
3 June
Main Body – Adm. Yamamoto
3 June
2nd Fleet – Adm. Kondo
3 June
IWO JIMA
Occupation Force – Adm. Tanaka
Close Support Group – Adm. Kurita
WAKE ISLAND
MARIANAS
SAIPAN
GUAM
KURE ISLAND
MIDWAY IS
320 miles from Midway
OAHU
HAWAII
JOHNSTON ISLAND
MARSHALL ISLANDS

4 June first light – Adm. Fletcher orders airstrike on enemy
Adm. Nagumo orders airstrike on Midway Island
12.00 hrs – airstrike on Adm. Nagumo from *Enterprise*, *Hornet* & *Yorktown*
Japanese carriers *Kaga*, *Akagi* and *Soryu* sunk

4 June 11.00 hrs -14.30 hrs – airstrikes from *Hiryu* sink *Yorktown*

2 June – TF16 & TF17 rendezvous

Task Force 17 – Adm. Fletcher
Task Force 16 – Adm. Spruance

3 June 9.00 hrs – Occupation Force sighted by PBY seaplane patrol

4 June 17.00 hrs – dive-bombers from *Enterprise* attack *Hiryu*
5 June 9.00 hrs – *Hiryu* sinks

0 miles 500
0 kms 800

Nimitz prospers in Pacific, June 1942. Battle of Midway turned the Japanese war

great 64,000-ton battleship *Yamato*, with its nine 18-inch guns; Admiral Nagumo's Carrier Striking Force, with its four fast fleet carriers, three battleships, two heavy cruisers, destroyer screen and 250 aircraft; and Admiral Kondo's 2nd Fleet embracing Admiral Kurita's Close Support Group of four heavy cruisers and destroyers; and Admiral Tanaka's Occupation force – all would head concurrently for Midway with the aim of arriving, undetected, within striking distance of the Island, also by 3 June.

Thereafter, on 4 June, it would be for Nagumo, flying his flag in the carrier *Akagi*, and his three counterparts in *Kaga*, *Soryu* and *Hiryu*, approach-ing from the north-west, to launch the aerial assault on Midway and knock out the air defences. The landings would then begin on the following day, 5 June.

That, then, was Yamamoto's proposed course of action for the capture of Midway. In pursuance of it, Nagumo's own operational instruction to the Striking Force on 4 June was another clear-cut and concise direction. The aim was: 'To execute an aerial attack on Midway ... destroying all enemy air forces stationed there.'

But standing between Nagumo's Striking Force and Midway were the US Navy's three 'flat-tops', *Enterprise*, *Hornet* and the newly-repaired *York-town* – all with the combined air component of some 230 aircraft – TBD Devastator torpedo bombers, SDB Dauntless dive-bombers and F4F Wildcat fighters. *Lexington*, lost in the Coral Sea, would be sorely missed.

Forewarned of the impending attack, Captain Cyril Simard, Midway's base commander, now ordered round-the-clock reconnaissances to be flown by the Island's PBY-5A Catalina seaplanes, supplemented by the Army Air Force's B-17s. With their duration of some thirty hours, the Catalinas were able to range far out over the 'nerve area' of ocean, sweeping widely over that sector of the compass lying between south-west and north-east.

Around 09.00 on 3 June, Ensign Jack Reid, a Catalina captain, was at the extremity of his westward patrol, at the point where the US code-busters had anticipated two of Yamamoto's Task Forces might well be found. A minute or two before turning for home Reid spotted, far ahead, a concentration of Nipponese warships heading east. 'Say,' he said to his co-pilot, sitting alongside him, 'do you see what I see?' 'You're damned right I do,' came the reply.

Using cloud cover for protection, Reid kept Admiral Tanaka's Occupation Force under continuous scrutiny for as long as he could, all the while radioing progress of the enemy's ships until lack of fuel forced a return

to base. Able to monitor the speed of the Japanese advance, all in Spruance's and Fletcher's Task Forces 16 and 17 were now alerted to the storm which must soon break . . .

The first exchanges in this supreme test of carrier warfare began soon after first light on 4 June when Admiral Nagumo's Task Force was some 240 miles out from the Island and moving towards it at speed. Land-based radar did not confirm the presence of the attacking groups until they were ninety miles from Midway; but, thereafter, their position was continuously plotted on the table.

Fletcher, in tactical command in *Yorktown*, now ordered Admiral Spruance, with aircraft from *Enterprise* and *Hornet*, to strike at the enemy. For Nagumo, this was the touchstone which triggered his re-

sponse as he let loose the full fury of his air component – from *Akagi*, *Hiryu*, *Kaga* and *Soryu* against Midway's air defences.

To Lieutenant Tomanago, Flight Officer in *Hiryu*, with his formations of thirty-six Kate torpedo bombers, thirty-six Val dive-bombers and escort of thirty-six Zeke fighters, fell the responsibility of leading the attack from all carriers. With the Zeros sweeping in ahead of the Strike Force, the three squadrons immediately engaged the defending fighters, scoring, initially, impressive victories over the obsolete Wildcats.

Lieutenant Yasuhiro Shigematsu, heading nine Zeros of the *Hiryu* Squadron, accounted for a remarkable eighteen Wildcats; his opposite number with the *Kaga* Squadron, Lieutenant Masao Iizuka,

Prelude to a mission: Val dive bombers aboard carrier *Soryu*. Carrier *Hiryu* in the background

leading another nine Zekes, claimed twelve of the defenders destroyed, while in the third wave Lieutenant Masaji Suganami and his Zeros from *Soryu* downed a further six of the intercepting fighters.

The opening exchanges were short-lived but intense, with the outcome favouring Nagumo's marauders. Against a loss of some forty of his own aircraft, his formations had destroyed about half the air force based on Midway either in the air or on the ground, with considerable damage being inflicted on the airfield and the surrounding installations . . .

Pilots returning from this successful initial foray reported that with one more heave . . . with one more assault by aircraft from all four carriers . . . the Island's air defences would be largely obliterated, thus paving the way for the troop landings on the following day. But the knock-out never came.

Admirals Fletcher in *Yorktown* and Spruance with *Enterprise* and *Hornet*, in a costly and yet brilliantly conceived counter-stroke, seized the initiative. Nagumo and his Striking Force, spurred on by the success of the early morning assault, was still heading for Midway with Yamamoto's and Kondo's forces lying off to the west, handily placed to offer support when needed. Further, the counter-attacks by US land-based Army, Navy and Marine corps aircraft against the Japanese force immediately after the first enemy raids were over, had proved to be singularly ineffective – lack of experience among the crews and obsolescent aircraft being, in part, to blame for the disappointing showing. All this did nothing to diminish Nipponese confidence.

Now it was squarely up to the carrier-borne aircraft from *Enterprise*, *Hornet* and *Yorktown* to turn the tables on the still dominant and aggressive enemy. Here came the crunch.

The opening attack against the Japanese carriers by *Hornet*'s unescorted torpedo-carrying TBD Devastators, led by Lieutenant Commander John Waldron, fared badly, the

Squadron being mauled by Zero fighters as it prepared to loose its torpedoes. Much the same fate attended the torpedo squadron from *Enterprise*, led by Lieutenant Commander Eugene Lindsey. Again without fighter cover, owing to a mix-up over the rendezvous, this second wave of Devastators was at once set upon by a superior number of Zekes as it manoeuvred for an attack on *Kaga*. Ten of the fourteen torpedo-bombers, including Lindsey's aircraft, were shot down into the sea.

This left the Devastators from *Yorktown*, escorted by Wildcats and led by Lieutenant Commander Lance Massey, to balance an inauspicious start. Once again, however, the attackers suffered grievously at the hands of the Zero pilots. Seven Devastators were clawed down by Nippon defenders before Massey, and most of his crews, had been able to release their torpedoes at *Soryu*.

Of the five aircraft which did loose their 'fish' at the carrier, another three were downed by Zeros.

It was a dreadful start to what was certainly a spirited retaliation. Of a total of forty-one torpedo-bombers dispatched from the three US carriers, only six lived to fight on and not one torpedo had found its mark. There was, however, another side to this tarnished coin. The attacks of the Devastators, although ineffective, had been pressed with undeniable courage; and this had caused the Japanese carriers to manoeuvre violently to avoid being hit. And this, in turn, meant that their own strike and fighter aircraft, used in the earlier attack on Midway that day, were still jam-packed on the flight-decks waiting to be refuelled and rearmed.

At this critical moment, first Spruance, from *Enterprise*, and then Fletcher from *Yorktown*, immediately dispatched every serviceable Dauntless dive-bomber which could be manned for a no-holds-barred, all-or-nothing onslaught against the now overloaded flight-decks of the enemy carriers. It was to be a maximum effort on the part of the US Navy pilots and their crews.

Led by Lieutenant Commander Clarence McClusky from *Enterprise*, with Lieutenant W. E. Gallaher's squadron giving support, thirty-seven aircraft came tearing down at an angle of 70° from around 16,000 feet, right down to 1,500, before releasing their bombs and plastering the crammed flight-deck of *Kaga*. Switching his squadron's attack to the carrier *Akagi*, Lieutenant R. H. Best repeated the tactics, pulling out only just in time to clear the ship's superstructure. As with McClusky's and Gallaher's attacks, his squadron's bombs also found their mark.

With both carriers and their aircraft blazing and creating mayhem on their flight-decks, Lieutenant Commander M. F. Leslie, with the Devastators from *Yorktown*, now turned the weight of his attack against the crowded deck of *Soryu*, driving home the onslaught right down to sea level. As fires broke out in the carrier, flames leaped from aircraft to aircraft until the flight-deck was an inferno. Seeing *Soryu* ablaze, the Captain of the US submarine *Nautilus*, Captain Elliott Buckmaster, lying off at a distance of some 3,000 yards, fired three torpedoes into the stricken carrier to administer the *coup de grâce*.

By noon on 4 June, three of Japan's latest carriers had either been disposed of or were destined soon to sink. Only the fourth, *Hiryu*, remained undamaged and still in play. A great naval/air battle was now in its final phase.

The losses on the US side, with half this historic day now gone, had not been light. *Enterprise* had suffered most heavily, losing fourteen out of thirty-seven dive-bombers, ten out of fourteen torpedo-bombers and a single Wildcat fighter. *Hornet*'s casualties were also severe, with all her torpedo-bombers perishing together with eleven Wildcats. As for *Yorktown*, she too had suffered with similar severity, all but one of her TBD Devastators being destroyed to add to the loss of two SDB Dauntless dive-bombers and three F4F Wildcats.

It was a dispiriting picture for the air groups of the three US carriers to

Midway toll: US Navy's Dauntless dive bombers leave the Japanese carrier *Mikuma* smoking

Four direct hits with 1,000-pound bombs started uncontrollable fires in the Nippon carrier. Gamely, she survived the night, but the inevitable end came at 09.00 the next morning, 5 June. Her captain, Captain Kaku, remained aboard as the waters closed over the enemy ship. The last of Nagumo's prize fleet carriers had gone.

Yamamoto, denied the full-scale show-down he had sought with Nimitz's Pacific Fleet, and no longer possessing any air cover after losing some 250 aircraft with the demise of the four carriers, now took, for him, the most painful decision – to retire westwards with the rest of his force.

The Battle of Midway Island, ever to keep its place among the epics of air–sea warfare, was over. Like the other two great island battles of World War Two – for Britain and for Malta – the victory shone forth as a paragon of resolve against the odds, of the meaning of airpower and of endeavour. In three memorable days, Chester Nimitz's forces had turned the Pacific war. The aircraft carrier had proved its worth . . .

Less than twelve months later, on 18 April 1943, Admiral Yamamoto fell a victim of US intelligence's code-breaking capacity, which had already contributed so significantly to the Japanese defeat at Midway. By decoding a message transmitted from the Admiralissimo's Headquarters, the US authorities had obtained advance warning of the C-in-C's impending visit to the Island of Bougainville in the Solomons: date and time of landing at Kahili airfield were known.

P-38 Lightning fighters of the 339th Pursuit Squadron of the Solomons Air Command, based at Guadalcanal, were waiting for Yamamoto as his aircraft approached the airfield to land. It was an unlikely way for a fighting admiral to go . . .

have to face. And yet when these losses were set against the immeasurable gain of three of Japan's foremost fleet carriers sunk, with the whole of their air component lost, the balance struck was undeniably in the United States' favour.

Only *Hiryu* now remained to be tackled. However, it quickly became clear that, far from making off, Rear Admiral Yamaguchi, an exceptionally able and experienced officer, was quite ready to stand and fight. The Samurai tradition still burned fiercely within him.

Between 10.00 and 14.30 on 4 June, the Admiral launched spasmodic attacks against *Yorktown* with his Val Aichi 99-1 dive-bombers and his Kate Nikajima 97-2 torpedo-carriers from his still intact striking force. Although heavily damaged, Fletcher's battle-torn flagship kept afloat until, later in the afternoon, two airborne torpedoes, delivered from short range, hastened the end, but not before the attendant destroyers had saved her crew.

Revenge for the loss of *Yorktown* was not long in coming, and soon after 17.00 twenty-four Dauntless dive-bombers from *Enterprise*, led by the irrepressible Lieutenant Gallaher, now found *Hiryu* one hundred miles or so north-west of Midway, making all of 30 knots and with Admiral Yamaguchi well satisfied with his day's work.

17 · COURT-MARTIAL OR VICTORIA CROSS

During the First War there were several instances from both sides where downed pilots were collected by their comrades and flown to safety. But during the Second War, because of the higher landing speeds and narrow undercarriages, there were very few occasions when shot-down pilots were picked up. The Americans strongly discouraged their fighter pilots from attempting pick-ups and threatened court-martial proceedings, but the British thought otherwise.

On 18 March 1945 George Green was flying his Mustang over Germany as wingman to his squadron commander, Pierce McKennon. The CO had nineteen destroyed and earlier had walked back from Fränce after being shot down. He now had a problem pilot – his wingman – in his outfit. Green had been grounded several times for various misdemeanours both on the ground and in the air. Recently, he had seriously transgressed the fighter code when he left his leader, 'Red Dog' Norley, and went after a German fighter. Alone, Norley had to fight hard to get back to Debden.

Norley was after Green's blood and wanted him posted from 335 Squadron, but McKennon decided to give him one more chance on this mission when the Mustang pilots strafed Prenzlau airfield, near Berlin. The flak, as usual, was heavy and accurate. McKennon's fighter was hit but he managed to climb to 4,000 feet and bale out – landing in the same field as his burning Mustang.

Flying low, Green saw his leader struggling out of his parachute harness and decided he would land in the rough field and collect his CO. He knew it had been done once before by a Thunderbolt, which had a roomy

cockpit, from a smooth field. Also, he knew that he faced death, captivity or a court-martial. He did not hesitate and judging the wind direction from the burning plane he selected wheels and flaps down and began his approach.

Descending to the meadow Green saw German soldiers and dogs heading for his CO. 'Take out those Germans,' he yelled to his circling comrades, and the Mustangs made a strafing run. For the time being the Germans retreated.

Colonel James Goodson, distinguished squadron commander in the Fourth Fighter Group, takes up the narrative:

Green came around again, dragging the plane in with full flap, and dropped it over the fence into the bumpy field. Mac ran to meet him and clambered on to the wing.

Green put on the parking brake and clambered out on to the other wing to get rid of his flying gear and parachute. It was the only way they could both squeeze into the tiny cockpit. Mac squeezed his six feet two inches frame into the seat. Green climbed in and sat on his lap. To get the canopy closed, Green's face was pressed against the gun-sight. Mac's face was pressed against Green's back.

Green had to do the flying. He took the plane back to the far edge of the field, stood on the brakes, opened up the engine to maximum power, and released the brakes.

The plane sprang forward and bounced and lurched over the rough field. He dragged it off after only about 300 yards. It fell back down, bounced hard, staggered back into the air, and wobbled over the trees at the end of the field. They had made it!

They still had plenty of problems. Mac was in agony from the weight of Green's

Two pilots in a P-51 Mustang! George Green at the controls, Pierce McKennon the passenger

body which pressed his legs against the sides and bottom of the cockpit.

They ran into fog, and, since neither of them could see the instrument panel, Green had to take it up to 15,000 feet. He was able to plug in his own oxygen tube, but Mac didn't have one. Finally Green felt Mac's body go limp. Squeezing his head around, he saw that he'd passed out. Taking off his mask, he placed it over Mac's nose and mouth. When he came to, Green took the mask back to keep himself from passing out.*

After two and a half hours they somehow made it back to Debden. Green called the control tower: 'Clear the runway!'

'Is this an emergency?' asked the controller.

'I guess so,' replied Green. 'We've got two pilots in this ship!'

On 21 December 1942 an Australian, Bob Gibbes, was leading six Kitty-hawks of 3 Squadron, Royal Austra-lian Air Force, on a reconnaissance flight to gather information about an enemy airfield for David Stirling's Long Range Desert Group. They found the airfield and since not a shot was fired when the Kittyhawks made their first attack and destroyed several aeroplanes, the squadron com-mander decided, against the rules, to go in again. This time they encount-ered some intense light flak, and once they were all safely through the bar-rage, Gibbes called for the flight to re-form: Bob Gibbes wrote:

To my horror and annoyance a RAAF officer who had very recently arrived in the Middle East, and who was to take over from me, not realizing the danger, led his number two in for a third attack. I urgently called for him to abort this attack, but he continued and unfortunately two of my other pilots followed him in. The result was inevitable. The second two aircraft were both shot down.†

Sergeant 'Stuka' Bee's Kittyhawk caught fire and he seemed to be attempting a belly-landing. The squadron commander advised Bee to climb and bale out, but the fighter struck the ground and burst into flames. Despite the circling Kitty-hawks an enemy ambulance crew

Bob Gibbes – recommended for the Victoria Cross

drove at speed to the crash but the pilot was dead.

Meanwhile Rex Bailey, the pilot of the second aircraft which had been hit, called up to say he was belly-landing about one mile from the air-field. After coming to a halt he called again to say he was OK. The CO answered and asked what the area was like for a landing. Bailey replied that the area was impossible and asked his CO to leave him.

Ordering the remaining three aircraft to keep me covered, and to stop any ground forces coming out to capture Bailey, I flew

down to inspect the area myself. I found a suitable place a couple of miles further out, and told Rex that I was landing and to get weaving out to me.

I was greatly relieved on touching down to find that my tyres had not been punc-tured and I taxied by a devious route for about a mile until I was stopped from get-ting any closer by a deep wadi. I stopped my motor, and realizing that I would have a long wait, and being in a state of abso-lute funk, I proceeded to take off my half-

* James A. Goodson, *Tumult in the Clouds* (Willam Kimber, London, 1983; Wingham Press, 1990).
† Johnson Papers.

168

full drop tank to lighten the aircraft. This proved very difficult. It was very heavy, and dragging it from below the fuselage and clear of the aircraft was extremely taxing.

My next action was to check on a possible take-off area into wind, as I was not sure that I could find the route which I had followed during the taxi in, and I wanted to get away as urgently as possible. I stepped out the best run and found it to be 300 paces only before it fell away into a wadi. I tied my handkerchief on to a camel thorn bush to mark the longest available take-off run and then returned to my machine and waited.

My covering aircraft continued to circle overhead discouraging any attempt to pick us up. After what seemed like an age, sitting within range of the Hun, Bailey eventually appeared, puffing and sweating profusely. He still managed a smile and a greeting. I had discarded my parachute and when he climbed into the cockpit I climbed in after him and, sitting on his lap, proceeded to start my motor. It was with relief that we heard the engine fire. Gradually, I opened throttle beyond all normal limits while standing on the brakes. When I had obtained full boost and revs, I released my brakes and, as we surged forward, I extended a little flap.

My handkerchief rushed up with alarming speed and we had not reached flying speed when we passed over it and shot down the slope of the wadi. With slight back pressure on the joystick I managed to ease the aircraft into the air, but we hit the other side of the wadi with a terrific thump. We were flung, staggering into the air, still not really flying.

To my horror I thought I glimpsed my port wheel rolling back below the trailing edge of the wing in the dust stream. The next ridge loomed up and it looked as if this was to be curtains for us as we could never clear it. I deliberately dropped my starboard wing in the hope of taking the bounce on the remaining wheel, and eased the stick back just enough to avoid flicking. To my great relief we cleared the ridge and were flying.

Retracting my undercarriage and the small amount of take-off flap, we climbed up. I was shaking like a leaf and I tried to talk to Bailey, but noise would not permit. The remaining three aircraft formed up alongside me and we hared for home, praying all the while that we would not be intercepted by enemy fighters, who would by now have been alerted. Luck remained with us and no one appeared.

On nearing our airfield at Marble Arch I

Rex Bailey

asked the Flight Lieutenant flying behind me to confirm that I really had seen my wheel bowling below me and proceeded to select my undercart down. He confirmed that I had, indeed, lost my wheel, and had not imagined it; and he also told me that the starboard wheel and oleo leg appeared to be undamaged.

At the time we were very short of aircraft and as every machine counted I wondered if I could save my Kittyhawk from further damage by carrying out a one-wheel landing. I felt that I would be able to accomplish this, but as it could prove dangerous, in fairness to my passenger I wrote a message on my map asking if he was agreeable. He nodded.

Calling up ground control, I asked them to have an ambulance standing by and advised that I intended coming in cross-wing with my port wing up-wind. Control queried my decision but accepted it. The Marble Arch airfield consisted of a large square area.

I landed cross-wind, holding my port wing up with aileron, and as I lost speed I turned the aircraft slowly to port throwing the weight out. When I neared a complete stall, I kicked on hard port rudder, and the

machine, swinging harder to port, remained balanced on the starboard wheel. Extreme luck was with me and the aircraft remained balanced until it lost almost all forward speed. The port oleo leg touched the ground and it ground looped rather mildly.

The port flap was slightly damaged and also the wing-tip, but the propeller and the remainder of the machine did not sustain any other damage. The port undercart was changed, the flap was repaired, the numerous small holes patched and the aircraft was flying again, six days later.*

For his great gallantry in rescuing a brother pilot so close to the enemy the AOC, Harry Broadhurst, recommended Squadron Leader R. M. Gibbes for the Victoria Cross, but somewhere along the chain of command it was downgraded to a DSO. At least, however, the Australian fared better than his US counterpart.

* Johnson Papers.

PART IV
SINCE WORLD WAR II

CHINA

Vladivostok

Chongjin

Yalu River

NORTH
KOREA

KOREA
BAY

Wonsan

Pyongyang

SEA OF
JAPAN

Kaesong

Inchon SEOUL
Suwon

SOUTH
KOREA

YELLOW
SEA

Taegu

Pusan

JAPAN

| 0 | miles | 100 |
| 0 | kms | 200 |

18 · KOREA: STANDING TOGETHER

At the beginning of the Korean War, in mid-1950, the US Far East Air Forces were in poor shape to stop the enemy's advance. For years their task had been the air defence of Japan and air–ground training had been neglected. Fortunately for the Americans the few obsolete Yak fighters of the North Korean Force

Left: Korea – rugged Far Eastern battleground of mid 1950s

Previous page: McDonnell Douglas F-15C, Eagle

Below: Korea: US paratroops drop north of Seoul . . .

were poorly flown and were soon driven from the sky by the far superior F-80s (Shooting Stars), which then tried to help the US 24th Division.

Largely because of the lack of tactical air power, such as we had seen in the Desert and Normandy, little could be done from the air to stop the Communists. The Americans, and some South Korean troops, were driven towards the bottom of the peninsula, where they set up a defensive perimeter round the port of Pusan. But they were still in danger of being pushed into the sea.

As usual, Uncle Sam soon got into his stride with an elementary joint operations centre, and radio-equipped jeeps called tactical air control parties – their equivalent of our contact cars. These jeeps patrolled the perimeter calling down fighter-bombers flying from Korea and Japan, but the high mountains reduced the range of their radio sets. The US Air Force filled this dangerous gap with light aeroplanes, called Mosquitos, whose pilots could talk to the operations centre, the tactical air control parties and the fighter-

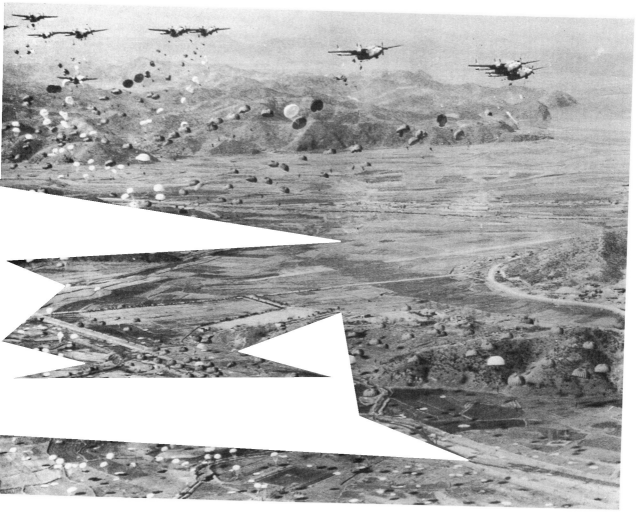

bombers. These Mosquito crews did a great job searching for and finding the enemy in that mountainous terrain, and co-pilots often helped the circling fighter-bombers by throwing smoke grenades from the rear cockpit. When there were no fighter-bombers they took matters into their own hands and hurled hand grenades at the enemy – sometimes with fatal consequences to themselves.

In July 1950 a United Nations Command was established and by early August the situation was under control. More tactical air-control parties and Mosquito aeroplanes were on hand. Communications were improved and radars moved in. F-84 (Thunderjet) fighter-bombers were on their way from the United States. A great airlift over the Pacific was established. Fighter reinforcements flew from Okinawa and the Philippines. The Americans were now ready to strike back, and, during September,

they broke out of the perimeter, mounted an amphibious assault near Seoul in the MacArthur tradition and advanced to the capital. From here, after some regrouping, they pressed to the north, joined forces with airborne troops and began to bed down before the tight fist of winter closed over the inhospitable terrain – which was to see another three years of combat before an uneasy truce ended the struggle.

Since South Africa was then a member of the Commonwealth, her Air Force sent their No. 2 'Cheetah' Squadron to Korea, whose thirty-eight Mustang pilots included some experienced and well-decorated veterans from the Desert and Italy. They were first based at Pusan East and, there being no air opposition, they were confined to armed reconnaissance missions. Finger-four sections of their ancient Mustangs checked in at the joint operations centre, which

directed them to one of the many tactical air control parties working with the ground forces who, in turn, passed them on to a forward air controller on the ground, or a Mosquito. Whenever possible the forward air controller marked the target with coloured smoke or the Mosquito fired small smoke rockets to mark their objective. The piston-engined fighters, like the jet-fighters, peeled off, bored in and attacked with bombs, rockets, machine guns and napalm fire bombs. Fighter pilots preferred to fly jets since, having fewer moving parts than the Mustangs, they could withstand more flak damage. Flak took a heavy toll of the South African fighter-bomber pilots.

On the early morning of 11 May 1951 four Mustangs of the Cheetah Squadron took off for a road interdiction mission north of Seoul. Jan Blaauw was leading and Vernon Kruger was his number three. Kruger hoped that on this day he would complete his tour of seventy-five missions and soon be on his way back to South Africa.

Having completed their first mission, landed, refuelled and rearmed at Suwan, they flew their second mission without incident. That afternoon they were airborne again for a road recce in the Kaesong area. This time Vernon Kruger was leading and Jan Blaauw was his wingman. It was Kruger's seventy-fourth mission.

There was not much enemy activity on the ground so they bombed a small dam hoping it would flood the road below. Then Kruger and Blaauw flew low looking for targets while the other pair provided cover. They spotted what appeared to be anti-aircraft guns and Kruger turned to take a closer look. Blaauw said the guns were firing at their Mustangs. Kruger attacked a 40-mm gun and plastered it with rockets and cannon. When about to open fire on his second attack Kruger was hit in the port wing which nearly turned the Mustang on its back.

The South African pilot pulled out of his dive, climbed and headed for the south and safety. But his port wing

B-29s over Korea

Accurate strike: good bombing of bridges across the Han River by the US Air Force

was on fire. It was time to go. When he jettisoned the canopy, flames were drawn into the cockpit, searing his hands and face. The next moments were vague as he tumbled through the air. Somehow, he managed to pull the ripcord, got the customary painful jerk and floated gently to earth.

The parachute was oscillating and Kruger's left shoulder hit the ground hard. As he struggled to release the harness, he realized his left shoulder was broken and he could only use his right arm. He hopped and hobbled towards a shallow donga painfully aware that, apart from his left arm, his ankle was also sprained, while his left hand and his forehead were badly burned. As he lay in the shallow depression he thought that if he was captured by the Communists his chances of survival were pretty slim. It was now about 16.00 hours and he could see movement in some nearby trees and heard the guns still firing at his three comrades overhead.

Every few minutes Jan Blaauw made a strafing run at the Communist soldiers which, the injured pilot realized, did not improve his chances of survival. But unbeknown to him, the American rescue service once again had been alerted, and a helicopter with fighter escort was soon on its way.

After thirty minutes or so, the three circling Mustangs were getting short of fuel. Two left the scene but Blaauw had decided to remain over his friend, guiding the rescuers, even at the cost of his own life.

As the shadows lengthened over the bleak landscape Vernon saw American jets overhead, but by this time Jan was almost out of fuel and he made a heavy crash-landing – the engine breaking from the fuselage – in a small paddy field close to his friend. Seconds later Vernon saw Jan running towards him. There was blood on his face and Vernon thought he had gone 'out of his senses' because he was shouting 'Klippe,

klippe' and 'darting about like a maniac picking up stones!' When Jan reached his friend he explained that the stones were required to adjust the centre of gravity position of the helicopter when it picked them up.

The enemy guns were still firing at the squadron of American jets overhead, and as they watched, and as daylight faded, Jan dressed his friend's burns. Then the beautiful S-1 helicopter arrived and strong hands helped them aboard. The stones were placed in the baggage compartment and they were away to a Forward Army Medical Unit.

Vernon was flown from Korea to a base hospital at Hiroshima and after three weeks Jan Blaauw came to see him. Vernon tried to thank this incredibly brave, resolute and steadfast Afrikaner who had been prepared to put his own life on the line for his brother pilot; but Jan brushed him aside saying: 'Vegeet dit. Ons vlieeniers moet mos saamstaad.' (Forget it. We pilots must stand together.)

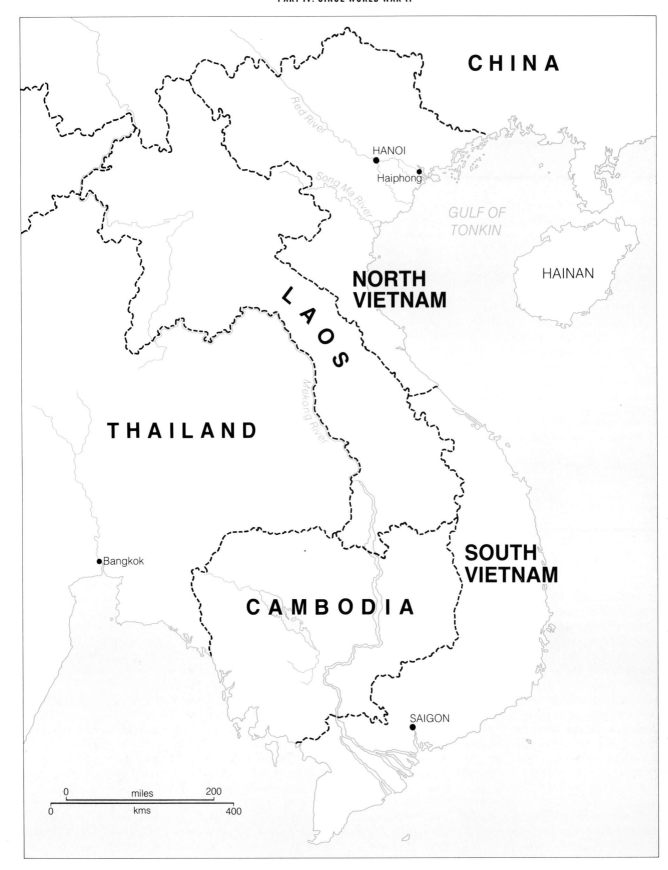

19 · VIETNAM

THE IN-COUNTRY WAR

In 1954 the former French colony of Indo-China was divided into North and South Vietnam, but Ho Chi Minh, Communist leader of North Vietnam and conqueror of the French in 1953 at the crucial battle of Dien Bien Phu, was determined to reunite the country; his tools were the regular North Vietnamese Army (NV) and their cadres in South Vietnam, the Viet Cong (VC). To supply the VC the elaborate Second World War system of mountain and jungle paths linking North Vietnam with guerillas in Laos, Cambodia and South Vietnam was re-opened and became the main supply route in this long war.

When, in 1954, the French departed, the Americans moved in and four years later they had more than half a million troops in South Vietnam. America under four successive Presidents, found herself more and more deeply involved in a distant futile war, which was never formally declared and never endorsed by the American people.

For America the war lasted ten years until her withdrawal in 1973. This long and often bloody struggle saw two separate campaigns – the In-Country War, the air–ground conflict against the enemy in South Vietnam, and the Out-Country War in the air against North Vietnam.

In the south, US fighter-bombers used some nasty weapons – napalm, white phosphorous, cluster bombs, rockets, 'smart' bombs and air–ground missiles – against the Viet Cong who harassed and terrorized the countryside. They were fierce, brave, resourceful, masters of the ambush and of the hit-and-run attack. When cornered, they fought hard and gave ground grudgingly. They were not well disposed towards American aircrew brought down by their automatic weapons and rockets, and the Air Force pulled out all the stops to rescue their downed aircrews. Speed, in such a hostile environment, was essential as a survivor's chances of

Left: Heavy drain on United States – war in Vietnam. *Below:* Ready to go. US pilots prepare for a mission

177

rescue from hostile territory were best within fifteen minutes. After thirty minutes his chances declined sharply. Lieutenant-Colonel Iceal E. Hambleton, navigator of an electronic EB-66, took somewhat longer to get out; his story has become a legend.

On the afternoon of 2 April 1972 two Douglas EB-66s were escorting a cell of B-52 Stratofortresses on a bombing mission when three Sam missiles were fired at Hambleton's aeroplane. One of the electronic warfare officers on board called a missile warning but the Sam hit the aeroplane and only Hambleton, of the six-man crew, managed to get out. As he drifted down his bleeper was heard by a forward air controller (FAC),

Captain Jimmie D. Kempton, flying on OV-10 Bronco, who established radio contact with the Colonel. The area was completely covered by cloud so Kempton let-down under the overcast and fortunately saw Hambleton's parachute on the ground.

A nearby rescue attempt had been cancelled and two piston-engined A-1E Skyraiders heard Hambleton's emergency calls and headed towards his position. Enemy troops were very close and the flak was heavy, but for the next two hours the Colonel directed the Skyraiders against his would-be captors, some of whom were within one hundred yards of his position.

Meanwhile, Jimmie Kempton had flown to the south making radio calls

for help. Soon he returned with four Army helicopters – two Cobra gunships and two passenger-carrying choppers. Approaching Hambleton's position two of the helicopters were hit by accurate flak and one was completely destroyed. The other managed to land and its two crewmen were rescued. As the light failed the two surviving choppers went home. The resolute Kempton stayed over the Colonel until relieved by another FAC whose precise Loran navigation and bombing equipment soon fixed Hambleton's exact position on the north bank of the Mien Giang River.

Throughout the night, FACS kept watch over Hambleton. At first light another Bronco, crewed by Captains Rocky O. Smith and Richard M. Atch-

Skyhawk landing on US Navy's carrier, *Enterprise*

inson, arrived over Hambleton, who was hiding in some bushes in the midst of a very large field. The Colonel reported that enemy troops were still close, but the bad weather prevented visual fighter-bomber attacks. Smith and Atchinson therefore relayed the co-ordinates of Hambleton's new position to the control centre where all the information was assembled for Loran (instrument bombing) air strikes. At the control centre a safety zone was established round the Colonel. Strike data was passed to the FACs and within hours fighter-bombers, using their Loran equipment, were placing their weapons between the Colonel and his enemies.

Later, on this second day of Hambleton's ordeal, a US Navy control ship in the Gulf of Tonkin, called a Sam launch but the FAC Bronco safeguarding Hambleton was over a layer of cloud and did not see the dust (from the launch) or the missile. The Sam blew the Bronco to pieces but Bill Henderson and Mark Clark were able to get out. Henderson was soon captured but Clark found cover not far from Hambleton.

Since the two survivors were directly in the path of a powerful North Vietnamese ground offensive there were many targets, and the FACs were very busy calling in the versatile fighter-bombers against tanks, transports, bridges and anything that moved on the ground. After several days of continuous attacks the area seemed quiet and on 6 April another attempt was made to bring out the two evaders.

Everyone knew the Jolly Green Giants, big and slow rescue helicopters, were vulnerable to ground fire and on previous rescue missions had paid a high price. Nevertheless all concerned in the rescue drama, from the Commanding General of the Seventh Air Force down to the aircrews and groundcrews, were determined to bring out their men; and so it was that on the fourth day a Jolly Green, escorted by Skyraiders, approached the rescue zone. Skyraider pilots saw intense flak from a

USAF Stand-out: Colonel Robin Olds

village, a Skyraider pilot shouted a warning, but heavy, multiple machine gun fire riddled the Jolly Green. Flames shot out below the main rotor and the stricken chopper rolled to the left and fell to the ground. All the crew were killed.

At their airfields US aircrews debated about the chances of another Jolly Green mission or an attempt by a light chopper at night. At one conference between FACs and US Army advisers a big, rugged, highly decorated Marine colonel joined the group, introduced himself and simply said: 'I understand you have people you want taken out?'

'Yes sir. We do.'

'Well, I have a full carrier of guys that would love to do that. When do we start?'

The airmen described the tactical situation and later the Marine colonel collected his team, and together with some South Vietnamese Rangers, went up-river after the two downed airmen.

Hambleton and Clark were told about the new arrangements. They began working their way towards the river. Clark was nearest to the river and swam and floated downstream, and was first to meet the Marines. Hambleton had to cross a minefield and took longer to reach the river. He hid by day and floated downstream

on a log by night. For three nights the Colonel made his slow progress downstream, always monitored, thanks to his bleeper, by the faithful FACs. On his fourth river-day he made contact with the Marines. Twelve days after being brought down Colonel Hambleton, against all the odds, but thanks to his fearless comrades and to the valiant Marines, was on his way home.

THE OUT-COUNTRY WAR: ROBIN OLDS

Flying P-38 Lightnings and P-51 Mustangs over north-west Europe, Robin Olds served a fighting apprenticeship to that great fighter pilot and leader, Colonel 'Hub' Zemke, commander of the illustrious 56th Fighter Group ('Zemke's Wolf Pack'). During the latter stages of the Second War, Robin accounted for twenty-four German aeroplanes and became an experienced and highly decorated squadron commander. More than two decades later he commanded the 8th Fighter Wing* at Uboa, in Thailand, where he found that a new generation of weapons were profoundly changing both the tactics and strategy of air fighting.

In Vietnam, for the first time in the history of air fighting, a fighter pilot could shoot down an adversary without physically seeing him; and the new 'smart' bombs, with their laser-guided pin-point accuracy, demolished, in three days, vital targets like the Dragon's 'Jaw' bridge over the Song Ma River and the Paul Doumer bridge spanning the Red River at Hanoi – objectives which hitherto had withstood countless attacks with the old 'iron' bombs.

Colonel Old's 'fighter jocks' flew the two-seater F-4 Phantom, the most versatile combat aeroplane in southeast Asia. It could participate in the different roles of air superiority, close air support, interdiction, air defence and long-range bombing. With two powerful engines it reached speeds

---

* Second War Fighter Groups later became Fighter Wings.

One confirmed

of more than 2 mach* and had a maximum altitude of nearly 60,000 feet. The Phantom's standard weapons were two 20-mm guns, four radar-guided Sparrow missiles and four heat-seeking Sidewinder missiles; with such a variety of weapons the Phantoms could fire at MiGs at distances ranging from about ten miles down to a few hundred yards.

He had to learn how to fight his heavy Phantom against the lively, lighter and more manoeuvrable MiG-21. Operating in pairs, MiG-21 pilots were steered by their ground controllers to a position behind the American fighter-bombers from which they made high-speed hit-and-run attacks. During the attack and breakaway they flew at 1.5 mach and used their superior speed to zoom away from the Phantoms. Because of the MiG's better manoeuvrability, Phantom pilots avoided the sustained, turning and twisting dog-fights of Mustang versus Messerschmitt.

The middle-aged Colonel found that the air war over Vietnam was more demanding, tougher and more dangerous than the war over Germany. So he began to re-learn the hardest way of all by flying 'tail-end Charlie', where Robin was always the last man to take off, the last man to attack in a dive-bombing or ground strafing mission, and the most vulnerable man in a dog-fight. Having learned to keep formation he moved to the number two, or wingman, position and then to number three where he led a pair of Phantoms. Eventually he led his Wing and describes a typical mission.†

We'd get the first order in the afternoon – there were about two strikes a day up north. We'd make up the squadron assignments and post an unclassified ver-

* The mach number is an aeroplane's speed expressed as a proportion of the speed of sound at that height and temperature.
† Edward H. Sims, *Fighter Tactics and Strategy* (Cassell, London, 1972).

F5 Tigers setting course

sion in the club. The kids would check the board there. When they saw they were on the morning mission they didn't show too much emotion. Maybe they'd have a drink at the bar, then supper, and enjoy our really great salad bar, then disappear from the club about eight o'clock.

At about two we'd go over to the club for breakfast, eggs and the best pineapples in the world. It was black outside. We could hear the Night Owl F-4s roaring off and see their glow and the floodlights on the flight line. We'd go down to wing headquarters in a van truck about 0245. There we'd get all the intelligence and learn about other forces and tactics and plot our maps and fill out our mission cards; we'd get tanker routes, times, rendezvous points, flak maps, navigation checks, speeds, bomb load, aim point, roll-in, sight picture, mill depression and so on and then the weather officer would give us a guess on the weather, intelligence would guess on the enemy and the communications guy would make his talk. The mission leaders would speak to the group. By then we'd know our pre-station time – fifty minutes prior to take-off. We took everything out of our pockets except the Geneva Convention and ID cards and sealed them in plastic. We put on G-suits and put a radio in one pocket and a brilliant cloth to wave in the jungle in the other. We stuck a two-pint bottle of

water in a knee pocket and a 38-calibre Navy Colt pistol on our right hip. Then we put on the Mae-West – two little packages which fit under the armpits, a survival vest with all kinds of things in it – food, a compass, knives, radio – and over all this a parachute harness. Then with helmet, map and mission kit we got in the trucks and started out to the birds. We had added forty-five pounds to our weight.

In the truck the guys were pretty tense – they knew it was going to be a hard one. At the aircraft we spoke to the crew chief but we didn't often fly the same plane. There was also the back-seater, who flew behind me and he was busy setting up the inertial guidance system while I checked the forms. The pre-flight inspection took about twenty minutes; we had to check the ordnance load, fuses, wires, and hundreds of other things. Then I climbed up the ladder. By now we were soaking wet. Sometimes the temperature was over 100 degrees. There was an elaborate strap-in procedure. The F-4 seat alone was more complex than the whole P-51! The F-4 was in a revetment and sometimes the fumes from the ground power starting unit were almost overpowering. Now came the pre-flight cockpit check. We checked everything and it took some time and then there was the elaborate ritual of starting engines. The crew chief is plugged in by telephone and talking to you. He tells you

whether the by-pass doors are closed, whether things move in response to your controls, and so on. The crew takes about ten minutes just removing pins. If everything goes right you move out ponderously, maybe carrying as much as 12,000 pounds of ordnance, taxi out with engine screaming; the kid in the back checks radar, missile control, the navigation system. We must take off on the second and rev up engines. We push 'em up to eighty per cent – that's all the brakes can hold – check the hydraulics, pneumatics, temperatures, fuel flow, rpm, generators, ramps, and then slam the throttle forward to full and then out and full forward again. That's the after-burner. She leaps forward and when you pass the 2,000-foot mark you must have a certain speed or abort then. At 175 knots (over 200 m.p.h.) you pull the stick back and she bounces and leaps off at 180 or 190 and then you form up and head for the tankers (KC 135s); after a time we refuel about thirty feet beneath them and drop down again and head north, over beautiful Laos. It's like Montana, a wild savage land, gorges, streams. Now the tension is up.

Soon we're crossing into Vietnam, the Black River, ahead is the Red River. Now all is business, you're in the Sam ring. We alter course and rendezvous with the 105s. From 480 indicated we increase to 500 and then up to 520, change course

Russian-built SAM

twice more, add more power, up to 540. We're heading to a target north of Hanoi. Our gear tells us they have us on radar, so we're constantly on the lookout for Sam sites. The only salvation is to see them coming. They'll kill you within 200 feet, so the key is dodging them. We hurtle on and now here come the Sams! The trick is seeing the launch. You can see the steam. It goes straight up, turns more level, then the booster drops off. If it maintains relatively stable position, it's coming for you and you're in trouble. You're eager to make a move but can't. If you dodge too fast it will turn and catch you; if you wait too late it will explode near enough to get you. What you do at the right moment is poke your nose down, go down as hard as you can, pull maybe three negative Gs up to 550 knots and once it follows you down, you go up as hard as you can. It can't follow that and goes under. In a two-minute period they once shot thirty-eight Sams at us. Sam sites are occupied one day, unoccupied the next. They're moved around. Going into Route Pack Six (a designated area in North Vietnam) was like going to the Ruhr. They had brought in all their guns. They knew we were coming and where we couldn't go and this kind of defense didn't allow us to stooge around. We got out as quickly as we could; we didn't strafe a truck, for instance, in the Hanoi or Haiphong areas.

Soon we approach the target and see flak – the 85s. When you've seen the muzzle flashes often enough you can tell whether that battery is aimed at your flight and you move a thousand feet to avoid the bursts. About this time here come the MiGs, from above. We keep our eyes on them and if they come in we break at just the right time and pull right back in and get in the stream. If we're not carrying bombs we go for the MiGs, of course. We have bombs on this mission and roll in together from a good height and dump the whole load as quickly as possible, through the 57 mm and 37 mm flak, going as fast as we can. Near Hanoi I've seen skies as black as those over Berlin and Magdeburg in the Second World War.

We're only over the target for seconds and after pickling our bombs we break and really get out. We know we might be bounced by MiGs again over the Red River and don't really breathe a sigh of relief until over the Black River. When we get back to base there's a maintenance debriefing which takes twenty minutes, an intelligence briefing which takes an hour and about two and a half hours after we land we're free. Then you can gauge the success of a mission by what goes on afterwards in the club. Sometimes it's quiet, if there were losses. If it's too quiet, it's not good. They're thinking about it too much. That's what it's like and it happens

twice a day. And there are twos and fours going to Laos and southern Vietnam and other places, and guys flying at night in the mountains, which is really tough!

MiG-21s flew from five bases in the Hanoi area which, because of political constraints, could not be attacked. Daily they attacked US fighter-bombers and it was decided that the F-4 Phantoms should stop dive-bombing and fly as fighter escort to the more vulnerable F-105 Thunderchiefs. The F-4 Phantoms flew lower than the F-105 Thunderchiefs to try and get at the MiGs before they attacked the fighter-bombers.

Robin's posse on this big operation consisted of fourteen flights of F-4Cs, six flights of 'Iron Hard' F-105s and four flights of F-104s Starfighters, supported ECM,* 'Big Eye' radar control and tanker aeroplanes. The MiGs reacted in strength and in the biggest air battle of this war seven enemy fighters were destroyed, including a MiG-21 by the Colonel.

On a later mission the Wing tangled with a bunch of MiGs and several were shot down, including another by Robin. On his way home, the Colonel saw an enemy fighter circling 'in the weeds' well below and, hoping that it would continue to orbit, he flew ahead for a few miles, letdown and, flying just a few feet above the rice paddies, stalked back for the MiG whose wary pilot saw him coming. The MiG turned and headed north, flying very low. Robin got behind him, but they were both so low that the American could not fire a missile. Robin's fuel was low but he hung on, knowing that sooner or later the MiG would pull up to clear a ridge, and when he did Robin slammed a Sidewinder into the MiG and headed south to find a tanker.

That evening there was a big party at Ubon to celebrate the Wing's victories and the Colonel's brace. From his young 'fighter-jocks' there were many toasts to Colonel Robin Olds, the outstanding fighter leader and folk hero of the air fighting over Vietnam.

* Electronic Counter Measures.

20 · THE FALKLANDS: 'THE NEAREST RUN THING...'

We fought this short contest 8,000 miles from home with one aircraft carrier, *Invincible*, already sold to Australia and another, *Hermes*, destined for the scrap heap; with Harriers never intended as air superiority fighters and Vulcan bombers temporarily reprieved from the boneyard. Our greatest deficiency – which could have been fatal – was the lack of an airborne early-warning (AEW) system. The Prime Minister and the Chiefs of Staff were fully aware of our vulnerability and took a calculated risk.

A rudimentary form of early warning was provided by the on-board surveillance radars fitted to most ships, but these were old and unreliable in heavy seas and there were large gaps, especially at low level, on our radar screens.

Fortunately, this quite inadequate early-warning system was supplemented by brave and resourceful SAS intelligence teams operating from the Argentine mainland, who reported enemy aeroplanes taking off, together with their estimated time of arrival over the fleet, and our nuclear submarines also provided valuable information; but these *ad hoc* arrangements did not close the radar gap because once enemy fighter-bombers were within fifty or sixty miles of the fleet they dived to sea level and faded from our screens.

Our lack of early-warning radar was tragically demonstrated on 4 May 1982, when a pair of Super Etendards, each armed with one Exocet missile, flew at high speed and low level towards the Task Force, probably assisted by a high-flying radar-

equipped aeroplane. *Sheffield*'s radar picked up a contact – probably an incoming aeroplane – approaching them from the west. This was an Etendard pilot who, emerging from the radar deadground, acquired *Sheffield* on his radar, transferred this information into the missile's computer, and, at a range of about six miles, fired the Exocet.

Sheffield was up against a flying bomb with a 350-pound warhead travelling at nearly the speed of sound, hugging the surface of the sea. The missile climbed slightly, just high enough for its own miniature guidance radar to lock on to the ship.

Up on the bridge the officer of the watch, Lieutenant Peter Walpole, was informed of a 'possible contact' but did not call action stations. Peering across the starboard bow, Walpole

Bleak Falklands scene, South Georgia

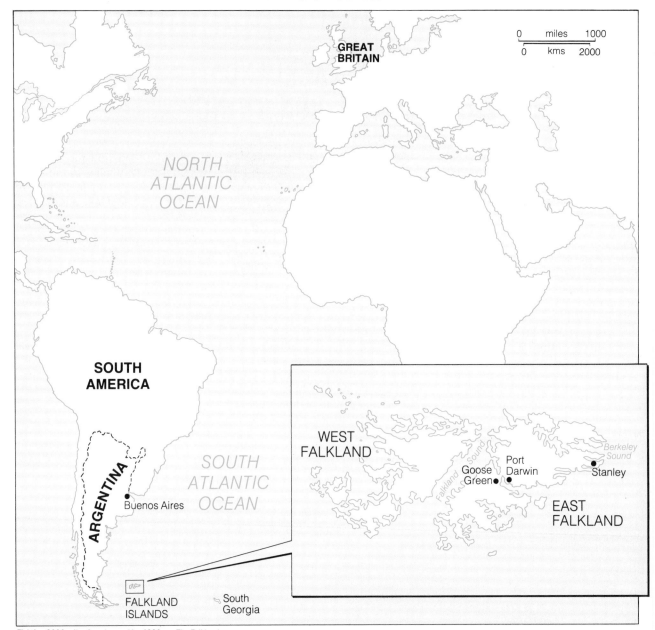

Fighting 8000 miles from home, May 1982 . . . The Falklands

saw a puff of smoke some distance away. When the missile was about a mile away Walpole and Lieutenant Brian Layshon, *Sheffield*'s helicopter pilot, shouted almost simultaneously, 'My God, it's a missile!'

Four seconds later, the Exocet hit Sheffield's starboard side amidships, eight feet above the waterline, and tore into the forward engine room where it exploded with tremendous force.

Fires started over a wide area and within twenty seconds the ship was filled with black, pungent, suffocating fumes. Four and a half hours later, with paint on the superstructure beginning to blister, the decks too hot to stand on and the magazines in danger of exploding, Captain Sam Salt gave the order to abandon ship.

On the night of Thursday, 20 May 1982, the liner *Canberra* and the assault ships *Fearless* and *Intrepid*, all protected by a screen of destroyers and frigates, steamed into the confined waters of Falkland Sound to spearhead the British invasion of East Falkland Island. On the other side of the island the aircraft carriers *Hermes* and *Invincible* were ready to launch their Sea Harriers at first light.

Port San Carlos was the objective of Marine commandos and paratroopers who since 04.00, had been ferried ashore, and, as the clear dawn broke, watchers on the bleak hills saw 'the White Whale', the liner *Canberra*, standing out like an iceberg against the drab grey blackcloth of the sea. Landing ships plied to and from the beaches, anti-submarine helicopters searched coves and inlets for two elusive Argentine submarines, while more helicopters buzzed overhead. Because of the sheer number of ships, helicopters and troops, it was an impressive and stirring sight but, as we had already found to our cost, the ships were vulnerable to determined enemy air attacks and one observer wrote: 'For the Argentine pilots it would not be a question of where the target is, but which target shall I go for.'*

On Friday, 21 May 1982, there was little doubt that the Argentine Air Force commander would throw the bulk of his 175 combat aeroplanes against the fleet. And so it proved. The air fighting went on all day – the sky painted with aeroplanes, shells and rockets. Only the failing light, with a great column of smoke rising from the doomed *Argent*, brought an end to the enemy air attacks. Some thirty Sea Harrier pilots had saved the day, destroying nineteen Argentine

Experienced Commander of the Fleet Air Arm's 801 Squadron: Lieutenant Commander 'Sharkie' Ward

aeroplanes, including nine Mirages and Daggers, five Skyhawks and three Pucaras, and driving off many others.

Perhaps our most experienced Sea Harrier pilot in the Falklands was Lieutenant Commander 'Sharkie'

Ward AFC, Commanding Officer of 801 Naval Air Squadron, Fleet Air Arm, based on *Invincible*. Known at the Royal Naval Air Station, Yeovilton, as 'Mr Sea Harrier', Sharkie Ward was leading his section of three Sea Harriers on his first combat air patrol when, towards the end of the mission, the controller on *Brilliant* advised that a low slow-moving target was some twenty miles to the south, and although low on fuel Ward replied that he would take a look. They dived towards the ground and Lieutenant Steve Thomas said, 'Boss, one Pucara left at eleven o'clock, very low.'

'Roger. You're nearest. You take him first,' ordered the leader.

Ward saw the twin-engine Pucara flying only a few feet above the ground, hugging the contours, and watched his two companions attack from the flank. Then with his Aden guns he opened fire at about 400

* *The Falklands Conflict* (HMSO, London, 1982).

The sinking of the *Belgrano*

yards and when he broke off at close range the Pucara had lost its left aileron and the starboard engine was on fire. On his second attack Ward came in with flaps fully down, at 280 m.p.h., so that he could get a long burst at his target; the port engine caught fire, but at some twenty feet above the ground, the stubborn pilot flew on. Wondering why the stricken aeroplane, with both engines on fire, did not crash, the squadron commander came in for his third attack and emptied his guns into the Pucara; the pilot ejected and the now blazing aeroplane crashed into the ground.

On their third combat air patrol, Sharkie Ward and Steve Thomas were flying at 500 feet over land west of Falkland Sound, 2,000 yards apart, when *Brilliant*'s controller said, 'Trident Leader. Got a problem. Being strafed by Mirages!'

Ward acknowledged, headed towards the line of ships in the bay and immediately saw two Mirages coming at him, head-on and very fast.

'Sharkie' Ward's wingman: Lieutenant Steve Thomas

The starboard Mirage fired a missile which streaked over the top of his canopy, and as he ducked beneath the two Mirages he thought the enemy missile was fired too close to lock on to his Sea Harrier.

Once clear of the Mirages, Ward reefed his Harrier into a tight starboard turn while Steve Thomas turned hard to port. The Argentine pilots, obligingly for Thomas, turned starboard and climbed, which placed Thomas astern of the two Mirages at a range of about two miles. His already armed Sidewinder 'growled' and the Navy pilot fired the missile which, after one small correction on course, hit the centre of one Mirage, which exploded into a spectacular fireball.

Seeing the fate of his companion, the remaining Mirage fighter hit his afterburners and headed for a solid layer of cloud some 2,000 feet higher. Steve Thomas, still within range and well inside the firing envelope, fired another missile which exploded just as the Mirage entered the cloud.

Harrier

Hovering above the Falklands: the helicopter came into its own – for both sides

Sharkie Ward watched his wingman's successful attacks, congratulated him, and suddenly saw a Dagger about fifty feet below and flying at right angles to him. He turned hard starboard after the Dagger, now very low over the land, manoeuvred into a good firing position about three-quarters of a mile astern and slightly higher, and fired a Sidewinder. The accurate and reliable missile streaked towards the Dagger, leaving the usual trail of white smoke, and seconds later the Dagger exploded. It was so low that the explosion and the balls of flames on the ground were almost simultaneous.

In the midst of these combats, Lieutenant Clive Morrell and his wingman, Flight Lieutenant John Leeming (on loan from 3 Squadron, Royal Air Force), were scrambled from *Hermes* and tried unsuccessfully to contact the controller on *Brilliant*. There was a lot of chatter on the radio and eventually Ward advised 'Spaghetti' Morrell about the general situation.

Clive Morrell saw the splashes of bombs near the Task Force, and soon after saw three light-coloured Skyhawks flying at low level and conspicuous against the dark-grey sea. He advised his wingman and, only a few feet above the sea, the Sea Harrier pilots chased the Skyhawks. Leeming wanted to arm his Sidewinders, but he had only flown the Sea Harrier fitted with AIM 9 Sidewinders once before, and could not find the right switches since they were quite different from those on the Royal Air Force Harriers. Frustrated, he tried everything he could without success, and eventually decided to attack with his two Aden guns. Opening fire at 800 yards he closed to about a hundred yards, firing short bursts all the time, and at this minimum range the Skyhawk exploded; as he broke away he saw another Mirage destroyed by a Sidewinder from Spaghetti Morrell.

Because the Task Force was dispatched without a proper AEW system the small Sea Harrier force could not protect the fleet adequately, despite brilliant flying; if such a system had been available, *Sheffield, Ardent, Antelope, Sir Galahad, Sir Tristam* and *Atlantic Conveyor* would not all have been lost. Other bombs hit the fleet and had they all exploded we could have lost fourteen ships.

This short, sharp contest was, as the Duke of Wellington said after the Battle of Waterloo, 'the nearest run thing you ever saw in your life, by God'. The calculated risk had paid off.

21 · DESERT STORM: VICTORY THROUGH AIR POWER

Whoever controls the Middle East controls a large proportion of the world's oil supplies; and whoever controls the oil can afford to buy weapons of mass destruction and hold the West to ransom. Thus, when Saddam Hussein invaded Kuwait for that very reason the Americans were quick to react and, as in Korea and Vietnam, demonstrated the great flexibility of their Air Force by reinforcing Gulf airfields with combat squadrons within hours. Once again the survival of freedom and democracy rested on the United States' broad shoulders, supported, to the best of her ability, by Britain, and later France, whilst the rest of Europe looked on.

Heeding the lessons of Vietnam – too little too late – America and her Allies went straight for Saddam's jugular, and on the night of 16/17 January 1991 sent the most powerful air fleet ever assembled against selected targets in Iraq and Kuwait.

Despite the vast technological strides in warplanes and their weapons, the basic principles of tactical air power, hammered out in previous contests, remain the same; these are air superiority, isolation of the battlefield and close support to the ground forces. Much target information, including the enemy's chemical and nuclear plants, had been provided by electronic surveillance from satellites, spy aeroplanes, AWACS (Airborne Warning and Control System) and drones, and reinforced by intelligence from Moscow and Tel Aviv. This knowledge was assembled by computer technology into the strike plan.

The air plan took shape in the Allies' air headquarters, a Riyadh basement called 'The Black Hole'. Here, Lieutenant General Charles 'Chuck' Horner, the air commander, worked with Brigadier General 'Buster' Glosson on their top-secret plans. Both generals had flown com-

bat missions over Vietnam and both took regular flights over the desert in jet fighters. A junior officer heard Horner ask Glosson how many warplanes might be lost in the first wave. Glosson thought they would lose a dozen. The official estimate was forty-five to fifty. In fact one FA-18 Hornet was lost to a SAM missile.

Their tools were a mixture of high and low technology F-117A Nighthawk Stealth fighters to rule the skies over Baghdad; the ageing yet indomitable F-4G 'Wild Weasel' Phantoms to suppress enemy radars; F-111 long-range fighter-bombers; F-15C Eagle air superiority fighters; and F-15E 'Mud Hens', lacking their target designators, were to attack other targets using old-fashioned 'dumb' bombs. With them came F-14 Tomcats, FA-18 Hornets, A-6E Intruders and A-7E Corsairs from six carrier battle groups; more Intruders, Hornets and AV-8B Harriers from Marines on land; and A-10A Thunderbolts, F-16 Fighting Falcons and the incomparable B52-G ('the Buff') from airfields in the UK, Spain, Turkey and Diego Garcia, in the Indian Ocean. This omnipotent American air armada was assisted by British, Canadian, French, Italian, Kuwaiti and Saudi fighter-bombers. Their crews came from seven nations, spoke four languages and it says much for Horner's planning that there were very few 'friendly fire' incidents.

The Daily Air Tasking Order detailed the targets and control was exercised through the utterly reliable E-3 Sentry AWACS who provided a constant stream of advice, often including the comforting call of 'picture clear!' EC 130Es, Airborne Battlefield Command and Control Centres, gave vital information about enemy tanks and armour.

Outstanding Commander: the USAF's brilliant Lieutenant General Charles 'Chuck' Horner

Night sky in the Gulf

At 23.40 GMT on 16 January 1991 the first of a wave of F-117A Stealth fighter-bombers released its laser-guided bombs against an important defence centre in Baghdad. Meanwhile, MH-53 helicopters carried brave men of the US Army Special Forces whose missions were to mark enemy early warning radars for attacks by heavily-armed AH-65A Apache helicopters and A-10A Thunderbolts.

Soon after powerful Allied 'strike packages', which had been assembling outside Iraqi radar cover, were 'topped-up' by tankers and headed for their targets. They were protected by fighter caps of F-15s, F-16s and F-18s who in Manfred von Richthofen's words about his fighters were free 'to rove in the area allotted to them!' 'Wild Weasel' Phantoms, with their HARM missiles to take out enemy SAM radars and EF-111s, to jam Iraqi radars, swept the area ahead of the strike packages.

Each strike package consisted of F-15s (sometimes Royal Air Force Tornadoes) flying in two 'card fours' immediately preceded by their own small force of 'Weasels' and EF-111s. Sometimes diversionary attacks took place as the F-15s rolled on to their targets.

The Tornado GRIs of the Royal Air Force had the most dangerous flying missions because, for some reason best known to the Air Staff, they carried the JP233 Airfield Denial Weapon which had to be dropped flying straight and level at 200 feet, and took seven seconds to deliver its considerable ordnance of concrete-cratering bombs and land mines. USAF fighter-bombers released their bombs from medium altitudes (15,000–20,000 feet), but after their last refuelling the Tornado pilots let-down in the pitch-black night to 200 feet and flew over the desert to their airfield targets. Wing Commander Jerry Witts,* CO of 31 Squadron wrote:

The aircraft lurches left as I reselect track hold on the autopilot. It all seems very unreal creaming along at 500 knots through the thick velvet darkness. The Head Up Display tells me we are at 180 feet above the desert but it could just as well be 18,000 feet because I can't see a thing ahead . . . Thank goodness it's flat – at least we think it is . . . We recite the litany of checks, just as we have done a thousand times before. But never like this. This time it's for real and ahead in only thirty seconds lies an Iraqi airfield . . . The aircraft vibrates rapidly as our JP233s dispense their loads. There's a pulsing glow from beneath the aircraft. Then, suddenly, two massive thumps as the empty canisters are jettisoned.

Intense triple A (flak to the veterans) brackets the Tornado . . .

The flashing lights become white stair rods arcing over and around us. Away to the right the sky erupts in orange flames, quickly followed by a curtain of incandescent white lights as more and more AAA barrage fires into the darkness . . . We rush onward. Homeward!†

* Wing Commander Witts was subsequently awarded the DSO.
† *RAF Yearbook Special: Air War in the Gulf* (RAF Publishing, RAF Fairford, 1991).

Fixed-wing aircraft

Tornado GR1
Fighter bomber
Max. speed: 690 mph
Max. range: 2,800 mls

Armaments: 27 mm guns;
various air-to-air and
air-to-ground weapons

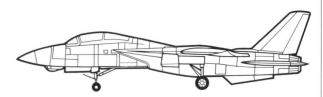

F-14A 'Tomcat
Carrier-based fighter
Max. speed: Mach 2.3
Max. range: 2000 mls

Armaments: 20 mm gun;
usually eight AIM-7 Sparrow or
AIM-9 Sidewinder air-to-air missiles

F-15C Eagle
Air-superiority fighter
Max. speed: Mach 2.5
Max. range: 3570 mls
(with conformal fuel tanks)

Armaments: 20 mm gun;
various air-to-air and
air-to-ground weapons

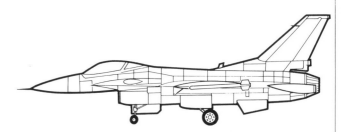

F-16C Fighting Falcon
Multirole fighter
Max. speed: Mach 2.1
Max. range: 2415 mls

Armaments: 20 mm gun;
various air-to-air and
air-to-ground weapons

F/A-18A Hornet
Strike fighter
Max. speed: Mach 1.8
Max. range: 2303 mls

Armaments: 20 mm gun;
various air-to-air and
air-to-ground weapons

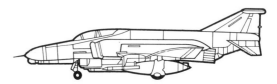

F-4G Wild Weasel
Air-defence suppression
fighter
Max. speed: Mach 2
Max. range: 1978 mls

Armaments: Various,
including AGM-88 HARM
anti-radar missiles

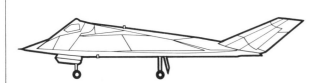

F-117A Stealth Fighter
Attack fighter
Max. speed: 691 mph
Max. range: 900 mls

Armaments: Various
air-to-surface, usually
two 2000-pound laser-
guided bombs

F111F 'Aardvark'
Long-range strike bomber
Max. speed: Mach 2.5
Max. range: 2925 mls

Armaments: 20 mm gun;
up to 25,000 pounds of bombs
on external pylons

B-52G Stratofortress
Strategic bomber
Max. speed: 595 mph
Max. range: 7500 mls

Armaments: Up to 50,000
pounds of bombs, twin
0.5 in tail guns

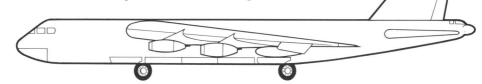

AV-88 Harrier 11
VTOL Attack fighter
Max. speed: 661 mph
Max. range: 2418 mls

Armaments: 25 mm gun;
various air-to-air and
air-to-ground weapons

A-6E Intruder
Carrier-based heavy
attack bomber
Max. speed: 806 mph
Max. range: 2740 mls

Armaments: Most air-to-
surface weapons, often 28
500-pound bombs

A-10A Thunderbolt II ('Warthog')
Close air-support aircraft
Max. speed: 439 mph
Max. range: 2454 mls

Armaments: 30 mm Avenger
anti-tank cannon; other
air-to-surface weapons

OV-10A Bronco
Low-altitude
reconnaissance aircraft
Max. speed: 281 mph
Max. range: 1437 mls

Armaments: Four 7.62 mm
machine guns; other air-to-air
and air-to-ground weapons

Rotary-wing aircraft

AH-64A Apache
Antiarmour attack helicopter
Max. speed: 227 mph
Max. range: 1057 mls

Armaments: 30 mm Chain Gun;
Hellfire anti-tank missiles

AH-1S Huey Cobra
Attack helicopter
Max. speed: 195 mph
Max. range: 315 mls

Armaments: 20 mm gun;
TOW anti-tank missiles;
other rockets

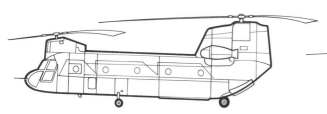

CH-47D Chinook
Transport helicopter
Max. speed: 188 mph
Max. range: 1279 mls

Armaments: None, but can
take 12-ton cargo load

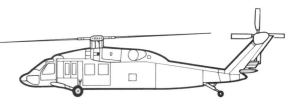

UH-60A Black Hawk
Assault helicopter
Max. speed: 184 mph
Max. range: 1380 mls

Armaments: Hellfire missiles;
7.62 mm machine gun

KURDISTAN

Aleppo

Mosul

Kirkuk

TEHRAN

SYRIA

R.Tigris

IRAN

LEBANON

Beirut

Damascus

BAGHDAD

Tel
Aviv

IRAQ

Amman

R.Euphrates

ISRAEL

Basra

JORDAN

SAUDI
ARABIA

KUWAIT

Kuwait City

PERSIAN GULF

Baghdad

International
Communication
Centre

Radio
& TV

Central
Railway Station

SADDAM'S
BUNKER
COMPLEX

DIMESHQ STREET

YAFA STREET

HAIFA STREET

RIVER TIGRIS

Zawra Park

Rashid Hotel

Haleb
Sq.

ZAITŪN STREET

Festival &
Parade
Ground

Dhahran

RIYADH

KINDĪ STREET

QADISIYA EXPRESSWAY

| 0 | miles | 200 |
| 0 | kms | 400 |

Other Tornado crews were not so fortunate as I* found out during a lively discussion at Royal Air Force Marham, Norfolk, with some of the crews of 27 and 617 Squadrons gathered together by Squadron Leader Graham Thwaites, acting CO of 27 Squadron.

The previous CO of 27 Squadron, Wing Commander Nigel Elsdon, and his navigator, Flight Lieutenant Max Collier, were both killed on the second wave of the first day when their Tornado was seen to crash after a low-level attack against the airfield at Shaibah.

On the night of 18/19 January 1991 it was decided that four Tornadoes would each 'loft' two 1,000-pound bombs, fused for an air burst fifteen feet above the gun emplacements, one minute before four more Tornadoes arrived with their JP233s. 'Lofting' means that the bomb is released

about three miles from the target as the Tornado climbs steeply and turns away, but the Tornado crewed by Flight Lieutenants Dave Waddington and Robert Stuart was tracked and hit by a French-made SAM; the pilot was knocked unconscious so Stuart used the command ejection system to throw both men clear only 180 feet above the ground.

During our debate in 27 Squadron's crewroom, Dave Waddington spoke about his time in the POW building when he heard the Stealth fighter-bombers and was impressed by the accuracy of their attacks which, on one occasion, removed a building believed to be the headquarters of the Ba'ath party only a few yards from his prison.

The young, highly professional pilots were surprised and shocked by the 'murderous' triple A which, together with SAMs, defended the mas-

sive Iraqi airfields. They were unanimous in their praise of General Horner and his planners and said the USAF command and control was excellent. They said that the Royal Air Force tankers were first-class and their 55 Squadron, also from Marham, had flown all its 199 tanker sorties without a hitch. They were pleased when after four days they were taken off their extremely hazardous low-level attacks and bombed from medium altitudes. They were proud of their sturdy Tornadoes; thought the JP233 was the right weapon against airfields, and all agreed with their Gulf AOC, Air Vice-Marshal Bill Wratten,† that it should have a stand-off capability.

* Johnnie Johnson.
† Air Vice-Marshal Wratten giving evidence to the Commons Select Committee on Defence. He was subsequently made KBE.

Left and below: Desert Storm – the manifestation of United States air power

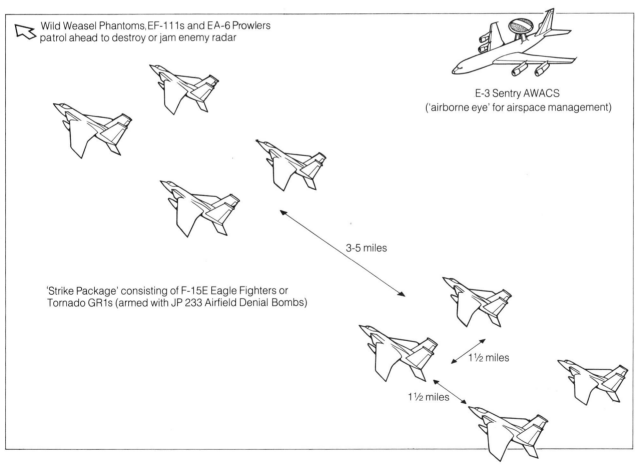

Wild Weasel Phantoms, EF-111s and EA-6 Prowlers patrol ahead to destroy or jam enemy radar

E-3 Sentry AWACS ('airborne eye' for airspace management)

3-5 miles

'Strike Package' consisting of F-15E Eagle Fighters or Tornado GR1s (armed with JP 233 Airfield Denial Bombs)

1½ miles

1½ miles

Tomcat taking off from USS *Kennedy*

At Dhahran, Captain Steven 'Tater' Tate, an ex-Marine who had shifted to the Air Force to 'see some action', and now of the 71st Tactical Fighter Squadron, was one of the Eagle pilots who had been in the Gulf since August and thought the Iraqis would fight. At 22.00 on the night of 16 January, Tate, on alert, got the order to 'lean forward and green up'. His four Eagles took off at 01.30 and after a lights-out, radio-out refuelling from a tanker, the Captain's flight, which was protecting four strike F-15E Eagles, arrived over Bhaghdad at about 03.05.

About an hour earlier, Tomahawk cruise missiles (at about one and a quarter million dollars a shot) and Stealth fighters had alerted the defences which threw up Triple-A and SAM missiles; and when Tate's formation arrived over the capital they saw a spectacular display of trac-

ers, flak and SAMs criss-crossing in all directions. 'Baghdad was like a huge blanket of Christmas lights,' Tate said. 'It was just sparkling all over.'

Tate, a few minutes ahead of the strike Eagles, set up a racetrack pattern orbit above the fighter-bombers and watched their bombs exploding below. Suddenly he picked up a radar contact coming up from the ground, and heard on his radio that Iraqi fighters were scrambling. Seconds later the blip on his screen was moving rapidly towards the tail of his number three who had just turned to the south. 'I was heading north-east on a different pattern. I didn't know if the bogie was chasing number three, but I locked him up, confirmed he was hostile, and fired a missile.'

The missile Tate fired was an AIM-7M Sparrow. The range was fifteen miles, and he was ready to fire again when the Mirage exploded into a huge fireball which the Captain thought was pretty exciting. He did not see the Iraqi pilot eject. Tate's was the only air-to-air victory scored by the First Tactical Fighter Wing.

Captain Ayed at Shamrani, Royal Saudi Air Force, was the first Allied fighter pilot to get two kills when a pair of Mirages, believed to be carrying Exocet missiles, were first detected by ships' radars. Led by Ayed

RAF Tornado

RAF Jaguar

two F-15 Eagles were then vectored some eighty miles by AWACS to intercept. The Saudi pilot fired two AIM-9 Sidewinders: 'I just rolled in behind them and shot them down,' he said. 'It was very easy.'*

Subsequently, the 'Gorilla' fighter-jocks of the 58th Tactical Fighter Squadron got seventeen kills but most of these were of the 'turkey shoot' variety when Iraqi aeroplanes fled to Iran and were easy targets.

Warrant Officer Steven L. Rucks, of the famed 101st Airborne Division, flew his AH-64A Apache helicopter from a Saudi base known as 'The Eagle's Nest'. Rucks and his gunner were highly trained to kill enemy tanks at night but on their first mission they were sent on a terrain-skimming approach against a concrete plotting centre for Iraq's air defence system. Steve watched as his gunner bent over his console display and lined-up on the concrete bunker some twenty miles ahead. Their target was already illuminated by a laser beam from a Special Forces soldier on the ground. Steve fired a brace of AGM-114 Hellfire missiles which sought out the core of light created by the shining laser and followed the

beam into the target. He only saw the explosion, purple and yellow, on his terminal display and thought how impersonal was modern war.

Throughout the world, television screens, especially Cable Network News (CNN), brought the air war not only into our homes but, according to *Newsweek*,† into 'the Black Hole' itself.

Horner and Glosson didn't know what to expect during those first thirty seconds over Baghdad. From the basement command post, Horner sent a subordinate upstairs to watch CNN ... Over a telephone line, the supreme air commander called to his scout, 'What are they saying?'

Back came the reply: 'Bernie Shaw's under the table and he's got the mike out the window.'

Horner checked his watch. At nine minutes past the hour Saddam's telephone exchange was due to be demolished. CNN needed the exchange to transmit its signal. At nine past, BARRROOOM.

'What's Bernard Shaw saying now?' Horner asked.

'He just went off the air.'

For Steve Rucks and his fellow Army Apache pilots the war took on a more personal note when supporting their ground troops in skirmishes

round the unoccupied oil refining town of Khafji. They killed tank after tank in the open desert. The pickings were so good that the Apache pilots shuttled to and from the combat zone, flying more missions than they were supposed to.

More personal still was a subsequent mission when Rucks and other Apache pilots actually captured several Iraqi troops with their low-flying Apaches by rounding them up like steers in true Western fashion and herding them to Allied troops.

Apache pilots also made special flights when they were refuelled on the ground by the big Chinook transport helicopters and flew deep into Iraq to destroy radar sites.

One of the most significant aeroplanes was the A-10 Thunderbolt, better and more appropriately known as the 'Warthog'. We have all seen pairs of Warthogs flying very low scanning the countryside and pulling up here and there to examine a likely

* It later became known that the AWACS aeroplane controlling this engagement deliberately held off US and Canadian fighters, which were closer to the Mirages, so the Saudis could have their own star.
† *Newsweek*, 18 March 1991.

Warthogs – stars of Desert Storm

to heat sources. The tank engines were running and the two pilots soon destroyed six; two more fell to their potent cannon whose 30-mm uranium-depleted rounds (each the size of a milk bottle) can penetrate the steel hull of a tank from up to 7,000 yards.

On 6 February, Bob Swain found some moving Iraqi armour in central Kuwait, dropped bombs and fired two Maverick missiles, knocking out at least one T-62, which threw a tread, spun round and burned furiously. The 33-year-old Reservist climbed away, evaded some gunfire and turned for home.

'As I was leaving the target', said Swain, 'I noticed two black dots running across the desert that looked really different than anything I had seen before. They weren't putting up any dust and yet they were moving fast and quickly across the desert.' He called Forward Air Controller Captain Jon Engle and said he thought he had a helicopter.

Engle spotted the helicopter with binoculars and fired two smoke rounds into the sand to mark the spot for Swain who fired an AIM-9, but missed. He made a second pass and fired 300 rounds from his powerful cannon: 'Some of the bullets ran through him, but we weren't sure if it was stopped completely. So I came back with the final pass, hit it and it fell apart. It was just in a bunch of little pieces.'

These first few days of highly successful air strikes, involving thousands of missions, gave some high-ranking commanders, and the media commentators, the feeling that the superior skills and technology of the USAF were about to provide a whirlwind victory, thus avoiding what we all feared – a bloody, drawn-out land battle.

As the days passed, however, it became clear that Saddam was far from finished for his Scud missiles continued to hit Riyadh, the Saudi capital, and Tel Aviv, the Israeli capital, in an attempt to drag the whole region into the confrontation. Patriot ground-to-

target. Unlike their fellow pilots flying the latest supersonic fighters armed with laser bombs and sophisticated radars, the Warthog pilots fly by stick and rudder, each pair over their own patch, and attack whatever they come across – the same as our low-level 'Rhubarbs' of the Second War.

For these gallant Warthog pilots there was both tragedy and triumph. There was tragedy when in one engagement two Warthogs were shot down within minutes – one pilot taken prisoner, the other killed. And

tragedy during the Khafji debacle when eleven Marines in two light armoured vehicles that had lost their bearings were killed by a Maverick missile fired from a Warthog.

Khafji was also the scene of triumph. On 30 January 1991, activated Reservist and Boeing 767 pilot Bob Swain, and some fellow Warthog jocks, found dozens of Iraqi tanks on the open desert. Swain led his wingman against the Russian-built T-62s and attacked with AGM-65 Maverick missiles. These detect and home in on

Stealth over the Gulf

air missiles, the most sophisticated computer-control weapons yet built, were hastily flown from the United States to defend both capitals, where they immediately passed their first operational test with flying colours. However, the enemy's still-strong flak defences continued to destroy Allied warplanes and the 'victory through air power' protagonists revised their original forecasts and some now thought that it might require 100,000 missions to get the job done.

Ever since the First War controversy has raged over the difference between what the airmen said they could do and what they actually achieved. 'Boom' Trenchard, 'Father' of the Royal Air Force, and its first Chief of Staff, argued that 'the bomber would always get through' and that sufficient air power would have avoided the slaughter at Verdun, the Somme and Passchendale where armies fought and died in the Flanders mud.

Between the two wars against Germany the same 'bomber' doctrine prevailed and thus, in the 1930s, most of the Royal Air Force's budget went on the bomber force rather than the fighter force which, by the narrowest of margins, defeated the Luftwaffe in the Battle of Britain.

In 1941, the then Chief of the Air Staff, Portal, was trying to convince the Prime Minister that, given a force of 4,000 heavy bombers, Germany could be defeated from the air alone; and in this mistaken view he was supported by a top American airman, 'Tooey' Spaatz, who, like 'Bomber' Harris, strenuously opposed any diversion of their mighty bomber fleets – such as bombing the German Army in Normandy – on the grounds that the end of the war by bombing alone was in sight.

Yet in 1945, when we of the Tactical Air Forces flew into Germany, we were amazed at the high morale of the civilian population and the extent of aeroplane production, which had remained high until the last months of the war. In the mid-1950s the draft of our Strategic Bombing Survey concluded that the results of the years of bombing had not justified the effort and the loss of so many young lives. The Chief of Air Staff at that time instructed that the report be 'watered down' to avoid a 'public outcry' from the relatives of the dead bomber crews.

At the end of thirty days of unparalleled bombardment from the air, involving some 70,000 missions, Saddam Hussein's air force was pretty well written-off, more than one hundred of his combat aeroplanes having been flown, for reasons unknown at the time, to airfields in Iran. But he still had some missiles and aeroplanes left, and we knew from the past that air superiority is not a condition that can be achieved once and for all. It must be won continually and maintained for as long as the Iraqis had any missiles or aeroplanes left.

After one month of such severe bombing we wondered how much longer the consistently over-rated Iraqi Army, said to number half a million, hunkered down in their bunkers outside Kuwait, could hold out. We knew that the despot's armoury was getting low and, thanks to our blockade, he had no re-supply routes. One-third of his armour and artillery pieces had been destroyed. His small navy had gone and his air force, our intelligence reported, had either fled or been destroyed. His infrastructure – power stations, oil refineries, road and rail communications – had gone too. How much longer could the Iraqi Army, includ-

ing the so-called élite Republican Guard, hold out in the barren, coverless desert? Perhaps, thought the armchair strategists, including the authors, 100,000 missions would see the job done without a bloody confrontation on the ground.

Although the Field Commander, the burly, able General 'Stormin' Norman' Schwarzkopf, had ample photographic and electronic evidence of enemy *matériel* destroyed, he could not look into men's hearts and minds and judge their will to stand and fight. He found his answer when on the early morning of 24 February 1991 he unleashed his considerable ground forces for the long-awaited ground battle. His deception plan was that the main assault would come from a big amphibious assault against Kuwait City, and another from Saudi Arabia into southern Kuwait. Instead the main thrust of British, French and US troops by-passed Kuwait, entered

Iraq to trap the occupying forces and prevent their retreat.

To move an army, largely by helicopter, in such a vast flanking movement from Saudi Arabia to the Euphrates, and to cut off Iraq's forces from retreat – to isolate and kill – was a classic demonstration of military skill and organization.

It was hardly surprising that after the heaviest air bombardment in history, including isolation of the battlefield by taking out the bridges over the Tigris and the Euphrates, there was little resistance from the defenders; and when they did stand and fight they were immediately set upon by Warthogs and Apaches. Fighter-bombers roamed ahead of our advancing columns and any counter-offensive threat by the Iraqis was immediately eliminated. Further afield, B-52s and F-111s continued to attack what few strategic targets were left and the famed 82nd Airborne Division was air-lifted to the north of Kuwait. Soon after, Kuwait City was surrounded, with tactical air covering any escape to Basra, the US Army safeguarding the way north to Baghdad and the US Marines attacking to the east. As 'Stormin' Norman' drew his net tighter, the Iraqis surrendered in large numbers.

As in previous wars, American search and rescue pilots flew courageously to bring back their downed comrades, and the recovery of Navy Lieutenant Devon Jones is a chronicle of outstanding leadership, teamwork and airmanship.

At about 06.50 on 21 January Jones's F-14A Tomcat was hit and destroyed by a SAM. Both Jones and his back-seater, Lieutenant Larry Slade, managed to eject. Slade was soon captured but Jones walked to the west and became anxious when his calls on his survival radio remained unanswered.

However a circling AWACS, code-named Yukon, knew of Slate 46's (Jones) plight, and soon a posse of one MH-53 Pave Low helicopter flown by Captain Tom Trask and his five-man crew, two A-10 'Warthogs' (Captains Paul Johnson and wing-

Destruction of Samawah Bridge over the Euphrates

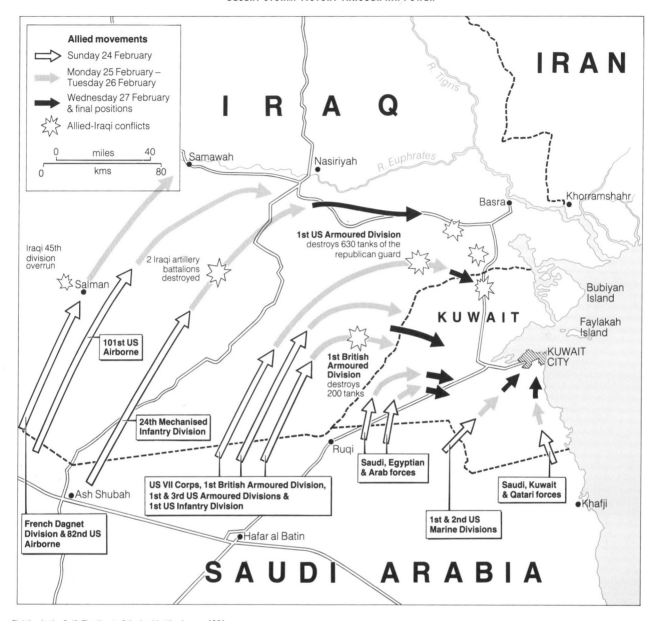

Fighting in the Gulf. The thrust of the land battle, January 1991

man Randy Goft) escorted by two F-15s, were crossing the 'fence' into Iraq. They had to fly 160 miles into hostile territory, and so Tom Trask held the big chopper at *fifteen feet* to avoid radar detection.

At 08.50 Yukon called the chopper to say that a fast-moving bogey was nearby. Trask dropped to *ten feet* and flew up a nearby wadi, but the F-15 leader reported that the bogey had turned north and disappeared. Shortly after Trask reached the fix given by Yukon, and although they

carefully searched the area for twenty minutes there was no sign of Slate 46. Since his fuel was running low Trask turned for the Saudi border leaving the Warthogs and F-15s to keep searching.

Just after noon the F-15 leader, who had briefly heard Slate 46, said they would have to leave for refuelling. Paul Johnson called again: 'Slate 46. Sandy 57. Do you copy?'

Devon Jones calmly replied: 'Sandy 57. This is Slate 46. Go ahead.'

Back at Arar airfield, where they

were refuelling, Tom Trask heard the conversation and told Yukon that he was returning north. Meanwhile the Warthogs were also running low on fuel, but before they left they had to get an accurate fix on Slate 46 so that the big chopper, operating at its maximum range, could fly straight to the survivor. The two Warthogs dropped to 3,000 feet and Johnson told Slate 46 to watch for flares he was about to release. The survivor said he was about four miles south, and seconds later he reported the Wart-

hogs were overhead. Johnson passed the co-ordinates to Trask, told Slate 46 that they had to leave for gas and would be back in thirty minutes.

At ten feet Trask crossed a four-lane highway full of enemy vehicles, and later was told by Yukon to fly east to avoid SAM radar detection. At about 13.50 the chopper and Wart-hogs joined together and headed north for the survivor. Five minutes later Slate 46 saw the chopper and called: 'One mile now. Ten o'clock'.

Everyone was elated that for the first time in this dangerous mission the chopper had voice contact with the survivor. But their delight was cut short when the chopper's left door gunner spotted an enemy truck and called: 'We've got a mover to the left.'

'Sandy,' Trask called the Warthog leader, 'where's the survivor?'

'The truck is going right at him,' replied Paul Johnson.

'Smoke the truck,' ordered the chopper's co-pilot.

'Roger,' acknowledged Johnson.

The Warthogs dived on the truck firing their powerful cannon. The enemy transport blew up in orange flames.

'Sandy,' called Trask, 'where's the survivor?'

'Fly right at the smoke,' Johnson replied.

'At the smoke?'

'Yes. Fly right at the burning truck.'

Trask reared the chopper on its tail and moved slowly towards the burning truck. To his surprise he saw a man in a green Navy flight suit climb out of a hole. 'The pilot stood there with his survival kit in one hand and his radio in the other, calm and still, like a young executive waiting for a commuter train.'*

Seconds later they had Devon Jones on board and at 15.15 he heard the co-pilot say: 'Sandy this is Moccasin 05. We're crossing the fence.'

Slate 46 was out of Iraq.

On 15 February, Captain Todd K. Sheehy and his wingman, First Lieute-

Top left: Puma

Left: Iraqi missile in the Desert

Captain Todd K. Sheehy and his A-10 Warthog

nant Ronald J. Keller, both of the 511th Tactical Fighter Squadron, were flying their A-10 Thunderbolts on an air interdiction mission when the Captain destroyed an Iraqi MI-8 'Hip' helicopter. Here is the narrative.

On February 15th 1991, while leading a formation of two A-10 aircraft on an air interdiction mission into western Iraq, Captain Todd K. Sheehy downed and destroyed an Iraqi MI- 'Hip' helicopter with fire from his A-10s 30mm cannon. On that date, Captain Sheehy and his wingman, Lt Ronald J. Keller were deployed to an airfield in Western Saudi Arabia in support of Operation Desert Storm and were assigned to the 354th Tactical Fighter Wing (TFW) Provisional.

Initial vectors to the target helicopter came from an E-3A Airborne Warning and Control System (AWACS) aircraft. Following the direction given to him by the Air Weapons Controller aboard the AWACS aircraft, Captain Sheehy led his flight towards the area of the reported helicopter. Due to the lack of an air-to-air radar aboard the A-10, acquisition of the helicopter was visual. Once spotted, Captain Sheehy dove at an angle of 45 degrees out of an altitude of 15,000 feet and began firing the 30mm cannon at 10,000 feet while approximately two miles from the helicopter which was flying at approximately 50 feet above the desert. After firing approximately 300 rounds of a mixture of 30mm armour piercing incendiary and high explosive incendiary ammunition at the helicopter, Captain

Sheehy recovered from the dive to avoid a concentration of enemy 23mm anti-aircraft artillery gunfire. As he climbed back to altitude, his wingman reported that the helicopter had been hit in the tail section and had stopped moving either hovering or having been forced to land, but was still intact. Captain Sheehy then made another pass at the helicopter firing approximately 250 rounds into the helicopter. It exploded and burned.

The most stirring rescue attempt was by Chief Warrant Officer Philip M. Garvey flying a UH-60 Black Hawk helicopter and his crew, including Flight Surgeon Rhonda Cornum.

On 27 February Captain William F. Andrews, 32, led four F-16s below cloud to look for Iraqi ground troops. Suddenly Andrews's F-16 was shaken by a violent explosion which threw it out of control. He closed his eyes, pulled the ejection handle and did not open his eyes until his parachute opened.

I talked to my flight on the radio as I was going down, telling them where I was. I hit the ground, wriggled out of the chute, and continued talking to my flight. We were trying to set up a rescue when I saw Iraqi soldiers only about a hundred feet away.

Meanwhile, Philip Garvey and his crew were at a forward operation location preparing to move troops

* Reader's Digest, June 1991.

over the battlefield. They were inside the helicopter, rotors turning, when operations called: 'You got Doc Cornum on board? Do you have all of your equipment? You have gas?'

Garvey replied: 'That's affirmative.'

'Well, we have a mission to go pick up a downed F-16 pilot.'

The Black Hawk lifted aloft in a swirling dust cloud and headed towards Andrews who, with a broken leg, was in bad shape: 'As they (the Iraqis) got within twenty feet, I saw a soldier launch a SAM at my flight. I grasped the radio and instructed my flight to use countermeasures to avoid getting hit. It worked. My wingman took evasive action and didn't get hit.' The Iraqis saw Andrews make the call, opened fire and blew his survival radio to bits with their AK-47 rifles.*

The Black Hawk helicopter was sixty miles inside Iraq and almost over Captain Andrews when it was shattered by ground fire and crunched into the sand. Major Cornum said later:

As we tumbled and rolled, I found myself underneath at least part of the wreck. I wasn't thinking clearly enough to know why I couldn't use my arms.† I used one foot to kind of push my way out from underneath this helicopter. By the time I got out the Iraqi soldiers were there.

Five of the eight people aboard were killed in the crash.

In less than four days it was all over. Nearly, but not quite, a 'walkover' for the ground forces; but certainly not a battle. Victory was won by air power. Mostly tactical air power, devised by the Germans in Spain, adopted by the British in the Western Desert, decisive in Normandy, updated with 'smart' weapons in Vietnam and employed to give a flawless performance in the Arabian Desert. The star of the show was the ugly duckling herself – the Warthog. From all aircrews there was high praise for the ever-present AWACS manned by courageous crews, specialists and controllers.

This short contest proved that today only the United States has the capacity to assemble tremendous military strength on the far side of the world at short notice. Only America could have destroyed Saddam's army, including his vastly over-rated Republican Guard, from the air. Today there is no other power, or combination of powers, which can stand against such an armoury – fashioned by President Ronald Reagan and deployed by President George Bush.

* Captain Andrews was later awarded the Air Force Cross.
† Major Cornum's arms were broken in the crash. Her husband, Major Mark Cornum, is also a flight surgeon and when home in the United States the two majors live on their ranch in Florida.

INDEX

V-2 rocket 103, 105, 108
Vampire 153
Veen, Lieutenant G. T. van de 77
Verdun 197
Verrall, Flying Officer L. A. 86
Vian, Admiral Sir Philip 82
Vickers Fighter 20
Victorious 118, 125, 126
Viet Cong (VC) 177
Vietnam War 11, 15, 177-82, 188
Vieux Chartes, Le 29
Voss, Captain V. 'Pops' 76
Vulcan bombers 15, 183

Waddington, Flight Lieutenant 193
Wainwright, Lieutenant-General Jonathan 158
Waldron, Lieutenant Commander John 165
Walker, Group Captain G. A. (later Air Chief Marshal Sir Augustus) 128
Wallis, Dr Barnes 118, 121
Walpole, Lieutenant Peter 183-4
Walther, Dr Erich 108
Ward, Lieutenant Commander 'Sharkie' 185-7
Warthogs 195-6, 198-202
Wasp 85, 86, 89

Waterloo, Battle of 13, 187
Webster, Lieutenant John 152
Weingartz, Lieutenant F. A. 77
Welch, Lieutenant George 152
Wellington, Duke of 187
Wellingtons 79, 94, 96, 128
Wells, Wing Commander W. G. 84
West, Flying Officer J. G. 86
West, Flight Lieutenant Ronnie 86
Western Desert 68-75, 202
Westmacott, Squadron Leader Innes 84
West Virginia 152
White, Air Commodore Harry 107, 108
White, Wing Commander John 107
Whiteman, Lieutenant George 152
Wigley, Squadron Leader Philip 84
Wildcats 118, 161, 163-5
Wilde Sau tactic 98, 105
'Wild Weasel' Phantoms 188-9
Willets, A. H. 97
Williams, General 'Bob' 102
Wilmot, Chester 134
Window 94, 96, 98, 99, 107
Witts, Wing Commander 189
Woodhall, Wing Commander A. B. 62-4, 87-8
World War I 12-13, 19-31, 37, 52, 59, 64, 68, 87, 103, 167, 197

World War II 11, 13-14, 28, 36, 45-169, 177, 179, 182, 196
Wratten, Air Vice-Marshal Bill 193
Wray, Air Commodore A. M. 97
Wright, Flying Officer 91
Wühlisch, Lieutenant von 19, 20
Wurzbach, Colonel Clemens 102

Yakovlev 145, 147
Yamaguchi, Admiral 166
Yamamoto, Admiral Isoroku 152, 158-9, 161-6
Yamato 163
Yarra, Flight Sergeant J. W. 'Slim' 86
Yates, Pilot Officer A. S. 86
Yom Kippur War 15
Yorktown 160-6
Yugoslavia 115
Yukon AWACS 198-201

Zekes 164-5
Zemke, Colonel Hubert 'Hub' 14, 94, 103, 179
Zeppelin raids 12
Zeros 164
Zuckerman, Sir (later Lord) Solly 140
Zuikaku 160, 161